New Strangers
in
Paradise

New Strangers
in
Paradise

The Immigrant Experience
and
Contemporary American Fiction

GILBERT H. MULLER

THE UNIVERSITY PRESS OF KENTUCKY

Publication of this volume was made possible in part
by a grant from the National Endowment for the Humanities.

Scholarly publisher for the Commonwealth,
serving Bellarmine College, Berea College, Centre
College of Kentucky, Eastern Kentucky University,
The Filson Club Historical Society, Georgetown College,
Kentucky Historical Society, Kentucky State University,
Morehead State University, Murray State University,
Northern Kentucky University, Transylvania University,
University of Kentucky, University of Louisville,
and Western Kentucky University.

Editorial and Sales Offices: The University Press of Kentucky
663 South Limestone Street, Lexington, Kentucky 40508–4008

03 02 01 00 99   5 4 3 2 1

Library of Congress Cataloging-in-Publication Data

Muller, Gilbert H., 1941-
    New strangers in paradise : the immigrant experience and contemporary
American fiction / Gilbert H. Muller.
        p.   cm.
    Includes bibliographical references (p.   ) and index.
    ISBN 0-8131-2134-5 (alk. paper)
    1. American fiction—Minority authors—History and criticism.
2. Immigrants in literature. 3. American fiction—20th century—History
and criticism. 4. Emigration and immigration in literature. 5. Ethnic
groups in literature. 6. Minorities in literature. I. Title.
PS374.I48M85   1999
813'.54093520691—dc21   99-24008

This book is printed on acid-free recycled paper
meeting the requirements of the American National Standard
for Permanence of Paper for Printed Library Materials.

Manufactured in the United States of America

For Laleh,
Parisa, and Darius

Contents

Preface

This book is about the interacting forces of migration and immigration, the global push and pull, the arrivals and departures that constitute a unique episode in the interrelationship of contemporary American fiction and the historical world. It covers a cultural and literary landscape that has been transformed since the Second World War by an increasingly large and diverse tide of immigrants to America's shores. Containing an introductory chapter that provides an overview of immigration as portrayed in recent American fiction, five chapters devoted to readings of seminal texts drawn from distinct immigrant cultures, and a concluding chapter, *New Strangers in Paradise* explores the relations of culture and power provoked by America's new immigrant tide. The book concerns itself with issues of race and ethnicity, multiculturalism and pluralism, postcolonialism and postmodernity, national and international conflicts. It explores the psychology of uprooted peoples, from the survivors of the Holocaust to the refugees of the Haitian boatlifts—the diasporic imagination in quest of the American Dream.

By focusing on writers as significant and diverse as Singer, Marshall, Kincaid, Mukherjee, Tan, Hijuelos, and others, this study demonstrates the ways in which American novelists and short story writers utilize the immigrant experience to erect new epics or national narratives for our times. Immigration has captured the imagination of numerous contemporary writers because it illuminates what Edward Said in *Culture and Imperialism* aptly terms the "contrapuntal and often nomadic" nature of American civilization at the end of the twentieth century. As Toni Morrison observes in *Playing in the Dark*, "American literature, especially in the twentieth century, and notably in the last twenty years, has been shaped by its encounter with the immigrant." Such literature rewrites the story of what it means to be American.

The aim of this book is to join cultural and literary experience in the first sustained study of contemporary American novelists and short story writers who explore this revolutionary "fourth wave" of immigration to America's shores. It seeks to be a broadly historical and cultural inquiry into selected paradigmatic texts that highlight the flowering of immigrant fiction today. By showcasing constellations of writers who deal with the immigrant experience from clearly defined ethnic and racial perspectives, this work demonstrates the ways in which such fiction reveals a common quest for American identity within a world of flux and change.

While extending the borders and thresholds of contemporary American fiction, the theme of immigration permits a dynamic convergence—especially in the era following the Immigration Act of 1965—of multiple heritages in one society. The overarching thesis of *New Strangers in Paradise* is that even as immigration since World War II remakes our world, it fosters or elicits new creativities in literature and life. These creativities are rooted in unique or alternative cultural experience and ethnic options, but they also suggest the need for a dynamic pluralism. The new immigrant experience in American fiction offers a vision that is at once diverse and inclusive. As such, today's novelists cross multiple borders in search of a single, shared national experience.

Immigrants have always engaged in nation-building, and the immigrants we encounter in postwar American fiction are emblematic of the transformation of our national mythology and of its literary canon. Such fiction argues for a polyglot nation, transnational connections, and new forms of cultural authority.

1

Promised Land: Postwar Fiction and the Immigrant Experience

> My mother believed you could be
> anything you wanted to be in America.
> —Amy Tan, *The Joy Luck Club*

Fiction and history in the era after World War II are interlocking journeys by immigrants to America's shores. This immigrant tide in contemporary American fiction is global, flowing across diasporas, borders, and postcolonial terrains. From the Holocaust to the Haitian and Cuban boatlifts, many of the departures and arrivals are reflections of recent historical traumas, creating in fiction what Bharati Mukherjee terms "odysseys of dislocation" (Woodford 2). Immigration for America's short story writers and novelists today is the representation of radically new desires by the world's uprooted peoples, an allegory chronicling the evolution of a multicultural nation-state.

The postwar strangers from near and distant shores who arrive in America constitute the latest wave in those major cycles of immigration that have characterized the nation since its colonial origins. However, they represent a unique historical conjuncture: instead of coming predominantly from Europe, these new strangers in Paradise have departed from all points on the global compass. Like F. Scott Fitzgerald's Dutch sailors in *The Great Gatsby*, who are counterpoised against Tom

Buchanan's nativist recitation of Stoddard's *The Rising Tide of Color*, they are part of the flow of providential history; they still gaze on America as the "fresh, green breast of the new world," but in their typically Third World origins, postwar immigrants provoke new perspectives on culture and social diversity—on what it means to be American in an increasingly pluralistic New World.

The idea of America as a New World, an Eden, an El Dorado, a Gold Mountain—the pure representation of desire—is embedded in all cycles of immigration history. In the postwar or postmodern period, however, the mythic assumptions about immigration to the Promised Land have changed, for postmodernism essentially implies a new set of social relations typical of late capitalism or postindustrial society. As Lyotard states, postmodernism involves "incredulity toward meta-narratives. . . . The narrative function is losing its functions, its great heroes, its great dangers, its great voyagers, its great goal" (xxiv). Transformed are the myth of Plymouth Rock, of America as the exclusive domain for Europeans seeking religious and political freedom; the myth of the Statue of Liberty, of the "huddled masses" and "wretched refuse" popularized in Emma Lazarus's poem "The New Colossus" (1883) who would find blessed sanctuary in America; and the myth of the Melting Pot, of nationalities and ethnic groups fusing into a unified nation. Plymouth Rock, the Statue of Liberty, the Melting Pot: this classic iconography is rendered ambivalently rather than lyrically by contemporary American writers. As Russell Banks writes in his magisterial novel *Continental Drift* (1985), the contemporary immigrant's eyes might be "peeled for the Statue of Liberty," but "when you get to America . . . you get . . . Disney World and land deals and fast moving high interest bank loans" (312). Today's boat people and airplane immigrants encounter a nation whose myths are in perpetual evolution and subject to persistent critique.

The contemporary immigrant experience retains at its core the mythology of the American Dream, but a dream that must contend with forces of psychic and cultural dislocation—with the reality that the new immigrants are "others" who because of race and ethnicity, caste and class, culture and religion do not fit comfortably into the traditional mythology of the Melting Pot. Immigration in postwar American fiction reflects a national myth or narrative undergoing transformation as the margin modifies the mainstream and cultural Others alter the ways in which both their identities and American identity are defined, for their

odysseys of dislocation are also odysseys of evolving national consciousness. Postcolonial and Third World immigrants remold the New World
and the narrative of America, forcing a dialectic on what was once a
common, largely Eurocentric cultural ethos. Whereas American fiction
once offered a microcosm of European immigration, it now projects a
frequently picaresque *tour du monde* in which the national landscape
actually becomes a microcosm of the world or, as Mukherjee writes in
Jasmine (1989), "an archipelago of ghettoes seething with immigrants"
(140). The world inside the American novel fuses with the "heteroglossia"
of the postmodern condition; in both fiction and fact, "the world becomes polyglot, once and for all and irreversibly" (Bakhtin 1981:2).

New Immigrant Nation

Fueled by postwar patterns of immigration, the epic of America, especially following the Immigration Act of 1965, also becomes polyglot,
multicultural, and transnational. Based on the 1990 census, almost nine
million legal immigrants came to America's shores during the 1980s, along
with two million undocumented immigrants. These immigrants ac-
counted for 28 percent of the population growth from 226.5 million to
248.7 million during the decade. Moreover, from 1990 to 1997, another
7.5 million foreign-born individuals entered the United States legally,
accounting for 29.2 percent of the population growth. This steady flow
of global immigration, which is traceable to changes in policy that began
during the Second World War, has transformed America's demographic
destiny. In fact, at a point midway into the twenty-first century, racial
and Third World ethnic groups will outnumber whites in the United
States: "Already one American in four defines himself or herself as Hispanic or nonwhite. If current trends in immigration and birth rates persist, the Hispanic population will have further increased an estimated
21%, the Asian presence about 22%, blacks almost 12%, and whites a
little more than 2% when the 20th century ends. . . . By 2056 . . . the
'average' U.S. resident, as defined by Census statistics, will trace his or
her descent to Asia, Africa, the Hispanic World, the Pacific Islands,
Arabia—almost anywhere but white Europe" (Henry 28). According to
the Census Bureau's revised 1997 estimates, there will be 96 million Hispanic Americans in the United States by 2050 in a projected total popu-

lation of 393 million, an increase of 237.5 percent. Similarly, the increase of Asians and Pacific Islanders to more than 34 million will be 412.5 percent. Within this demographic context, postwar immigration functions as a trope for an altered myth of America that was Eurocentric in origin but today reveals the outlines of an incipiently "universal" nation.

The migration of European and Third World peoples to the United States during and after World War II has a striking historical and literary significance. Émigrés and displaced persons, political refugees and golden exiles, illegal aliens and legal beneficiaries of increasingly generous immigration policy, the immigrant heroes and antiheroes who populate contemporary American fiction are the products of a raw, almost primordial global energy that casts groups from continent to continent in the postwar, postcolonial era. Russell Banks captures this global scattering of peoples across diasporas in *Continental Drift*, whose very title serves as a paradigm for the movement of people on the margins of other continents to the metropolitan centers of America: "It's as if the creatures residing on this planet in these years, the human creatures, millions of them traveling singly and in families, in clans and tribes, traveling sometimes as entire nations, were a subsystem inside the larger system of currents and tides, of winds and weather, of drifting continents and shifting, uplifting, grinding, cracking land masses" (34). Banks posits new conditions of postwar historicity by embedding global patterns of human movement within a process or continuum that equates the push and pull of contemporary immigrant experience with the geological contingencies of the planet. Peoples are likened to continents, moving and colliding, drifting on the crustal plates of the earth. In centuries of time some peoples are thrust over other peoples; some are subducted under others. *Continental Drift*, a canonical novel of migration and immigration that will be treated in greater detail in the concluding chapter, traces in alternating chapters the calamitous forces that push Bob Dubois down the coast from his native New Hampshire to Florida and pull Vanise Dorsinville from her small village in Haiti to the same destination. Banks's novel is a new form of national narrative—one that modifies heroic or canonical myths stressing America's glorious past and replaces these myths with a reconstituted epic that delineates the fragmentation of national life as peoples move from other countries and continents to the United States. Texts like *Continental Drift* are counter-hegemonic, constituting in Edward Said's words a "strategic formation" and possessing "mass, density, and referential power among themselves and thereafter in the culture at large" (*Orientalism* 20). The very resistance of such novelists as Russell Banks, Isaac Bashevis Singer, Amy Tan, Oscar Hijuelos, Bharati Mukherjee, Jamaica Kincaid, and dozens of other contemporary novelists to a traditional, unitary, or hegemonic American epic forces a redefinition and reconstruction of an authentic national narrative for the postwar period. To encounter postwar narratives of immigration is to recognize new, distinctively diverse articulations of nation and identity.

These multi-voiced "musings on nation and identity" (Cook 10) can be traced in a direct major line of historical influence to World War II and the altered patterns of immigration growing out of that historical watershed. The Second World War resulted in the repeal of the Chinese Exclusion Acts; the negotiation of the Bracero Program for wartime labor with Mexico, Barbados, Jamaica, and British Honduras; Presidents Truman's 1945 executive order admitting refugees from eastern and southern Europe; the passage of the India Bill and the War Brides Act in 1946 and the Displaced Persons Act in 1948; and additional provisions liberalizing immigration policy. What these changes in immigration policy suggest cumulatively is the gradual erosion of exclusionary attitudes toward Third World peoples as well as peoples from eastern Europe. The fiction of immigration becomes a prototypical cultural form—a cosmopolitan metanarrative—precisely because it captures and illuminates the shifting national and global terrains of worldwide migration caused by World War II and the consequent breakup of Empire. Contemporary American fiction, shaped significantly by its encounter with the immigrant, is more diverse than in earlier periods of literary history because decades of unparalleled global turmoil and change during and after World War II, converging with radical shifts in immigration policy, notably after 1960, have broadened multicultural contestations for space on American soil.

The myriad changes in immigration policy and population flow caused by World War II (including the internment of more than 110,000 Japanese Americans on the West Coast) constitute a historical drama that would prove irresistible to American writers of fiction. Despite the passage over Truman's veto of the restrictive McCarran-Walter Act in 1952, which erected a quota system favoring the nations of northern and western Europe, a new wave of Mexican Americans and Asian Americans in the 1950s reduced the total flow of immigrants from Europe to 50 percent. Between 1961 and 1970, more than half the immigrants arriving in the United States came from Cuba, Mexico, and South America. The 1965 amendments to the McCarran-Walter Act abolished national-origin quotas and were followed by the 1969 Hart-Cellar Act, which expanded immigration from countries such as China and India whose quotas had been small. Today, Europeans account for only 12 percent of all new immigrants: the series of visa programs, such as the 1993 Diversity Immigrant Visa Lottery aimed at countries "adversely affected" by past immigration controls, continues to expand the contemporary immigrant tide as people from Latin American, Caribbean, and Asian countries alter the drama of American civilization. These new tides of immigration offer fresh metanarratives for American writers, who from their typically ironic-parodic perspectives trace the intersecting cultural geographies now competing for authority at the end of the century.

Even those texts that treat the immediate postwar experience from a Eurocentric perspective eschew conventional approaches to the American epic—to the myth of the nation as Eden. A decidedly Eurocentric author, Vladimir Nabokov nevertheless recognizes in his contemporary classic, *Lolita* (1955), the fading, fragmented light of the traditional myths and verities of immigration in the postwar era. Humbert Humbert, that "enchanted traveler" traversing an "elected Paradise" in *Lolita*, possesses the typical nonconforming tendencies of immigrant protagonists confronting the contradictions inherent in the idea of America after World War II. Despite his injunction in the afterword to *Lolita* not to read for didactic intent or social criticism but rather for "aesthetic bliss," Nabokov takes us on a Cook's tour of postwar America in the late 1940s, training his parodic gaze on the absurdities of small town life and roadway culture. Nabokov's self-styled "creature" is an awkward immigrant, an Old World aesthete and pedophile who possesses an outsider's perspective that pinpoints both the promise and the limitations of American culture. When this representative of the decadent Old World links his destiny to a nymphet that is the New World embodiment of a banal national culture, we see in their primal contestations a struggle between mutually alien world visions that is a central issue of immigration in the postwar period.

Humbert Humbert leaves for the United States, that "country of rosy children and great trees" and his imagined Eden, at a time when "the gloom of yet another World War had settled upon the globe" (34). The Second World War, creating tens of millions of displaced persons, produced one of the greatest population shifts in history, an uprooting of peoples that constitutes a watershed in the narrative of immigration. Humbert is the fictive avatar of the more than 350,000 displaced persons admitted to the United States between 1945 and 1950, despite a national origins quota system that was unfavorable to the dispossessed of the world. He departs "the old and rotting world" (Nabokov himself left Paris for America in 1940) for a Paradise of Poe-like nymphets. Roaming and rutting in rich national soil, this postwar pilgrim embarks on a picaresque "joy-ride" across the United States. Using his protagonist as a reflection of the author's own need to "invent" America, Nabokov in *Lolita* explores parodically those power relationships and contestations—linguistic, sexual, social, and political—provoked by postwar patterns of immigration to the New Eden.

Nabokov's *Lolita* recapitulates formally and stylistically a range of postmodernist aesthetics, especially in its involution and spirit of play, but the dynamics of cultural production posited by the text are of equal significance. *Lolita* is typical of those novels created by a galaxy of postwar writers who enter into a dialogic relationship with readers over the impact of immigration on the contemporary American experience. These writers, as Nabokov asserts in his afterword to *Lolita* are "faced by the task of inventing America" (314). The immigrant women and men in this fiction share a sense of confusion, error, loss of identity, isolation, possible oppression, and defeat. At the same time, these voyagers to America's cities, shores, and towns recreate identity even as they transform the national narrative. In navigating the vagaries of cultural life in the postwar era, immigrants confirm Anthony Giddens's thesis in *The Consequences of Modernity* (1990) that the fragmented and discontinuous reality of contemporary America, its fissures and dissonances, produces paradoxically a sense of possibility.

Offering narratives of uncertainty, confusion, and dislocation as a context for certain globalizing tendencies, American novelists who illuminate the immigrant experience give vigorous expression to the fragmentation of contemporary cultural experience. Whether it is the frantic mutations of identity seen in the Holocaust survivor, Herman Broder, the protagonist of Isaac Bashevis Singer's *Enemies, A Love Story* (1972), or the endless self-transformations of the heroine in Mukherjee's *Jas-*

mine, immigrant characters in contemporary fiction find themselves surrounded by an acute dissonance of cultural messages, caught in the contradictions of American myths and realities. These discontinuities are central to what Giddens terms "the condition of post-modernity." According to Giddens, post-modernity "is distinguished by an evaporating of the 'grand narrative'—the overarching 'story line' by means of which we are placed in history as beings having a definite past and a predictable future" (2). As the prototypical cultural form of the Age of Empire, it is not surprising that contemporary fiction should be preoccupied with precisely those phenomena—the scope and pace of change, the global flow of information, the concomitant movement of peoples across space and time, the radical breakdown and transformation of modern institutions—that suggest a rupture in the grand narrative, a movement into a new age, whether termed postmodern, post-European, or postcolonial, following World War II.

Postmodern People

One of Giddens's central concerns in *The Consequences of Modernity* is to demonstrate the process whereby the "juggernaut" of modernity, an intrinsically hegemonic, Eurocentric phenomenon, becomes a heterogeneous and polyglot global force that is remaking our times. Thus the "modern" is reconstituted either as the "post-modern" or as "radicalized modernity," depending on one's perspective on the New Age. Giddens, who terms himself a utopian realist, prefers the condition of radicalized modernity, wherein diversity, fragmentation, dispersal, mobility and differentiation on a global scale, which are all potentially catastrophic tendencies, actually become positive forces in the reorganization of institutions. Giddens asserts that the very discontinuities of the postwar era create those conditions that contain emancipatory features. Ultimately modernity, as Giddens conjectures, "turns out to be enigmatic at its core" (49) or, as Habermas maintains, is an unfinished project worth revitalizing.

There is, of course, little question that post-World War II patterns of immigration reflect precisely those dialectically connected forces of fragmentation and possible integration that Giddens finds central to postmodernist discourse. The shifting contours of immigrant identity, as people of color redefine the relationship of the Third World to the First World and of the margin to the center, promote the radicalized version of American democracy that I hope to elucidate in this study. Contemporary multicultural America *is* the product of specific global developments reflected in the arrival of immigrants from Europe, southeast Asia, the Middle East, the East and West Indies, and Central and South America as the demographic boundaries of the United States expand to embrace, however unevenly, the promise of a multicultural, inclusive nation-state.

Immigrants enter the realm of contemporary American life as voyagers from both pre-modern and modern diasporas: from the ashes of wartime Poland to the killing fields of Mao's China; from the rural frontiers of Mexico, Haiti, and India to the urban centers of Havana, Tehran, and Santo Domingo. Exiles, refugees, émigrés, they harbor memories of underdevelopment *and* development, gathering on American soil in a concatenation of languages and cultures that is more hybrid than at any previous time in United States history. How does one construct narratives that capture this epochal, chiasmatic drift of peoples across continents to a nation whose very idea of itself is being altered by these post-Holocaust, postcolonial migrants, these wandering peoples?

One prototypical immigrant of the postwar era is Yifeng ("Love Fortune"), who as the Americanized "Ralph" in Gish Jen's *Typical American* (1991) leaves the "wreckage, and inflation, and moral collapse" (4) of China in 1947 and travels to "the complete other side of the world"— New York City—to pursue his dreams. China experiences its own Holocaust following the war with Japan. Manchuria falls to the Communists as Ralph Chang embarks on his American odyssey. "It's an American story," writes Jen at the outset of the novel, but it is a story that plays upon certain utopian concepts central to the national mythology. *Typical American* shares formal, mythological, and ideological characteristics common to the fiction of contemporary immigration. The immigrants in this fiction typically bring Third World dynamics to the First World, reconstituting the national allegory in multicultural form. Moreover, to the extent that Third World protagonists seek new destinies in a First World setting, they serve as corollaries to Fredric Jameson's thesis (1986) that "the story of the private individual destiny is always an allegory of the embattled situation of the public third-world culture and society" (69). The protagonists in this fiction make pilgrimages from distant parts of the globe to their imagined America—their sanctuary of freedom and opportunity—seeking the best that their new Eden has to offer. Like Ralph, whose carefully listed goals for self-improvement are a play on Benjamin Franklin's prescriptions for a virtuous, productive, and successful life, these immigrant protagonists confront a new embattled situation and are forced to wonder: What is America's purpose, its strategy, its plan? What promissory note—family, ancestral traditions, religion—should one offer in exchange for the American Dream?

The more the heroes and heroines of this fiction question America as it is, the more they sense personal and national contradictions. Paul Ricoeur observes that "to take part in modern civilization, it is necessary at the same time to take part in scientific, technical, and political rationality, something which very often requires the pure and simple abandonment of a whole cultural past" (27). In Ralph's case, the immigrant hero spouts mantras that parody the Protestant ethic of the way to wealth. He believes the sky's the limit, that anything is possible. Ralph sits down at the table of American culture and transforms himself from immigrant to permanent resident to citizen. Yet becoming an American, as the author hints in this sharply satirical, comic novel, is a complicated business, and never without haunting memories of heritage and homeland.

The hero of *Typical American* contends with the perils of contemporary life and the loss of heritage, but it is his "good fortune" to be the beneficiary of changes in immigration law that enable him to contest for cultural space and a new destiny in the United States. Approximately 25 million people entered the United States between 1880 and 1924, the vast majority from Europe. Although the Chinese had built America's railroads and worked its gold mines in the mid-nineteenth century, the Chinese Exclusion Act of 1882 eliminated this source of labor. Congress extended the act indefinitely in 1902, and it was not until 1943, after China had become an ally of the United States against Japan, that the Chinese Exclusion Act was repealed. We see the intersection of history and fiction in a character like Ralph, the first foreign-born Chinese in more than sixty years eligible for American citizenship. The Nabokovian joyride Ralph takes in a commandeered convertible at one stage in the novel is a metaphor of mobility (similar to Humbert's automotive odyssey in *Lolita*) suggesting the entry or re-entry of Asian Americans into the national landscape.

The predominant narrative voice in such contemporary novels of immigration as *Typical American* and *Lolita*—cool, ironic, distancing—is one major feature distinguishing them from earlier counterparts. For all their narrative sweep and powerful social and political commentary, Upton Sinclair's *The Jungle*, Willa Cather's *My Antonia*, and Henry Roth's *Call It Sleep* depict the grim, naturalistic verities of immigrant history. Largely absent from this earlier fiction is the willingness of authors to subordinate potentially harrowing historic realities to the comic, often fantastic and liberating discords of contemporary experience. Nowhere in the earlier fiction of immigration—or, indeed, in fiction written prior to 1950—is there a figure like Herman Broder, the Jewish immigrant in Isaac Bashevis Singer's *Enemies, A Love Story*. Singer's novel ostensibly is about the impact of the Holocaust on its immigrant survivors, but, because of its absurdist narrative tone, the text also functions as a comic meditation on the convoluted cycles of modern American and global history. Singer (along with other American writers who will be discussed in the next chapter) confronts in *Enemies, A Love Story* the essential dilemma of how an artist deals with an event as horrendous as the Holocaust by creating what Linda Hutcheon (1988) terms "historiographic metafiction." In treating the Holocaust in *Enemies*, Singer reveals the power of fiction to articulate traumatic historical events in a way historical record cannot. Herman, arriving in New York like millions of immigrants before him, is the contradictory element in a joyful and victorious postwar world that imagines American society as an extension of carnivalesque Coney Island. Unable to forget the destructive currents of history, Herman starts out as a ghost writer for a prominent rabbi and ends, after a series of picaresque vicissitudes, as a prototypical invisible immigrant, disappearing into the New World vastness, perhaps "hiding somewhere in an American version of his Polish hayloft" (280). Herman, especially in his antic relationships with women, constructs and reconstructs himself in the course of the novel: from ragged Holocaust survivor to downtrodden worker and serial lover to deranged isolato riding the subway while imagining demonic incarnations of Hitler lurking in the urban shadows. His dislocated odyssey, culminating in his disappearance at the end of the novel, like a voyager seeking a new life elsewhere in Eden, offers a vision of the American future, a death and rebirth that other characters in the novel, notably his all-suffering wife Yadwiga, also seek as a form of transcendence from those cataclysmic historical processes unleashed by the Second World War.

In his curiously postmodernist mutability, Herman reminds readers that to define oneself as an immigrant within existing contemporary American institutions is an active project, a reworking of identity that has no predictable outcome. Immigrants walk a tightrope between their own valued cultural and linguistic heritage and the dream of American mobility and success. For them, America is not "a gigantic mistake" (a word E.L. Doctorow attributes to Sigmund Freud in yet another postmodern novel of immigration, *Ragtime*), nor is it a pristine earthly Paradise, but rather a land where marginalized peoples might seek, as James Clifford states in *The Predicament of Culture* (1988), "specific paths through modernity" (5). Their ability to create and recreate immigrant identities derives precisely from the primal reality that they enter a New World from the Old World or the Third World, rushing toward a future of freedom and psychic reinvention. Toni Morrison suggests that this dream of the New World offers immigrants "a once-in-a-lifetime opportunity not only to be born again but to be born again in new clothes. . . . the new setting would provide new raiments of self" (34). This active reconstruction of immigrant identity transpires in an American landscape that is not only a mythic platform—the Promised Land—but also a concrete national setting.

The sheer exuberance and momentum of immigrant lives and cultures colliding with this American newness creates the carnivalesque pace and atmosphere of so much contemporary fiction. Indeed, it is the diasporic power and carnivalizing energy of postwar immigration that has captured the collective imagination of many of our finest contemporary novelists, who see in today's wandering exiles the apotheosis of what Edward Said in *Culture and Imperialism* (1993) terms the "contrapuntal and often nomadic" nature of American civilization at the end of the twentieth century (xxv). Typical of this wild, diasporic energy is Christine Bell's picaresque, postmodernist novel, *The Pérez Family* (1990), whose disjunctive structure, consisting of sixty-four brief chapters of comic, cartoon-like narrative, captures the contrapuntal rhythms of contemporary immigrants struggling to reconstruct identities and lives in the New World. Bell's bizarre, crisply written novel chronicles the refugee dislocation caused by Fidel Castro's 1980 decision to let loose a flood of working class Cubans, along with political prisoners and mentally disturbed inmates from Cuban institutions, to the United States—the infamous Mariel boatlift to Key West, Florida. Typical of the novel's tragicomic heroes is fifty-seven-year-old Juan Raul Pérez, who had been imprisoned for twenty years for selling advertisements for a pro-Batista newspaper. Juan is condemned to oscillate between the Third World, signified by his authentic but lost Cuban family—his wife and daughter who had escaped to Miami when Batista was overthrown—and the new American world of improvisation and invention suggested by the makeshift family he becomes a part of as a Mariel exile.

Within the carnivalesque arena inhabited by the Mariel refugees (they are housed initially at the Orange Bowl Refugee Camp, a former Junior League stadium), Juan becomes part of a new Pérez family being invented or constructed by Dorita (subsequently Dottie). Dottie is a surreal Mother Courage figure in her forties who latches onto Juan, subsequently adding a senile man named Caesar Pérez as her "father" and a "son" Felipe Pérez, a former Marielito and Miami street punk, to complete her "family," thereby moving up from 134 to 7 in the favored relocation placement listing of the Immigration and Naturalization Service. Dottie is the parodic epitome of the immigrant in quest of the American Dream. "I am not here for political asylum," she declares early in the novel. "I came here for nail polish and rock and roll and for men like John Wayne. I want everything you say I can't have" (19). Dottie ultimately finds her partner in America in Juan, the John Wayne antithesis who for his part rediscovers but ultimately rejects his original wife, Carmela, comfortable but spiritually dissatisfied in her middle-class existence, knowing that Dottie is more attuned to the wild uncertainties and curiously redemptive possibilities of life in America.

Bell's novel is typical of the new cultural diversity found in postwar fiction as large numbers of Third World refugees enter the United States under special laws, especially after 1960. Prior to this period, all of the displaced persons and refugee relief acts—notably those of 1945, 1948, 1953, and 1956—had resulted in a largely European influx of immigrants. With the world depicted in *The Pérez Family*, however, a narrative shift from monoculture to multiculture occurs as literary production and immigration history intersect in the Cold War era. Foreign policy considerations, fueled by an anti-Communism whose most visible and immediate incarnation in the 1960s was Castro's Cuba, led to the entrance of more than one million Cubans into the United States between the time Castro assumed power on January 1, 1959, and 1994. Cuban immigrants—the first of the world's boat people—arrived in successive waves, representing all races, classes, and castes of society, and settling mainly in Miami and the New York metropolitan area. The Mariel group of 1980 was the last of these major waves, but unlike earlier Cuban refugee waves, it was working class in origin. In Bell's novel, Dorita had earned her livelihood in Cuba by handling laundry, by cutting sugar cane, and possibly by prostitution. As Dottie, she possesses both Third World survival skills and a hodgepodge of postmodern cultural styles that serve her well as she searches in America for "a second chance to live the way she dreamed life should be" (20).

New Strangers in Paradise

As postcolonial societies experience political disruptions that send millions of exiles on journeys to America from the nearest and farthest shores of the Third World—the Caribbean, Asia, the Middle East, Africa—the fiction depicting this global turbulence reflects the multicultural diversity characterizing postmodern literature, with novelists and short story writers viewing immigration through the filter of race and ethnicity. In essence, these postcolonial voyagers are on missions of discovery to the New World. New strangers in Paradise, as captivated by El Dorado as Columbus and Ponce de León, they are the colonized counterparts to the earlier European explorers. Bringing their otherness to Flushing and San Francisco and numerous locales in between, these immigrants lead lives governed by old phantasms and contemporary revelations. Often they seem like the displaced natives of ethnographic romance. They are the world's postcolonial subjects or natives in a new national habitat.

The influx of so many Third World immigrants to the United States in the postwar era creates what Gordon Lewis (1978), speaking of the English experience, terms "colonialism in reverse" (304). Large subgroups of immigrants coming to America harbor memories of the battles and contestations of imperialism whether in Cuba, Barbados, the Dominican Republic, India, or Vietnam. They bring with them cultural narratives that must coexist with the mythic national narrative—the traditional story of America as the Promised Land—on an equal basis. At times these dual narratives are complementary and overlapping, as in the fundamental desire of the new immigrants for jobs, freedom, property, mobility, and educational opportunity. At other times, the immigrants' rival histories of colonial subjugation and racial discrimination confront the verities underlying the American national experience. In their new imperial habitats in the United States, those immigrants who were formerly colonized challenge the myths and symbols of the nation. Their heterogeneous otherness and racial difference force an interrogation of American identity and accepted national norms.

By engaging in a critique of dominant culture, such texts as Paule Marshall's *Brown Girl, Brownstones* (1959) reveal a transformation of the grand narrative of America—the evolution of a more ecumenical or transnational myth across borders and geographic terrains. Marshall's novel, whose narrative begins in 1939 and moves through the war years, traces the efforts of Barbadian immigrants to leave behind patterns of colonial exploitation and surmount new forms of racism in the United States. The Boyce family occupying the center of the novel and other "Bajan" families settling in Brooklyn during the Depression are like "a dark sea nudging its way into a white beach and staining the sand" (4). Selina, the young heroine in *Brown Girl, Brownstones*, is in a pervasive condition of cultural uncertainty as she struggles to find a path between her mother's desire to succeed in "The City of the Almighty Dollar" and her father's romantic impulses to transplant a colonial, patriarchal lifestyle in the New World or, even better, to return to the West Indies. Selina learns at an early age that race, class, and gender are the determinants of destiny as the industrious, resilient, acquisitive members of the Barbadian community (who significantly are women) pursue the American Dream even as they reconstruct their African and colonial past, reworking language, folklore, and cultural memory into a usable fabric for survival in "this man country." Contrary to bell hook's assertion that "too many red and black people live in a state of forgetfulness, embracing a colonized mind so that they can better assimilate into a white world" (191), we see in Selina and the women in *Brown Girl, Brownstones* a conscious rather than unconscious effort to contend with America on their own terms. At the end of the novel, Selina has not yet found a way to integrate the dual knowledge of her African-Caribbean heritage and the ways of the New World, but she has learned to emancipate herself from both the constraints of colonial culture and the threats of American cultural conformity. By leaving the New World to rediscover the old, she reveals the hybrid movement of cultural styles across borders that offers essential clues to the formation of immigrant and national identity in the contemporary period.

Immigrant heroines like Selina are a postcolonial prototype: they refuse to be robbed of their native or traditional identities even as they struggle to possess their new American world. Selina's search for a viable culture and identity, tempered by her marginalized condition as the child of African-Caribbean immigrants, creates those contrapuntal lines of development that Said elucidates in *Culture and Imperialism*.

Although Said devotes much of *Culture and Imperialism* to the British experience, his thesis that the novel is the prototypical cultural form of modern Western empires has relevance to the American literary culture. "Curiously," he writes, "so influential has been the discourse insisting on American specialness, altruism, and opportunity that 'imperialism' as a word or ideology has turned up only rarely and recently in accounts of United States cultures, politics, history" (8). Said asserts that American literature must be read contrapuntally against a "specific history of colonization, resistance and finally native nationalism" (51). American identity "is too varied to be a unitary and homogenous thing; indeed the battle within it is between advocates of a unitary identity and those who see the whole as a complex but not reductively unified one" (xxv). It is precisely this alignment of identity across cultural borders and frontiers that promotes the pluralism or cosmopolitanism that is so prominent in the postwar fiction of immigration.

By validating or legitimizing a complex cosmopolitanism, texts like *Brown Girl, Brownstones* assert a new period in literary history in which immigrant protagonists and mainstream America converge on the borders and internal spaces of competing cultures—in what James Clifford terms "a culturally defined place where peoples with different culturally expressed identities meet and deal with each other" (24). Just as the exclusionary immigration policies of the late nineteenth and early twentieth centuries fostered a monoculturalism that nourished by extension a Melting Pot mystique, the post-World War II era produces narratives depicting "inconceivable aliens" (to rework a phrase used by Henry James in *The American Scene*) or hyphenated Americans—"Mexican-Americans," "Chinese-Americans"—whose cultural differences push American national identity from Melting Pot to mosaic or collage. By extending the frontiers of culture and moving away from the social codes of traditional European immigrants, the new immigrants in American fiction offer fresh models of national identity.

The radical cosmopolitanism that typifies postmodernist literature, positing that there is no longer a unified vision of American culture but rather competing domains or centers of culture drawn inward from the borders toward a confrontation with mainstream American culture, finds distinctive expression in the rise of contemporary schools of ethnic fiction and, concomitantly, of new definitions of American literary history. A case in point is the history and literature of Mexican Americans, which is a narrative of frontier people uprooted, displaced, and marginalized by multiple conquests. However, in the contemporary era beginning with World War II, this tale alters or transforms itself into a story revealing a new consciousness or group awareness of the need to promote Mexican-American culture and lifestyle even as the *movimiento* sought economic, social, and political parity—as well as a degree of acculturation—with Anglo civilization. Although *La Raza* or *La Causa* in the broadest context signifies a political movement dedicated to promoting Chicano culture, since its inception in the 1960s the movement has emphasized the importance of literature as a discourse strategy promoting a renaissance in Mexican-American consciousness. Stressing their salad-bowl heritage as Amerindians or *mestizos*, their contrapuntal movement back and forth across the Mexican and United States borders, their history as immigrants, *mojados*, and *braceros* subject to prejudice and exploitation, Chicano novelists and short story writers move beyond marginality by decentering the American literary experience to reveal the contours of a rich culture—one embracing more than 13 million people in the United States today—searching for a common identity.

As with other immigrant groups, World War II was a major force in the evolution of Chicano culture and the broader decentering of traditional literary and cultural authority. The *bracero,* or temporary worker program established during the Second World War, combined with a massive flux of *mojados,* or undocumented aliens throughout the contemporary era, creates a new Mexican-American diaspora. The massive migration of Mexicans to the Southwest and also to the urban barrios in Los Angeles, Chicago, and elsewhere, which during the war years required workers for America's military industries, generated a new consciousness among Chicano writers who singly and collectively began to erect alternate cultural centers in their fiction. The effort of Tomás Rivera, for example, to present in his novel . . . *y no se lo trago la tierra* (*And the Earth Did Not Devour Him,* 1971) a social and political history of Chicano migrant workers in South Texas between 1945 and 1955, is a major decentering effort. By chronicling the lives and documenting the folk pathways of a largely unknown or anonymous migrant and immigrant population in *Tierra,* Rivera creates, in a technically innovative short story "cycle," a spiritual history of *La Raza*—the people—imparting to this community a distinctive cultural voice. Works like *Tierra* do not diminish the "grand narrative" of America but rather enhance and internationalize it, making traditionally marginalized populations visible to the whole society.

Ethnic and racial difference in the immigrant fiction of writers like Rivera, Marshall, Bell, Jen, and Banks alters America's grand narrative by bringing marginalized groups into contact with American culture in such a way that the specific features of these groups become a distinctive aspect of postmodern life. In other words, the subject of contemporary immigration might be culturally specific—an illumination, for example, of the Chicano experience—but it also reveals the central dynamics of American and indeed Western life today, which is marked by the powerful shaping force of shifting, multicultural populations. That the tensions between the "colonists" and the "colonized," between "us" and "others" have shifted from Third World settings to the borders and barrios of the American landscape itself suggests also that the skirmishes of postcolonialism force both immigrants and mainstream Americans to reassess their identities. Assuredly, Third World immigrants in the United States are not colonial subjects in the same way that Native Americans, black slaves, or defeated Mexicans were during earlier phases of American history. The circumstances of life for contemporary immigrants, whether in the larger American society or in the more restricted metropolitan domain, is typified by far greater social and physical mobility and educational participation than their counterparts who remain postcolonial subjects in their own lands. Nevertheless, there is validity in insisting on a Third World perspective in assessing the constituent racial groups—the peoples of color representing *le tiers monde*—that typify immigration to the United States in the postwar era. Robert Blauner in *Racial Oppression in America* (1972) offers a trenchant assessment of the connections between colonized peoples and immigrant minorities in

contemporary America. "The economic, social, and political subordination of third world groups in America is a microcosm of the position of
all people of color in the world order of stratification. . . . Racial domination in the United States is part of a world historical drama in which
culture, economic system, and political power in the white West has spread
throughout virtually the entire globe. . . . The oppression of racial colonies within our national borders cannot be understood without considering worldwide patterns of white European hegemony" (15). As Blauner
suggests, there is a linkage between the Third World without and the
Third World within. If colonialism is viewed as a process involving exploitation, domestication, and management of peoples as well as the
transformation of the nation's mind to Western perspectives, it is clear
that this colonizing experience or structure has always existed on American soil.

Still, it is the national frontiers and interior regions of America
rather than overseas territories, the developed rather than the underdeveloped world, that determines objective realities for postwar immigrants. And it is precisely at the intersection of the experience of
colonialism that many immigrants bring with them to America's shores
and the reality of America's evolving institutions that a certain metamorphosis of immigrant identity occurs. For example, the heroine in
Jamaica Kincaid's novel *Lucy* (1990), is a nineteen-year-old immigrant
from the West Indies who comes to North America to serve as an *au pair*
for a white family. She could be doomed to replicate ages of servitude in
urban America but instead wars against both her ancestral history and
her colonial status within a "perfect" American family that disintegrates
slowly under her cool, ironic, judgmental eye. Lucy jumps from tropical shores into the whirlpool of life in the United States, shedding sexual
and cultural constraints and rejecting her adoptive American family
for the uncertainties of postmodern existence. Near the end of the novel,
she alludes to the precarious but necessary metamorphosis of self caused
by her leap into postmodernity: "I understood that I was inventing
myself. . . . I did not have anything in mind, but when the picture was
complete I would know" (134). Lucy rejects all colonizing structures
and imperatives; her complementary project is to create for herself what
might be termed a postmodernist immigrant style—self-reflexive, indeterminate, emergent, ultimately unassimilable. Lucy's journey to and
through contemporary America is an allegory of immigrant mutation

and transformation as the protagonist explores the shifting boundaries of self in her encounter with the West.

The Floating World

Cynthia Kadohata likens these new immigrant encounters with America to journeys through a "floating world," a striking metaphor used as the title of her first novel. This floating world defines the permeable space within America where nations and cultures meet; it is the liminal ground of the postmodern experience. Immigrant inhabitants of this liminal or marginal landscape sense that they are neither entirely "here" nor "there." Representing disparate races and diverse origins, they challenge the notion of both a common heritage and fixed boundaries so central to the grand narrative of the American state. Instead they wander or float contrapuntally across cultures, nomads who reject established frontiers and boundaries and embrace instead the intermediate space between cultures.

This dissolution of fixed frontiers and a common cultural ethos creates an instability in the notion of the Eurocentric American nation—a nation that until recently was central to American literary history and to canon formation. As the United States absorbs waves of Third World immigrants, the traditional hegemony of a privileging white country also dissolves. The quintessence of the nation thus becomes heterogeneous—an America exemplified by a mix of racial, ethnic, and linguistic styles and cultural traditions. The very myth of the American nation experiences a transformation and regeneration. If the story of America at the end of the twentieth century is of rival, overlapping, and ultimately interdependent cultural histories, it is the myriad configuration of writers who themselves represent diverse origins—Banks, Mukherjee, Marshall, Rivera, Tan—that illuminate the boundary wars of recent immigrants who seek a viable place within the grand narrative.

The liminal space existing between immigrant culture and mainstream American society gives birth to the possibility of reinventing the self that is a central motif in the postwar immigrant literary canon. At the beginning of Mukherjee's *Jasmine*, the young heroine, a native of Hasnapur, falls from a banyan tree while arguing her fate with an astrologer. (Trulong Ann, the Vietnamese heroine of Nina Vida's *Goodbye*,

Saigon, also fights a fortune teller's ominous prophecy that she was born under an unfavorable sign. Like Jasmine, her immigrant struggle in America reveals that the grand narrative has not lost its totalizing power.) Jasmine punches a starshaped wound in her forehead—a clairvoyant third eye—that ultimately permits her to "see" and also to manage her fate as an exile. She moves from India to Europe, to Florida, to Flushing, to Baden, Iowa, and ultimately beyond, reinventing her life in America as a physical and spiritual vagabond, a refugee whose primal dream is simply to keep moving westward across the North American continent. She feeds off what she sees as "the speed of transformation, the fluidity of American character and the American landscape" (138), gaining strength from the very violence and disruptiveness endemic to this postmodern Eden. She does not assimilate into the dominant culture in any traditional sense of the term as much as read this culture intertextually, appropriating from the sheer grotesquerie of her life in America those archetypal energies which, compounded by her Hindu sense of destiny and reincarnation, turn her into an amalgamated immigrant, *both* alien and American, perpetually evolving as she seeks yet another frontier.

Jasmine's odyssey in the New World casts her as a multicultural American Eve—the corollary to R.W.B. Lewis's more Eurocentric American Adam, that frontier hero inhabiting "the area of total possibility" (91). But Brahma, Vishnu, and Shiva—Jasmine's new "trilogy" or trinity—compound mythically her immigrant power. By inhabiting that zone between immigrant culture and the more commonplace American landscape, the new frontier where peoples intermingle, Jasmine is able to discern what is intrinsic and essential about her new Eden. She grafts her role as Shiva to the components of American culture, traversing this marginal zone, immersed in but transcending America's perverse propensity for violence, seeking always a glimmering Eden that seems over the next horizon.

The marginal zone illuminated by the contemporary immigrant experience becomes a trope for this new American Paradise. The very myth of the nation alters from one of shared values to one of values that have yet to be charted in the new Eden. Moreover, these "myth-texts," to borrow a useful phrase from Clifford Geertz (1988:45), reflect the quest for a changing, perhaps transient, elected Paradise. What Geertz terms "the international hodgepodge of postmodern culture" (82) turns the older, absolute contours of the American Eden with its cultural and economic hegemony into a more mysterious, lesser known ethnographic landscape. The Lucys and Jasmines of immigrant fiction today create a *tristes tropiques* on America's own shores, a literature of the once-colonized who, because of race, language, gender, geographic origin, and cultural tradition, redefine the national essence, enriching the myth or the allegory of America as Eden.

If contemporary fiction of immigration is treated as a series of myth-texts, the messages embodied in these texts reveal a quest for an American Dream or New World Eden that is more fluid than fixed. However, the fiction of the dream—of America as a landscape of possibility—fuses ultimately with the polyglot fluidity of the immigrant heroes and heroines of contemporary fiction as they seek to redefine themselves in this country. In fact, the promise of Paradise is valorized in the effort to reinvent the self—to enter a magical realm of transformative possibilities that would not have been possible in the more rigid and hierarchical societies that the immigrant protagonists left. Jasmine might have remained an anonymous figure in a peasant population in India; hurled into the tumultuous and phantasmagoric flux of an advanced industrial nation which for her is an entirely new historical setting, she now claims the right to be whatever she wants to be. For the new immigrants, the American Dream thus becomes the opportunity to retain a bifocal perspective on existence, one that might or might not preserve older cultural habits and beliefs but which assuredly permits a reexamination of identity, an exploration of possibilities in the New Eden.

By insisting on the interpretative space permitted by a bifocal perspective, the new immigrant—this product of postwar and postcolonial historical shifts—provokes a reconstruction of American reality. Up to World War II, restrictive immigration policies tended to rigidly define the American experience, circumscribing this reality with Eurocentric features. As already suggested, the second half of the century reveals a transnational reordering of American reality that is a reflection of the postwar, postcolonial territorial reorganization of the globe. No longer are Third World peoples or people of color peripheral to the American experience but rather the source of national promise. As Homi Bhabha (1990) observes: "Once the liminality of nation-space is established, and its 'difference' is turned from the boundary 'outside' to the finitude 'within,' the threat of cultural difference is no longer a problem of 'other' people.

It becomes a question of the otherness of the people-as-one. . . . The great contribution of Foucault's last published work is to suggest that people emerge in the modern state as a perpetual movement of the 'marginal integration of individuals'" (301).

In the wake of the Second World War, the American nation begins to assume a new shape as families, peoples, and national groups from around the globe come to America in search of opportunity. The very essence of postmodernism is this multicultural, polyglot internationalization of civic life, especially in the United States. In the postmodern era, there is a real and metaphorical dissolution of borders and a refiguring of culture under the onslaught of air transport, satellite communication, labor migration, high-tech transnational banking, and international marketing—the entire juggernaut of interdependent processes that make all national borders permeable. America's postwar immigrants are thus heterogeneous voyagers—postmodern explorers and entrepreneurs who because of their multiple differences redefine the United States as a collective frontier for private and public transformation.

Persistently in the postwar era, the way in which American novelists and short story writers structure their immigration narratives reflects the duality inherent in the contemporary American experience. The new immigrant experience, steeped in alterity, cultural independence, and multivocal musings on identity, clashes with the univocal, assimilative, universalizing tendencies of the traditional national experience. The textual dynamics inspired by simultaneously diverging and converging ethno-linguistic forces provokes a radical transformation of national experience arising "from the disparity in cultural histories and needs of the heterogeneous population of this country" (Lauter 29). Bharati Mukherjee explains this unique transformation: "Society forces me to deal with my complexion, race, and religion. I am always being 'otherized' and that's why my battle is to convince the dominant culture that we're here to stay. The culture has got to think of itself as having melded and become a third thing" (Baker 16). This "third thing" is the kaleidoscopic new America, a pluralistic Promised Land of growing racial and cultural diversity that embraces multiplicity, flux, and constant reinvention as the essence of the nation.

At no time in American history has the dominant culture had to contend with the powerful centrifugal impulses that have been provoked by those forces of global and largely Third World immigration groups arguing for a certain linguistic-cultural independence, which in turn provoke, in Homi Bhabha's words, "counter-narratives of the nation" that "continually evoke and erase its totalizing boundaries" (300). These new immigrants share a fundamental national loyalty to the principles of political, economic, and religious freedom; they benefit immediately from the inalienable-rights ethos embedded in the American national myth and codified by constitutional law. Their arrival on America's shores reminds us of those longstanding historical conflicts that have characterized all waves of immigration to the United States. Such conflicts, as John Higham argues most persuasively in *Strangers in the Land: Patterns of American Nativism 1860–1925*, have tended to create an evolutionary enrichening and modification of the national experience. Today, however, immigration precipitates not so much national modification as national transformation. Third World immigration, predominantly Hispanic and Asian, has created bilingual societies in many of America's cities, in large parts of the Southwest, and in Florida and California. With declining industrial bases, decrepit schools, and decaying infrastructures, American cities in particular no longer serve as the urban arenas for assimilation that characterize earlier epochs of immigration history. Similarly, entire economic sectors in rural areas—as exemplified in fiction by the poultry farms populated by Japanese and depicted so graphically by Cynthia Kadohata in *The Floating World*—have become exclusively Asian or Hispanic. In short, those structural forces that once nourished assimilation and the cultivation of the Melting Pot mystique have weakened. Moreover, the pace of postmodern change in transportation, telecommunication, and media transmission enable the new immigrant groups to sustain and replenish their linguistic and cultural identities, even as they establish their discrete place in a transmuted national landscape where the old cultural or metropolitan center no longer holds.

Nowhere is the ethno-linguistic independence of the new immigrant in American fiction more apparent than in those texts that incorporate words, locutions, and syntactic structures from the native language. This deliberate narrative strategy, seen in novels of immigration as diverse as Rudolfo Anaya's *Bless Me, Ultima*, Isaac Bashevis Singer's *Enemies, A Love Story*, Paule Marshall's *Brown Girl, Brownstones*, and Amy Tan's *The Joy Luck Club*, creates impediments and challenges for mainstream readers approaching these texts, for such readers now find themselves in a referential field that is multicultural and linguistically bipolar; such readers, experiencing a new textual dynamics, have to decipher this field, pierce the impenetrability of the Other's culture, listen carefully to the contestatory voices, and ultimately accept this otherness as an essential component of the kaleidoscopic nation. When, for example, Auntie Ying Ying St. Clair in *The Joy Luck Club* accuses her daughter of having no "chuming" or internal wisdom, Amy Tan invites monolingual American readers to be textual ethnographers contending with—and hopefully coming to understand—the uniqueness of the Other's domain. Put differently, mainstream readers must move to the linguistic and cultural margins or borders delineated by such texts, into precisely that arena of conflicts and crosscurrents within the immigrant culture itself. The "aunties" in *The Joy Luck Club* who prefer Chinese, the mothers in *Brown Girl, Brownstones* who speak Creole, the older people in *Bless Me, Ultima* who only speak Spanish, reaffirm the integrity of their marginalized world, while the children, typically bilingual and bicultural, must traverse the margins of immigrant and mainstream culture, mediating their passage across transnational domains. Indeed, the motif of generational conflict, often embedded in bilingual and bicultural tensions, serves as a collective subtext in this fiction as today's immigrants and their children interrogate their fate.

Contemporary American fiction's canonical encounter with the immigrant demonstrates the emancipatory elements inherent in a nation where notions of Eurocentric hegemony yield progressively to a tacit acceptance of cultural difference. Because of postwar patterns of immigration, the United States today is a polyglot Paradise that seems light years removed from the vision of Israel Zangwill, who in his four-act melodrama, *The Melting Pot* (1908), popularized the myth of a Eurocentric Eden: "America is God's Crucible, the great Melting-Pot where all the races of Europe are melting and re-forming. . . . Germans and Frenchmen, Irishmen and Englishmen, Jews and Russians—into the Crucible with you all! God is making the American!" The Immigration Act of 1924, which made the Third World "ineligible for citizenship," preserved this Melting Pot mystique until World War II, when immigrant history and immigrant narratology, as we have seen, began to forge an alternative mythology of a metropolitan nation of globally overlapping cultural subjectivities.

The discourse and text-building strategies of today's novelists and short story writers focus on the immigrant as the symbol of America's radically altered demographic destiny. Today the Golden Door is open to the entire world. The Immigration and Nationality Act of 1965, which ended the blatantly racist national-origins quota system codified in the 1924 law, reconstituted Eden for immigrants coming from developing countries in Asia, Africa, Latin America, and the Caribbean. Despite the parodic proclivities of its writers, the United States today is still the embodiment of the American Dream for the world's immigrants. Moreover, the dream has assumed a striking planetary consciousness. As Miss Noi, a former Saigon bargirl performing on Bourbon Street in Robert Olen Butler's extraordinary story, "Fairy Tale," part of his short fiction cycle about Vietnamese immigrants, *A Good Scent from a Strange Mountain* (1992), observes, "I like the way fairy tales start in America" (45). Once upon a time, the Founding Fathers came to America from Europe for religious freedom, political self-determination, economic opportunity. Today, the world's immigrants, mothers and fathers alike, recreate this primal tale. In turn, America's writers explore those pathways through which their contemporary immigrant protagonists discover and nurture a new Garden of Eden— an even more pristine Paradise—the world's first universal nation.

2

Haunted by the Holocaust: Displaced Persons and the American Dream

Where are the Nazis? What kind of a world is this without Nazis?
A backward country, this America.
—Isaac Bashevis Singer, *Enemies, A Love Story*

Holocaust survivors in postwar American fiction are displaced persons estranged from all national narratives. Like the protagonist in Saul Bellow's *Mr. Sammler's Planet,* they meditate on the relationship between the Earth, the Moon, and Planet Auschwitz. And if Auschwitz, as Theodor Adorno suggests, is the central event of our age, this primal catastrophe, which ushers in the postwar era, separates and estranges the survivors of the Holocaust from the myths of the American nation. The uprooted souls depicted in the fiction of Bellow, Singer, Styron, Malamud and other contemporary American writers are haunted by the Holocaust, unable to embrace the "cheerful countenance," as Tuveson observes in *Redeemer Nation,* that serves as "a sign of one's recognition as a citizen of the country" (31). They lead erased lives in America, unwilling to assimilate or find faith either in their new adoptive nation or in older systems of belief. With their prewar civilization all but obliterated, Holocaust survivors resist the paradisaical inscriptions of the American Dream. For these displaced persons, the grand narrative of America simply collapses when confronted with the utter destruction of absolutes caused by the Nazi terror.

27

Prior to World War II, the fiction of immigration made sense of events—even those events that were harrowing or destructive for those generations who departed the Old World for the New. However, post-Holocaust novelists had to make room for the inexplicable and invent strategies—typically comic or grotesque—to represent events that seemingly defied rational explanation. Bellow's *Mr. Sammler's Planet*, Isaac Bashevis Singer's *Enemies, A Love Story*, William Styron's *Sophie's Choice*, and other novels and stories depicting immigrant survivors of the Holocaust tend to interrogate the allegorical power of the American experience—the nation's ability to transform or salvage lives shattered by the Nazi era. Old, introspective Sammler; the compulsively concupiscent Herman; the haunted, guilt-ridden Sophie: these survivors are figures in a postwar American landscape who continue to walk on the edge of historical catastrophe. As they conduct their daily lives in postwar America, they carry with them a historical calendar that is adjusted to Auschwitz and the Nazi horror. Their exile in America offers provisional solace but rarely salvation. Reliving the horrors and absurdities of history, they seem to be hiding from themselves in the Promised Land, the prisoners of Holocaust memories. Like Reuven Tamiroff, the Holocaust survivor in Elie Wiesel's *The Fifth Son* (1985), they seek anonymity in America, usually in New York, where the "city is made to order for misanthropes" (59). Tamiroff feels he is part of "an extinct race, an extinct species" (23). Postwar America suits such an individual, for the nation's emerging culture of homogeneity permits Holocaust survivors, as the protagonist of Wiesel's novel attests, "to blend with the masses" (194).

Holocaust Survivors

The immigrant survivors of the Holocaust journey to an America that had denied special refugee status to Europeans during most of the Roosevelt era, but which by the end of World War II had started to alter its official attitude toward these displaced persons. As Europe in 1944 and 1945 lay prostrate beneath the crush of converging Allied armies and the collapse of the Reich, millions of displaced persons—a continental epic of wartime migration unmatched in previous history—moved back and forth across the blighted landscape. This apocalyptic procession of refugees, numbering more than ten million people, included displaced Germans; Russian prisoners of war; forced laborers; Lithuanians, Latvians, and Estonians; and countless other migrants. They were joined by 60,000 Jewish survivors of the concentration camps and an additional 200,000 Jews who had endured in hiding to survive Hitler's Final Solution.

Between 1945 and 1950, almost 350,000 displaced persons arrived in the United States, the beneficiaries of a mixed and contradictory national welcome that had been made possible by the efforts of the American Jewish community as well as a growing anti-Communism in the postwar political realm that recognized the value of accepting refugees from Eastern Europe. In 1946, American Jewish groups, concerned about the plight of Holocaust survivors in Europe, joined with Catholic and Protestant church, business, labor, and educational leaders in a grassroots campaign designed to pressure a reactionary, strongly anti-Semitic Congress to change immigration law in order to admit displaced persons. The efforts of these groups to alter the prevailing pattern of restrictive immigration policy that had persisted throughout the late nineteenth and twentieth centuries occurred during a period when anti-Semitism, as David Wyman, Leonard Dinnerstein, and other scholars have documented, was at high tide. The implications of this American anti-Semitism for European Jewry were disastrous. As David Wyman indicates, "the Nazis wished to be rid of the Jews, but until 1941 this end was to be accomplished by emigration, not extermination. The shift to extermination came only after the emigration method had failed, a failure in large part due to the lack of countries open to refugees" (35). The racist, anti-Semitic, generally xenophobic platform of the America First Committee, formed in 1940; the anti-Semitic speeches of Charles Lindbergh; the virulent anti-Semitism of America's "radio priest" Father Coughlin; the powerful unwillingness of such senators as Nye, Bilbo, and Wheeler to consider the plight of European Jewry: all indicate that the United States during the war years was an intolerant nation whose attitudes and policies prevented it from acting forcefully to prevent the Holocaust. Even after news of the concentration camps began to filter into the national consciousness, there was little public interest in opening the country's doors to Jewish refugees. Public opinion polls of American students and workers consistently revealed a pattern of antipathy to Jews that was second only to intolerance toward American blacks. As late as 1946, a survey conducted by the American Institute of Public Opinion revealed that a scant five percent of Americans favored increased Jewish immigration, while a majority of the public preferred to reduce or eliminate immigration completely (Bouscaren 7). It was only when President Roosevelt, in the last year of his life, was presented with incontrovertible evidence by his long-time friend, Secretary of the Treasury Henry Morgenthau Jr., of American indifference to the Holocaust that he established the War Refugee Board to save what was left of European Jewry—in the words of his innocuous directive, "to develop positive new programs to aid the victims of Nazism" while pressing the Allies and neutrals to take forceful diplomatic action in their behalf.

After Roosevelt's death in 1945, it fell to President Truman to develop a displaced persons policy and, in the process, create from evolving political and historical realities the context for new literary myths about immigration. Under pressure from a coalition of American Jewish groups concerned about the deplorable conditions for death camp survivors in European DP camps, Truman in July, 1945, dispatched Earl Harrison, a former Commissioner of Immigration, to "inquire into the condition and needs of displaced persons in Germany who may be stateless or non-repatriable, particularly Jews" (Loesser 4). Moved by Harrison's stark depiction of life in the camps and his powerful arguments to open immigration to the persecuted survivors of the Holocaust, Truman on December 22, 1945, issued a directive to provide visas for 39,000 displaced persons, to be "distributed fairly among persons of all faiths, creeds and nationalities" in central and Eastern Europe and the Balkans. This directive fell short of European realities, for by 1946 almost 200,000 Jews seeking protection from a renewed outbreak of anti-Semitism had poured into the American zone in Germany. Spurred by the well-orchestrated campaign of the Citizens' Committee on Displaced Persons, a national umbrella group whose leadership consisted of such board members as Eleanor Roosevelt, Herbert Lehman, and Fiorello LaGuardia, the refugee issue was forced on the conservative 80th Congress that convened in 1946 with control of both the House and Senate in Republican hands. Between 1946 and 1948, numerous anti-Semitic restrictions were added to the final Displaced Persons Act that emerged from this Congress. As Dinnerstein (1982) summarizes:

> There was a double irony in the 1948 DP Act. Not only did it
> discriminate against Jews but it undercut the advantages that

had accrued to them under the provisions of the Truman
Directive. Between May 1946, when the first boatload of refugees to be given preference under the President's order arrived, until June 29, 1948, Jews constituted about two-thirds
of the 41,379 people admitted under the program. On July
1, 1948, when the new law went into effect, 23,000 European
DPs (mostly Jews) who had received preliminary approval
to enter the United States had their priorities wiped out because the act had specifically repealed the Truman Directive. (181)

Only in 1950 was a revised bill eliminating the 1948 restrictions that
discriminated against East European Jews passed by Congress, thereby
opening to European Jewry more of the 341,000 slots for displaced persons authorized to enter the United States.

For postwar American writers, the task of representing the Holocaust through its displaced immigrant survivors forced them to deal with
a series of national and international forces surrounding this apocalyptic moment in history, including the forces of displacement inherent in
the lives of the survivors. The concentration camp and slave camp survivors of World War II, who in the words of Aharon Appelfeld had been
reduced by the Nazi murderers to "anonymity, a number, a creature with
no face" (2), brought the horrors of the Holocaust with them in their
postwar passage to the United States. Trying to get some sort of grip on
postwar experience in America, they find themselves physically removed
from the threat of cataclysm but still marked by the wounds of the Holocaust experience. In American fiction, the refugees and concentration
camp survivors adopt numerous disguises—monasticism, assimilation,
self-punishment, debauchery, suppression of memory—to cover these
wounds, but they are brought back inevitably to the inferno still raging
in the self. Their dark night of the soul clashes with postwar American
euphoria, forcing the juxtaposition of buoyant national experience against
apocalyptic experience that in turn produces cultural representations of
a new epoch that is, as Singer suggests by the title of a posthumous novel,
meshugah—crazy, senseless, insane. Their own status as refugees or displaced persons—emblematic DPs—signifies the acute dissonance and
disjunction central to their lives as their history competes with the triumphant narrative of their adoptive nation.

Three Allegories

Three representative short stories—Bernard Malamud's "The German Refugee," Flannery O'Connor's "The Displaced Person," and Philip Roth's "Eli, the Fanatic"—capture the complex national ironies and metaphysical dissonances that drive the narratives of departures and arrivals stemming from the Nazi era. These stories measure the texture of American life as well as those special spiritual or allegorical claims made by the American national project against the more immediate allegory of the Holocaust. The allegorical figures at the center of the stories by Malamud, O'Connor, and Roth are the penultimate DPs ushering in the postmodern era: they remind America and its grand narrative of a specific legacy of evil, of other broken covenants, and of the radical rupture of history and tradition. How can immigrant survivors in the wake of Kristallnacht and the camps start a new life in America? How can the American Dream and other privileging myths be the same for them as it was for previous generations of immigrants?

Bernard Malamud, who largely ignored the Nazi era in his fiction and whose sad, burdened ghetto immigrants more typically remind readers of an earlier tradition of Jewish immigrant fiction, acknowledges in "The German Refugee" the undeniable psychic and cultural deracination caused by Hitler and the impending Nazi genocide. Malamud's story, which is the last selection in his collection *Idiots First* (1963), implies an intrinsic connection between the historical catastrophe caused by the rise of Hitler and the dislocations sensed by immigrants escaping the Nazi terror on the eve of World War II. Told from the retrospective first-person position of a narrator who at the time of events in 1939 was a twenty-year-old college senior offering tutoring lessons to the burgeoning refugee community in New York City, "The German Refugee" operates as a gloss on Jean-Francois Lyotard's assertion that the postmodern project 'GonzoToGo, Inc. "presents the fact that the unrepresentable exists" (78). As Sidra Ezrahi observes in her study of the Holocaust in literature, "in fiction the realist's or naturalist's respect for details which comprise the fabric of historical processes is defeated by facts which can hardly be integrated into any preexistent system of ethics or aesthetics" (3). That Malamud should select an aesthetics of black humor to depict the impact of the Nazi terror on the American experience typifies the standard approach of American writers to this literary challenge of representing the Holocaust. It is the task of the narrator, Martin Goldberg, to teach a famous Berlin critic and journalist, Oskar Gassner, a sufficient amount of English so that he can lecture on "The Literature of the Weimar Republic" at New York's Institute for Public Studies. Martin, who becomes Gassner's guide and mentor during the summer of 1939, attempts to create a comprehensible American reality, embracing certain Whitmanian myths, for his German refugee: "Here I was palpitating to get going, and across the ocean Adolph Hitler, in black boots and square mustache, was tearing up and spitting out all the flowers" (195). In the course of this ambitious seven-part story, both the narrator and the refugee succumb to the mounting and totalizing catastrophe in Europe whose very magnitude in terms of terror prevents the baffled refugee from reinventing himself on American soil.

As with O'Connor's Displaced Person, Malamud's German refugee is both a realized character and an allegorical figure suggesting the presence of the Other in America during the World War II era. Malamud recreates the New York summer of 1939 in the colors of a peaceful and orderly urban pastoral—of days capped by the "tail end of sunsets over the Palisades (203)"—that is juxtaposed against the impending European conflagration. The New York of Walt Whitman, America's bucolic bard, who functions as a mythic national presence in the story, also serves to elevate the narrative allegorically above the more prosaic march of history chronicling the mobilization for war, the Soviet-Nazi nonaggression pact, and the invasion of Poland that serves as the backdrop for the tale. Indeed, the narrator attempts to reinvent his German refugee in the mold of Walt Whitman, for his student curses German literature and language, which he can no longer function in or write about. But it is Oskar who recognizes the unreconcilable disparity between Whitman's transcendental humanity—the *Brudermensch* that intrigued German poets—and the incompatible "German earth."

Oskar temporarily overcomes his creative and spiritual block to write and deliver his lecture in English in October of 1939, incorporating Whitman's lines from *Leaves of Grass* into his presentation.

> And I know the spirit of God is the brother of my own,
> And that all the men ever born are also my brothers,
> and the women my sisters and lovers,
> And that the kelson of creation is love. (211)

As the German refugee speaks, Warsaw has fallen, and two days after his lecture, Oscar receives notification that the wife and child he had left behind had been transported from Germany to the border of Poland by Hitler's Brown Shirts: "There, it is rumored, she is shot in the head and topples into an open tank ditch, with the naked Jewish men, their wives and children, some Polish soldiers, and a handful of gypsies" (212). Faced with this reality, Oskar commits suicide—by gassing himself in his apartment. Whitman's transcendental refrains—so central to the myth of America as the Promised Land and as the realm of democratic vistas—exist contrapuntally with the personal tragedy of the German refugee and the collective tragedy of the impending Holocaust.

Whereas the Holocaust functions in "The German Refugee" as an impending prophecy of doom, it is the paradigm controlling events in Flannery O'Connor's "The Displaced Person," the last story in her classic collection, *A Good Man Is Hard to Find* (1955). O'Connor's complex, richly allegorical three-part story reflects in its title those radically altered post-Holocaust realities the United States experienced in the era after World War II. The author found the locus of this story in contemporary events and also in the situation on her family's farm in Milledgeville, Georgia, where her mother had taken in a Polish refugee family. In the story, the Guizacs—the DPs—are immigrant survivors brought to the Georgia farm of Mrs. McIntyre by a charitable priest, Father Flynn. The Guizacs enter a rural community consisting of the white tenant farmers, the Shortleys, and two black laborers, Astor and Sulk; collectively they form a microcosm of the changing postwar world as well as a vision of a postmodern paradise, for Mrs. McIntyre in her vanity believes that the industrious Mr. Guizac (who throughout the story is likened to Christ) will be her savior.

Although narrative perspectives in O'Connor's remarkable story are filtered through the minds of Mrs. McIntyre and Mrs. Shortley, it is the Displaced Person who occupies the allegorical center of the tale, for the author essentially is concerned with the loss of grace and the breaking of spiritual covenants in the contemporary world. Guizac, the refugee who in the course of the story becomes a sacrificial Christ figure, is the embodiment of the horrors unleashed on humanity by the Nazi era. Images of the grotesque world of the Nazi concentration camps permeate the text, as in Mrs. Shortley's vision of this historical and spiritual watershed. "Mrs. Shortley recalled a newsreel she had seen once of a small room piled high with bodies of dead naked people all in a heap, their arms and legs tangled together, a head thrust in here, a head there, a foot, a knee, a part that should have been covered up sticking out, a hand raised clutching nothing" (200). Old Father Flynn, somewhat forgetful but possessing nevertheless a refined sense of the fallen condition of humanity, tries to convince Mrs. McIntyre of the imminence of Purgatory, but she disdains religious arguments. "Think of the thousands of them," Father Flynn intones, "think of the ovens and the boxcars and the camps and the sick children and Christ Our Lord" (245). But Mrs. McIntyre, always practical, retorts that there are no ovens or camps in America. The courtly, reserved Displaced Person, at first efficient and industrious and seen by Mrs. McIntyre as her "salvation," gradually becomes a prophetic force of displacement in her Arcadia, for he wants to rescue a young female cousin who is languishing in a European refugee camp by marrying her to one of the black farmhands. Viewed suddenly as a threat—the Other or Alien in this pastoral landscape—Guizac is renounced and abandoned by the farm's inhabitants, who watch conspiratorially as he is crushed beneath the wheels of a runaway tractor.

Every major story by Flannery O'Connor is a revelation, and with "The Displaced Person" she illuminates the universality of displacement in a grotesque, post-Holocaust world. Following the deaths of Mrs. Shortley (whose paroxysms during a fatal stroke mimic her memories of the victims in the newsreel) and Guizac, and the departures of Mr. Shortley, Astor, and Sulk, Mrs. McIntyre, debilitated by a stroke and dependent, also is seen as a displaced person bereft of spiritual vision. O'Connor, in her introduction to A Memoir of Mary Ann, observes that in the absence of faith or even tenderness (which might substitute for faith), "the logical outcome is terror. It ends in forced-labor camps and in the fumes of the gas chamber" (227). She reconstructs the Holocaust as a spiritual rupture and suggests that the failure of Americans to save and nurture its survivors perpetuates a legacy of evil tantamount to the broken covenant that ended the biblical promise of paradise.

The concept of a broken covenant—and the implications for postwar America—is also central to Roth's "Eli, the Fanatic," which is the last story in his collection Goodbye, Columbus (1959). Whereas the action of Malamud's story unfolds in an urban setting and O'Connor's in a rural one, Roth's story takes place in the suburbs, that emerging demographic phenomenon characterizing life in postwar America. The story also investigates the ambivalent nature of assimilation in postwar American life, as the suburban Jews in "Eli, the Fanatic" attempt to both escape from the urban ghettoes of their parents and suppress if not renounce their specifically Jewish identities.

"Eli, the Fanatic" is a seriocomic satire on Jewish-American assimilation into the middle class suburbs, but also another allegory of guilt and provisional redemption in postwar America. John Higham, in *Send These to Me: Immigrants in Urban America* (1984), traces the Jewish acculturation process and the attendant population shift as a postwar generation moved to the suburbs: "While American culture became more receptive to Jews, they in turn were becoming more fully Americanized. By the 1950s about three quarters of American Jews were native born, and most of these were third-generation Americans. . . . The center of gravity in postwar Jewish life shifted to the suburbs, where settlement was frequently more dispersed than it had been in the cities. The suburban Jews made and spent their money in much the same way as their gentile neighbors" (174). The Jews depicted by Roth in "Eli, the Fanatic" are the quintessential middle class secularists of America's emerging postwar consumer society. They are fully integrated into the mass culture of their suburban paradise, Woodenton ("Wooden Town"), a bucolic town outside New York City that seems light-years from urban realities. Having peacefully suppressed their Jewish identities, they also believe themselves to be light years removed from the Holocaust. Consequently, they experience cultural shock when a yeshiva composed of a small group of Holocaust survivors occupies an old house on a peaceful knoll above the town. (Roth's sly inversion of the Puritan concept of America as a "city on a hill" is in keeping with the satiric thrust of the story.) Eli Peck, an attorney, is designated by his peers—Ted Heller, Artie Berg, and Harry Shaw—to evict the displaced persons in their midst for violation of local zoning laws. They do not want to be reminded of their ethnic and religious origins, gladly renouncing Diaspora memory for a placid existence in their middle-class Promised Land.

> "A Yeshivah!" Artie Berg had said. "Eli, in Woodenton, a Yeshivah! If I want to live in Brownsville, Eli, I'll live in Brownsville."
> "Eli," Harry Shaw speaking now, "the old Paddington place. Old man Paddington'll roll over in his grave. Eli, when

I left the city, Eli, I didn't plan the city should come to me."
(269)

Disoriented by the apocalyptic vision of hundreds of little yeshiva boys
and "goddam fanatics" out of the twelfth century ruining their "modern
community," Peck and his crusaders conspire to eliminate the aliens in
their midst. Yet as Roth makes clear in his suburban satire, it is only the
assimilated Jews who are terrified of Leo Tzuref, the director of the yeshiva, and his children; the gentiles in the community pay them scarce
attention, even the bearded, black-frocked young man with his black
Talmudic hat who wanders through the town on various errands.

In their denial of Tzuref and his "tribe," the assimilated community
of Jews in Woodenton try to deny not only their Jewish identity but also
the Holocaust. Nevertheless, the Holocaust hovers over the postwar landscape, for it is the survivors from their vantage point on the hill, engaged
now in their own errand in the wilderness, who crystallize for Eli that
old diasporal history, the old culture, the old ways, the old spirituality
that he must recapture if he is to save himself. Eli, who has a history of
nervous breakdowns, has so ceased to be Jewish that he is afflicted with a
primal angst. Gradually, however, he is led by Tzuref (whose name echoes both the Yiddish word for "trouble," *tsuris*, and the Hebrew word for
"participation" or "joining," *tsaref*) and his associate, the mysterious young
stranger in black, to a religious understanding of the "law" that transcends his secular role as an attorney. Tzuref and his wards are "tired" (a
decidedly understated word connoting their condition as Holocaust survivors) and want to call Woodenton, with its golden stores along Coach
House Road, its suburban trees and lawns, their home. The Talmudic
scholar gradually and patiently converts Eli from secular conspirator to
a fanatic, a lawyer for the defense of persecuted Jewry. In a letter to Tzuref,
Eli acknowledges for the first time their European history and the vic-
timization and "persecution of the Jewish people." Subsequently, in a
bizarre role reversal, Eli donates his best suit to the "greenie" and in turn
dons the young Hassidim's black outfit, even the ritual undergarment.
Parading through town in his new raiment and into the hospital, where
his wife gives birth to his son, Eli is reborn as a "fanatic." In the end, an
attendant calling him "rabbi" administers an injection: "The drug calmed
his soul, but did not touch it down where the blackness had reached"
(313).

By renouncing personal and collective assimilation into a vast post-war Melting Pot, Eli reverts to a more spiritual state. Eli becomes Elijah, which in Hebrew means "Lord." He learns about the "blackness" of the Holocaust and the blackness of his dress, which links him with Tzuref and his children. Instead of invoking Crevecoeur's vision of America as an arena where "individuals of all nations are melded into a new race of men," Roth posits in "Eli, the Fanatic" a competing vision that is more millennial and resonant with Old Testament themes. Eli is only partially sedated at the end of the story: the essential core of his being acknowledges the Holocaust and recognizes orthodox Judaism, so much at odds with the immigrant dream of assimilation and the suburban dream of conformity. Even with his new round of impending "therapy" (Roth pokes fun at the postwar generation's embrace of Freudian remedies for the troubled American spirit), Eli will pass on to his son a knowledge of Old World horrors and Talmudic verities.

The Cannibal Galaxy

The America that Holocaust survivors like Guizac and Tzuref journey to is not so much an Edenic landscape as a purgatory where the reality of their European hell—in Lawrence Langer's apt phrase that "bizarre limbo of atrocity"—competes with the elusive promise of their new paradise. Whether in Brooklyn or Manhattan, Georgia or the Catskills, Middle America or Miami Beach, these immigrant survivors harbor memories of destruction in even the most benign American settings. Essentially the bizarre limbo of the Nazi catastrophe destroyed for the immigrant survivors any illusion of civilization. Jean-Paul Sartre in *What Is Literature?* (1949) was one of the first intellectuals to trace the historical rupture caused by the Holocaust. In Sartre's words, the West was suffering from a collective historical and ethical amnesia: "the notion of Evil . . . had been abandoned" (211). In the aftermath of Dachau and Auschwitz, the world learns again "Evil is not an appearance." The evil of the Holocaust produced a rift in civilization as well as a more specific rupture in European Jewish history and Yiddishkeit culture. For the immigrant survivors of this inexplicable evil, even the myths of American civilization function ambiguously, for their sense of evil prevents them from embracing the United States as a reconstructed paradise. At best, postwar

America offers immigrant survivors a banal limbo of its own, a bizarre purgatory of dislocations and distortions. For example, the vision of America nurtured by Joseph Brill, the protagonist in Cynthia Ozick's *The Cannibal Galaxy* (1983), is scarcely paradisaical. Brill, a French Jew who survived the war by hiding in a church basement and then in a hayloft, is the principal of a private school in the Midwest. He views the United States as a land of mediocrity: "He saw himself in the middle of an ashen America, heading a school of middling reputation . . . beleaguered by middling parents and their middling offspring. All of this was a surprise in his late middle age, but a surprise of only middling size. He was used to consorting with the Middle" (5–6). Brill's ontological journey from the Old World to Middle America—to him the middling excrescence of the new—is cast by Ozick in mock-heroic terms. Imagining himself destined by the sheer fact of his having survived the liquidation of French Jews to create an academic oasis that would link the best of the intellectual traditions of Europe and Jerusalem, Brill in his vanity and obtuseness becomes a minor academic dictator trying to fashion a "Sorbonne grown out of an exiled Eden" (36).

Creating a tenuous and banal existence on the rocky shores of the Great Lakes, Brill ironically finds that he still resides in an apartment fashioned over a renovated gymnasium that is labeled the Hayloft by the wealthy American benefactress who subsidizes his school. Even the stolid brick buildings, lined up symmetrically on the campus like boxcars, remind him of the trains that took many of his family members from Paris to Poland and their destruction: "So innocently American was the architect of the new wing that he had not dreamed, Joseph Brill was certain, of boxcars, but boxcars rolling eastward had taken away Joseph Brill's mother, father, his brothers Gabriel and Loup, his little sisters Michelle and Louise … his baby sister Ruth, and released their souls into an ashen field" (17). The ashen world of Brill's Middle American existence offers the protagonist his own field of fatuous pedagogical and philosophical dreams, but his "secret cynicism" prevents him from perceiving the talents of a quiet girl enrolled at the school by her famous mother, a philosophical linguist, whose brilliance and integrity remind Brill over the years of his own worthlessness. Preoccupied with the breakdown of civilization and envisioning himself trapped in a cannibal galaxy, a "megalosaurian colony of primordial gases that devours smaller brother galaxies" (69), Brill in later age takes an American wife, rears a family, and retires to middle class existence in Florida. His life reads like a parody of the American Dream he had tried so assiduously to avoid, for he understands all too well the uncommon middleness of his sojourn in America.

Another Ozick character unwilling to accept the notion of America as Eden is the concentration camp survivor Rosa Lublin in the two-part novella *The Shawl* (1980). Rosa, who in the brief first section titled "The Shawl" had witnessed her daughter thrown against an electrified barbed wire fence by a concentration camp guard during World War II, finds herself thirty years later in the extended section "Rosa" "a madwoman and scavenger" (13) in a Miami Beach environment seemingly populated by grotesque humanity. Tortured by her own "cannibal dreams" (15) and exiled earlier from New York City after having destroyed her antique shop, Rosa incarcerates herself in a seedy hotel room, writing letters to her long-dead daughter, treasuring her daughter's shawl like a talisman, and attempting to remain detached from the world of the living. In one scene, disoriented on the beach of an opulent Miami hotel, she finds her exit blocked by barbed wire fencing that reminds her of her daughter's European fate. The hotel manager, a Jew, is not concerned by her horrifying memories of incarceration and loss triggered by the barbed wire, thereby confirming Rosa's skepticism about the Promised Land. As she observes cynically of her niece Stella, another Holocaust survivor, "Stella Columbus! She thinks there's such a thing as the New World" (42). From her Edenic prewar existence, Rosa believes that she has "fallen" into an America that she equates with Sodom and Gomorrah: "Blue stripes, barbed wire, men embracing men . . . whatever was dangerous and repugnant they made prevalent, frivolous" (53). Only at the end of the novella, after having been pursued throughout the narrative by a bumptious, irrepressibly optimistic and amusing older suitor, does she actually reclaim her daughter's shawl, while persistent thoughts of her own cannibal galaxy—her way of remembering the Holocaust—merge with a provisional commitment to the world of the living in her grudging acceptance of a comic suitor who has courted her throughout the second section.

It is clear that the immigrant survivors who come to America persist in viewing life as a litany of extreme situations and that American writers treat the Holocaust as a watershed in the national experience. Saul Bellow (1969) places the Shoah in its American context:

Just what the reduction of millions of human beings into heaps
of bone and mounds of rag and hair or clouds of smoke beto-
kened, there is no one who can plainly tell us, but it is at least
plain that something was being done to put in question the
meaning of survival, the meaning of pity, the meaning of justice and of the importance of being oneself, the individual's
consciousness of his own existence. It would be odd, indeed,
if these historical events had made no impression on American writers, even if they are not on the whole given to taking
the historical or theoretical view. (160)

American fiction actually reveals the historical and theoretical view precisely in that body of fiction tracing the displaced souls who survive the
Holocaust and find themselves as refugees in the United States. Utilizing
oblique, ironic, often absurdist techniques to render Holocaust consciousness within an American setting, novelists and short story writers mine
the constituents and tropes of post-Holocaust experience, what Langer
(1975) terms "the displacement of the consciousness of life by the imminence and pervasiveness of death . . . the assault on physical reality; the
disintegration of the rational intelligence; and the disruption of chronological time" (xii), to produce their own versions of Cynthia Ozick's cannibal galaxy. Indeed the metaphor of the cannibal galaxy can serve as a
generalized trope for the American world immigrant survivors inhabit.
Dorothy Bilik offers an astute assessment of their condition.

The immigrant survivor is more a *luftmentsh* (one who lives
on and in the air) than were his predecessors. In this he is not
only the product of a literary context that values myth and
the absurd over the realism and socioeconomics of earlier
times. Modern history as well as literary modernism is responsible for the lack of corporeality of some postwar fic-
tional immigrants. They come as remnants of a murdered
culture rather than as fragments of an atrophying one. They
come out of a European past they have been forced to abandon to confront an American scene far more complex that
the one encountered by earlier immigrants. (48)

Earlier Jewish immigrants like those depicted in Henry Roth's melancholy *Call It Sleep* did not have to contend with the magnitude of Auschwitz in their lives. In fact, the young protagonist in Roth's novel, David Schearl, has a near-death epiphany at the end of the narrative that fuses immigrant longing with a vision of the Golden Land that is virtually impossible to locate in post-Holocaust American fiction. David's revelation, his spiritual rebirth, propels him into a world of diversity but also brilliant national unity—"of the glint on tilted bricks, of the uneven shine on roller skates, of the dry light on gray stone steps, of the tapering glitter of rails, of the oily sheen on the night-smooth rivers, of the glow on the outstretched open palms of legions upon legions of hands hurtling toward him" (598). Here is the Whitmanesque catalog of national virtues—what Roth at the onset of *Call It Sleep* invokes as "that vast . . . land, the land of freedom, of immense opportunity, that Golden Land" (12)—that immigrants coming to America out of the ashes of the Holocaust cannot comprehend. They seem to live in air, devoid of epiphanies, experiencing a loss of identity that becomes a basic characteristic of the postmodern period. As George Steiner (1987) writes, "Auschwitz would signify on a collective, historical scale the death of man as a rational, 'forward-dreaming' speech organism. . . . The languages we are now speaking on this polluted and suicidal planet are 'post-human'" (55).

Singer's Suicidal Planet

Nowhere are the contours of this suicidal planet, this cannibal galaxy, expressed more graphically and successfully than in Isaac Bashevis Singer's *Enemies, A Love Story* (1972). Singer's novel along with *The Penitent* (1983) and his posthumous *Meshugah* (1994) comprise a post-Holocaust trilogy in which protagonists attempt to exorcise the millions of ghosts created by Hitler's apocalypse. The plot of *Enemies, A Love Story,* which integrates the Nazi past and the American present, as well as millennial Jewish history and secular Western philosophy that serve as the foundation for the author's cyclical view of time, begins with a mordant author's note: "Although I did not have the privilege of going through the Hitler Holocaust, I have lived for years with refugees from this ordeal." Combined with the novel's quirky title, the author's observation suggests the discordant, tongue-in-cheek tonalities that prevail throughout the narrative. Singer cautions readers that his refugee characters are in no way "typical" but rather exceptions to the rule; in fact, the novel embodies those elements of the fantastic and grotesque that typify Singer's fictive universe. In this novel, the main refugees—Herman Broder and his three wives—lead a picaresque existence in New York City. Herman, bouncing between Yadwiga, his plodding and devoted gentile wife; the beautiful and suicidal Masha; and his first wife, the intellectual Tamara, who reappears in New York out of the ashes of Europe, resembles a spectral figure trying to reembody himself in America. The entire novel is haunted by echoes and premonitions of an immediate past that continues to operate in the present for the wartime survivors.

Singer, who left Poland for the United States in 1935, dramatizes in *Enemies, A Love Story* the difficulty of transmitting a cultural and religious past as well as a specific European Jewish identity to the United States in the aftermath of the Holocaust. The upheavals of the Second World War prevent easy assimilation or acculturation in the Promised Land. Herman, his three women, and several other secondary characters who are immigrant survivors, embody a people's historical consciousness that coexists uneasily with the dominant metaphor or myth of America as Eden. Like Brill in Ozick's *The Cannibal Galaxy*, Herman survived the Nazi Holocaust in Poland by hiding for more than two years in a hayloft, attended by his family's gentile servant, Yadwiga. Subsequently, thinking his first wife and their two children have perished, Herman takes Yadwiga as his second wife in America. In turn, Yadwiga recreates in their apartment in Brighton Beach an urban Eden for her husband, whom she dotes on like a protective and compliant Eve. Herman is also involved with another immigrant survivor, the tempestuous Masha, who lives in the Bronx with her mother, Shifrah Puah. And when Tamara miraculously reappears and takes up residence in Manhattan, Herman's frenetic existence assumes ludicrous dimensions as he shuttles across three boroughs, an American Don Juan trapped in his own sexual hell. With women in three boroughs—a demographic division suggesting Singer's playful presentation of the Freudian schema of superego (Yadwiga), ego (Tamara), and id (Masha)—Herman is subjected to a hurricane of warring passions and commitments, a virtual holocaust of the senses, that push him to the edges of traumatic experience mirroring those historical terrors he continually relives.

Although Herman persistently reinvents himself in America, deceiving Yadwiga for example by pretending to be a traveling book salesman while working in actuality as a ghost writer for the sly, pragmatic, "dynamic," and thoroughly Americanized Rabbi Milton Lampert, he is incapable of that ultimate metamorphosis into an American citizen that would permit him to embrace the realities of the New World. When Herman mournfully tells the tolerant Lampert that he "is no longer a part of this world," Lampert replies that these words are cliches: "I know hundreds of concentration camp survivors. Some of them were practically on their way to the ovens—they're right here in America, they drive cars, they do business. Either you're in the other world or you're in this world" (25). Rabbi Lampert, who has no congregation and who is the archetypal American huckster, skillfully marries Judaism to Mammon and revels in his success in the Golden Land. By contrast, Herman attempts to establish a refuge for himself, imagining that Nazis are still operating in the United States.

Herman's quest for a diasporal refuge, a peaceful home in America, clashes with his essential vision of the world as a universal concentration camp. The pristine, almost Edenic apartment the devoted Yadwiga keeps for them in Brighton Beach, filled with sunlight off the ocean, the smells of coffee, baking bread, and the foods Herman had loved in his pre-Holocaust childhood, recreates for the protagonist a prelapsarian world, a transposed paradise with an "East European flavor." Yet this Promised Land along Mermaid Avenue contains for the obsessive Herman sinister overtones of the Nazi era: "Sunlight fell on crates and bushel baskets of oranges, bananas, cherries, strawberries and tomatoes. Jews were allowed to live freely here! On the main avenue and on the side streets, Hebrew schools displayed their signs. There was even a Yiddish school. As Herman walked along, his eye sought hiding places in case the Nazis were to come to New York" (17). Even the most bucolic days on Coney Island are compromised for Herman by a "primeval" reality, "a stench of putrefaction," the memories and metaphors of extermination that signify the Age of Auschwitz.

Whether in an urban or rural setting, Herman encounters postwar America as a mildly deranged immigrant survivor who is estranged from the grand narrative and trapped by wartime memories. In fact, Singer positions the competing narratives of Europe and America most strikingly in the two episodes where Herman takes Masha and then Tamara upstate to the Adirondacks and the Catskills. The juxtaposition of pristine rural imagery and the tropes of the Holocaust are simply an exten-

sion of Herman's consciousness. In the pastoral Adirondacks, while gaz-
ing over the hills and lakes, the psychotic Masha, who shares Herman's
temporal dissociations, asks, "Where are the Nazis? What kind of world
is this without Nazis? A backward country, this America" (110). Similarly, Herman can find little solace in the Edenic subtext Singer inscribes
in the Adirondack scenery: "The birds had announced the new day as if
it were the morning after creation. Warm breezes carried the scent of the
woods and the smell of food being prepared in the hotels. Herman imagined that he heard the screech of a chicken or a duck. Somewhere on this
lovely summer morning, fowl were being slaughtered. Treblinka was everywhere" (112). Herman resists any reconciliation of the Holocaust and
his postwar American experience, thereby preventing any formation of a
new national identity. He senses historical trauma and disruption on
every street and by every lake in America. His post-Holocaust world is
also post-traumatic, and thus he can never achieve the full reintegration
of personality that would permit him to be a comfortable immigrant in
his new nation.

Nevertheless, the dynamics of American life are such that Herman
can hide in America at the end of the novel, for this has become his
predisposition and his destiny. After Masha commits suicide, Yadwiga,
who bears Herman's child, joins with Tamara to create their own survivors' universe in America, setting up home and shop in an inherited Jewish bookstore that suggests, however anachronistically, the fusion of the
Old World and the New. Although a comic nihilism and carnivalesque
action pervade Singer's post-Holocaust universe in *Enemies, A Love Story*,
he seems to suggest that America does offer some victims of the Nazi era
a provisional context for survival. Even if individuals cannot form a new
national identity, they can reconstitute cultural identity, for there aren't
enough Nazis in postwar America to prevent this project.

Singer's chronicle of Holocaust survivors expands with his novels
Meshugah and *The Penitent,* which reflect the juxtapositions and contrapuntal narrative rhythms typical of the postmodern fiction that attempts
to deal with the Nazi era through what Lyotard calls in *The Postmodern
Condition* "new presentations, not in order to enjoy them but in order to
impart a stronger sense of the unpresentable" (79ff). *Meshugah*, the more
impressive of the two novels and closer in its antic narrative rhythms
and tragicomic tone to *Enemies, A Love Story,* appeared in the 1980s in
serial form and in Yiddish in *The Forward.* Its original title, *Lost Souls,*

was expressive in itself but Singer changed it to *Meshugah*, which the author is careful to remind readers is a Yiddish word meaning "crazy, senseless, insane." Both the final title and the earlier variant capture the essence of the postwar period for Holocaust survivors, for there can be no American innocence for immigrants who have experienced the demonic forces of the Nazi era. The narrator of *Meshugah* is a partial incarnation of Singer himself at an earlier age: Aaron Greidinger is a writer and radio personality in his late forties who writes serial novels for *The Forward*. A pre-Holocaust refugee who is famous for his depictions of earlier European Jewish life and who is revered by New York's radio listeners for his homespun advice on everything from love to the occult, Aaron is essentially a postwar Miss Lonelyhearts content to inhabit a modest upper West Side apartment, publish his fiction, and engage in occasional dalliances with admiring women. Like his counterpart Herman Broder, he seeks a small place and a separate peace, but he is drawn as if by destiny (Singer observes that there is no word for mere coincidence in Yiddish) into a whirlwind of postwar complexity that brings him back to the Holocaust—that specific moment of crisis that transformed history, culture, and postmodern relationships.

Into the narrator's office at *The Forward* comes an old prewar acquaintance, Max Aberdam, who materializes like a "lost soul" from the Holocaust universe. If Aaron is a likable schlemiel, then Max is the schlimazel who plays cultural tricks on the narrator, uprooting him from his vague postwar American sublimity and his nostalgia for old Poland, and reminding him of another "master" narrative—the Holocaust—that subsumes all other national narratives. Max, a gargantuan figure who at sixty-seven becomes Aaron's devilish *doppelganger*, also plays the role of an outsized Miss Lonelyhearts, investing money for legions of refugee women who, in turn, love him for his devotion to their financial affairs. Unlike Aaron, however, Max has a refined sense of the world's essential lunacy in the wake of the Holocaust. A wartime wanderer to Bialystok, Vilna, Kowno, Shanghai, San Francisco, and finally New York, he perceives his odyssey of dislocation as a metaphor for the Jewish people: "I experienced the full range of Jewish woes." Yet Max is also a vital life force whose zany advice and gallows humor bind psychological wounds. One of Singer's most engaging skeptics, he declares, "I owe nothing to the Almighty: as long as He keeps sending us Hitlers and Stalins, He is *their* God, not mine" (5). Max's ethos, which he embraces and imparts joyfully, is that "the whole world is an insane asylum" and that New York City in particular is "eternal bedlam." Nevertheless, he acknowledges that "America is our last refuge" (28). Happy to be "reaping shovelfuls in the land of Columbus," Max speaks an irreverent and iconoclastic brand of post-Holocaust humor: "Our Jews are always first in line of fire. They simply have to redeem the world, no more and no less. In every Jew resides the dybbuk of a messiah" (42).

As Aaron's corpulent, worldly, concupiscent double, Max serves to center the narrator in the postmodern universe rather than in the nostalgic and faded world of prewar European Jewry. Max also offers Aaron the key to postmodern salvation—his own mistress, the twenty-seven-year-old concentration camp survivor, Miriam Zakind. Miriam, who is married to a deranged American poet but who loves both Max and Aaron, treating them as her two true husbands, also has a refined sense of the absurdity in the post-Holocaust world. Quite literally engulfed in Holocaust horrors and betrayals, she functions as the decidedly ambiguous moral center of this world. Late in the novel, Aaron discovers that Miriam had been a prostitute for the Nazis and had ultimately collaborated with them as a young *kapo;* as such, she is a challenge for Aaron, who discovers her secret past from a concentration camp survivor while on a trip to Israel. Temporarily renouncing Miriam and returning to New York, he feels like "a fossil of a long-extinct epoch" (218). In a remarkable act of affirmation by Singer, the author contrives a wedding—a civil ceremony— for the couple following Max's death, "the quietest wedding since the one between Adam and Eve" (228).

If the postmodern world for Holocaust survivors is indeed *meshugah*, a constant attempt to make sense of inexplicable horrors and moral compromises, it is little wonder that Singer's complacent schlemiel, Aaron, gradually construes contemporary life as a chronicle of destruction. Late in the novel, he ruminates: "The Hitler and Stalin catastrophes demonstrated that humanity's dreams of permanent peace and a united mankind were unreal. Dozens of new nations had sprung up, and everywhere there was strife and warfare. The world's hatred of the Jews did not diminish even after Hitler's Holocaust, and Israel was engulfed with enemies" (154–55). With his increasingly apocalyptic sense of history, Aaron learns to confront the human condition *in extremis*. His trip to Israel, where he encounters the polyglot survivors of the Holocaust, ends in an epiphany triggered by full disclosure of Miriam's past. Geoffrey

Hartman has observed that the Holocaust challenges the credibility of redemptive thinking; in this context, it is a challenge for Aaron to love Miriam, who had assumed complicity in the destruction of her own people. Nevertheless, his union with her is a quiet, provisional redemption, a marriage between a tortured Adam and a tainted Eve, the new emblems of postwar civilization.

Whereas America offers Aaron and Miriam the national space to revise their lives and deal with the terrors of recent European history, the protagonist in Singer's *The Penitent* renounces his American paradise for another Promised Land, the nation of Israel. Joseph Shapiro, wildly successful in America, tells his tale in 1969 to a frame narrator who readers can imagine is Singer himself. Shapiro, who fled Warsaw in 1939 and experienced continental horrors and wandering during the war, arrived in the United States on a visa in 1947 and proceeded to enact a rags-to-riches ritual so central to America's grand allegory. "All the refugees envied us—what luck to go to the Golden Land" (12), he states, and indeed his dream of becoming a successful American is realized. A real estate mogul, Shapiro nevertheless witnesses his American Dream going awry as he lapses into infidelities and is overcome by a sense of spiritual purposelessness that precipitates his decision to leave all of his American possessions behind and fly to Israel in quest of his cultural and religious inheritance.

Shapiro's embrace of American materialism, his desire for assimilation, and his complicity in the moral relativism of the postwar era had resulted in the disintegration of his identity as a Jew. Only his nightmares serve to stimulate traumatic memory. In one dream, he imagines he is hiding in a cellar with his parents and other Jews, but when a match is lighted he sees that he is dressed "as a Nazi in a brown uniform and a swastika" (27). Shapiro gradually senses the destruction of his identity as the "Evil Spirit" gains ascendancy in his consciousness. In a narrative of reverse immigration, he flees the Golden Land for Tel Aviv, escaping "a civilization that is a slaughterhouse and a brothel" (63). However, he discovers that Tel Aviv, with its worship of Mammon and its sinister sensuality, has become an extension of America. Whether it is Tel Aviv or New York, the world is still *meshugah*, devoid of religious and cultural knowledge. It is only in the orthodox section of Jerusalem, Meah Shearim, that Joseph becomes a Penitent in this simple allegory by Singer: he refines and purifies his life, marries a virtuous and orthodox woman, and settles forever in Israel. Alan Berger has observed that the "only authentic Jews in Singer's work are either dead, or survivors. The best among the latter are authorally removed to Israel" (81). This is the case in *The Penitent*, a minor parable among Singer's more distinguished body of work, and atypical of the author's persistent comic skepticism concerning the world after the Holocaust. In his author's note at the end of the novel, Singer does distance himself from the saga of Joseph Shapiro, who "finally made peace with the cruelty of life, and the violence of man's history. . . . Joseph Shapiro might have done so, but I haven't" (168). For Singer, the odds against finding any secure place in the postwar era are long; in this ominous world, he asserts, rebellion against the degeneration of civilization is just as beneficial as prayer.

Bellow's Post-Holocaust Everyman

The degeneration of postwar civilization is a major motif in the fiction chronicling the fragmented lives of Holocaust survivors in America. In Saul Bellow's *Mr. Sammler's Planet* (1970), the protagonist, a survivor who is in his seventies, trains his mordant intellect and one good eye (the other eye had been destroyed by the butt of a Nazi's rifle) on an urban American landscape that is less an Eden for refugees than a postmodern wasteland. Artur Sammler, whose damaged eyesight and austere philosophical vision make him a postmodern amalgam of Tiresias and Oedipus, a sort of post-Holocaust Everyman, gazes on the bizarre New York City culture of the 1960s through the informed lenses of the numerous "historians of civilization" whom he has devoted a lifetime to reading. A Polish Jew who had risen persistently from the ashes of a dying civilization—first by crawling from an extermination pit that claimed the life of his wife; then by hiding in a mausoleum to escape Polish partisans committed to the Nazi vision of *Judenrein*, or a world free of Jews; and finally resurrected "out of the DP camp in Salzburg" and brought by his nephew, Dr. Arnold Gruner, to the United States in 1947—Sammler perceives his "planet" as being on the verge of disintegration. New York City, in fact, is Sammler's metaphor for this global demise: the city "makes one think about the collapse of civilization, about Sodom and Gemorrah, about the end of the world" (307–8).

If civilization is on the verge of collapse, or perhaps merely repeating itself in an entropic cycle (and fair-minded Sammler is prepared to consider this variant proposition), then New York City in the decade of the sixties is the apotheosis of this cyclical degeneration. Just as in Singer's *Meshugah* the world is presented as a "vast madhouse," Bellow's protagonist views urban culture as a carnivalesque arena of human vice and folly. Sammler, an unreconstructed Anglophile who thinks of New York as a Third World quagmire, "an Asian, and African town" signifying the "barbarous world of color," is both a detached, philosophical observer of his alien environment and a participant who is drawn irresistibly toward its "confused styles" (11). For he is also a "refugee in Manhattan," part of the polyglot flow of contemporary immigrant history. With his "screwy visions," he is a latter-day Whitman delighting in profuse catalogs of the urban scene and its bizarre inhabitants; he is simultaneously repelled and enthralled by the "artistic diversion of the streets," even as these diversions tend toward the excremental and sexual.

At seventy-two, Sammler is beyond sex (as a rude student anarchist reminds him when he delivers a dull history recitation at Columbia University), a decidedly dry but droll old man in a dry season, lamenting the paganism governing his postmodern Sodom and Gomorrah. Although *Mr. Sammler's Planet* reflects the increasingly ruminative style of Bellow's fiction (similar extended discourses on the decline of Western civilization and urban culture can be found, for example, in *The Dean's December*), the novel actually possesses a comic brio as the protagonist considers the panorama and parody of humanity parading before him. Despite his apocalyptic musings and his affinity for the religious writers of the thirteenth century—notably Meister Eckhardt, who for Sammler is the epitome of his beloved Augustinian tradition—the protagonist also enjoys his quasi-journalistic role as the chronicler of his infernal city. New York City in the 1960s, which Sammler in his role of urban ethnographer traverses from Union Square to Columbia University, using his West Side apartment as the locus of operations, is to the protagonist a landscape of the grotesque. It is a disjunctive universe populated by a wildly disparate assortment of humanity, including several younger relatives. Bellow devotes extended paragraphs and entire pages to catalogs and descriptions of these carnivalesque Americans: "What one sees on Broadway while bound for the bus. All human types reproduced, the barbarian, redskin, or Fiji, the dandy, the buffalo hunter, the desperado, the queer, the sexual fantasist, the squaw; bluestocking, princess, poet, painter, prospector, troubadour, guerrilla, Che Guevara, the new Thomas à Beckett" (151). Although there is a Swiftean edge to Bellow's delineation of the sixties scene, and a distinctive repugnance for the unwashed, un-educated, promiscuous youth of the period, the author (as well as his protagonist) recognizes the fascinating ability of Americans to "mytholo-gize" or "legendize" themselves. These new Americans, so unlike the Ger-manized culture of Sammler's privileged Polish childhood or the effete Bloomsbury universe of his prewar decades in London as a journalist hobnobbing with Wells, Keynes, and others, have the pioneering power to reinvent themselves endlessly. They thrive on "the anarchy of the streets." They are "a crazy species," but a species nevertheless that treats its madness as a "masquerade, the project of a deeper reason, the result of the despair we feel before infinities and eternities." Americans might be "acting mythic" like a pack of Hollywood extras, but their very urge and ability to reinvent themselves cast them paradoxically "into chaos, hoping to adhere to higher consciousness, to be washed upon the shores of truth" (153).

Artur Sammler, this old man in a dry season, this shadowy Other who roams the bright kaleidoscopic universe of sixties America, is drawn as if by destiny into the cultural condition of his New World. A disci-plined intellectual and amateur biographer (his mildly demented daugh-ter urges him to complete his study of old friend H.G. Wells) exploring cultural and historical "truths," Sammler seeks continuities within the complex, disjunctive, compelling modes of personal reinvention he en-counters in urban America. Central to Sammler's own moral progress is his three-day odyssey around New York City (a restricted time frame that Bellow skillfully pushes outward into other narrative frames that ultimately embrace the totality of Western history and thought) that is governed by the old man's encounter with a black pickpocket. The pick-pocket practices his craft aboard Sammler's Fifth Avenue bus. Likened to a gorgeous and powerful animal, a puma, he reminds Sammler of "the breath of wartime Poland" (9). He is the predatory principle in human history—what Saul Friedlander terms the "modes of domination and terror" at the core of the Holocaust. In the course of the novel, Sammler will be hunted by this urban predator: in a primal scene, the thief traps Sammler in the lobby of Sammler's apartment building and exposes his powerful penis to his pinned quarry before leaving without speaking a word. The thief is a far more complex figure than critics—especially recent critics who have charged Bellow with racist stereotyping—acknowledge. At the conventional metaphorical level, the thief "picks" Sammler's pocket by triggering the old anxiety of the Holocaust. But he also triggers Sammler's survivalist instinct. After all, Sammler is a man who escaped from a mass grave and then survived a pogrom by the very Polish partisans he was fighting with against the Nazis. He has knowledge of the world of violence, capriciousness, death.

Bellow deepens the connection between the pickpocket and Sammler by rendering the black man as the immigrant survivor's sartorial double. Almost item for item, he mimics Sammler's Old World style of dress, a similitude that is not missed by the refugee: like Sammler, the "pickpocket himself wore dark shades. He was a powerful Negro in a camel's hair coat, dressed with extraordinary elegance, as if by Mr. Fish of the West End, or Turnbull and Asser of Jermyn Street" (9). Sammler senses that although they are binary racial opposites, both of them are cultural Others within American society. Just as the black man has been "savagized," Sammler too has been demonized within a Western political scheme of good and evil. Both the black man and the Jew are what Adi Ophir terms "archetypes of negation," existing in opposition to a dominant culture that insists on such binary terms as superior-inferior and pure-impure, thereby forcing Others to a "conceptual borderline" where they may be excluded or exterminated (63–65). When Sammler prevents his estranged, psychotic son-in-law Elsen, a death camp survivor, from beating the pickpocket to death, he begins his own final psychic regeneration by aligning himself with the black man against the fierce weight of Western historical oppression. Once, in Samosht Forest, Sammler had killed a German soldier who was begging for his life. In a second life-and-death situation in America, the old man, an understanding Job, reinvents himself on the streets of New York as a messenger of distributive justice.

In confronting the reality of his Otherness through his *doppelganger*, Sammler reconnects with the polyethnic urban world—with his America—that he would have preferred to view in a detached fashion as "a kind of philosopher." Sammler cannot simply "watch" the world's lunacies unfold like some "registrar of madness." He must also bear witness to it and recognize that he has and will continue to participate in it. Likened variously by the secondary figures in the novel to a sacred person, a confidant, a curate, he attends to his neurotic daughter, Shula, who survived the war in a convent and is now a bagwoman in New York City; to the dysfunctional son and daughter of his mentor, Dr. Gruner; and ultimately to Gruner himself, who is dying of a brain aneurysm. Attending to one man's death out of the legacy of the Holocaust and the Six Day War (which the protagonist covers as a journalist in a quixotic but nevertheless necessary encounter with a new generation of corpses), Sammler experiences a renewed reverence for life, a reaffirmation of "this droll mortality." His improvised Kaddish for Gruner in the last pages of the novel is a prayer of love for his relative and benefactor. This prayer permits him to experience, as he once observed, "some order within himself," and it enables him to restore the civil margins of existence in Planet America.

Sophie's Choice *and the Age of Anxiety*

Old Sammler shares with the young protagonist in William Styron's *Sophie's Choice* (1979) a preoccupation with "this droll mortality" that grows out of the Holocaust experience. The narrator of Styron's controversial novel, who comes of age in the postwar years largely through his association with the Polish Catholic concentration camp survivor, Sophie Sawistowska, is an American innocent who learns slowly about the absurdity of life after the Hitler era. That Styron selected Sophie as the focus for his investigation of the Holocaust has occasioned rather severe censure from novelists such as Cynthia Ozick and critics who suggest that the novel reflects a thinly disguised anti-Semitism: "*Sophie's Choice* . . . fails to comprehend the Jewish specificity of the Holocaust. Ahistorical in method, Styron's novel deals not so much with an epic-making event, but with human existence in extremity, sexuality, slavery, and stereotype. This kind of Holocaust novel encourages trivialization by ignoring the interconnection between the destiny of Judaism and the fate of Western civilization. Styron draws the incredible conclusion that Jews are insensitive to the Holocaust" (Berger 33). Such *a priori* rejection of the novel misconstrues Styron's objectives. The author acknowledges that Sophie "is not a Jew, she went to Auschwitz, and she is a victim. I had to say to myself from time to time that this is not the pattern, that Jews were the major victims, but I also had to face the fact that there were other victims and I was determined to put that down" (West 235). The novel, which grew out of a "revelation" that Styron had about a Polish woman, an Auschwitz survivor, whom he had known in Brooklyn in 1947, and which took him four and a half years to write, including a haunting trip to Poland and Auschwitz, is in fact deeply historical rather than ahistorical in design. Consciousness of the Holocaust, often rendered in documentary form, becomes transposed upon American soil in the form of Sophie, one survivor who happens to be Christian, as were eighty percent of the displaced persons coming to the United States in the postwar years.

Sophie's Choice, which was researched meticulously by Styron, is unique in the canon of American fiction illuminating the America experienced by Holocaust survivors in that it provides a triple perspective on the event: the crushingly real knowledge of the event by Sophie; the acquired knowledge of the event by the twenty-two year old narrator, Stingo, who senses in the Holocaust a modern metaphor for the South's own legacy of slavery; and the obsessive conjuring of the Nazi era by Sophie's lover, the brilliant, schizophrenic, suicidally doomed Nathan Landau. Taken together, this trio comprises a set of postwar polarities: of the Old and New Worlds; of North and South; of Catholic, Protestant, and Jew. For Stingo, who is a scarcely disguised avatar of Styron himself, the haunting events of the summer and fall of 1947, when all three characters inhabited a Brooklyn boarding house—the Pink Palace—propel him into the world of love, death, and vocation as a writer. These events also center him in the postwar Age of Anxiety, "these unending years of madness, illusion, error, dream, and strife" built upon "the black edifice of Auschwitz" (514) that would influence his maturation through the decade of the sixties, the vantage point in time from which he reconstructs the earlier events.

It is Sophie, of course, who possesses the firsthand knowledge of the Final Solution. Coming to America from a Swedish DP camp, she entwines her elusive but gradually revealed European life with the lives of the rural Southerner Stingo and the urban Northerner Nathan. Just as Stingo, the migrant to New York City, is "a young Southerner wandering in the Kingdom of the Jews" (4), Sophie finds her destiny embedded once again in Jewish culture in the form of Nathan, her lover; Dr. Blackstock, her employer; Yetta Zimmerman, her Flatbush landlady, and others who define the margins of exile in postwar America. Sophie does not arrive in America with any deep faith in the immigrant's capacity to create a new beginning for herself. For her, knowledge of *l'univers concentrationnaire*—a phrase that the mature narrator invokes from his reading of George Steiner—persistently erodes the "newness" of the American experience. Stingo might recall the halcyon rhythms of his Brooklyn days—"sunny and mild, flower-fragrant, almost as if the days had been arrested in a seemingly perpetual springtime" (3)—and in fact the trio spends bucolic days at Coney Island, at Prospect Park, and in their rooms in the Pink Palace. Ultimately, however, a palpable sense of horror and doom floats over this urban pastoral as if one mythic narrative is competing with another for ascendancy.

Both Stingo in his youthful naiveté and the somewhat older Nathan in his obsessiveness gain knowledge of *l'univers concentrationnaire* through Sophie. From his sanctuary in the "huge Jewish arrondisement" of Flatbush, Stingo pursues his chosen vocation as a writer by entering into Sophie's tortured life as a friend and confidant. His ability to forego employment is facilitated by a recently revealed legacy, the discovery and sale of gold coins that had been received by his Southern ancestors from the sale of a family slave. Stingo's father unwittingly links the Southern past to the present in a letter implying that the old evil has a resonance in "the recent revelations of the horrors of Nazi Germany" (30). At the outset of the novel, evil for Stingo, who is comically preoccupied with the need to lose his virginity, seems to exist in another country. From his writing desk, he can gaze out the window at the fresh green breast of the New World: "It was such a placid and agreeable view I had of the park, this corner known as the Parade Grounds. Old sycamore trees and maples shaded the sidewalks at the edge of the park, and the dappled sunlight aglow on the gently sloping meadow of the Parade Grounds gave the setting a serene, almost pastoral quality" (36–37). By the end of the novel, awareness of evil has entered his American Arcadia: "Someday I will understand Auschwitz," he underlines in a fragment from a diary that he would later largely destroy. His characteristically American innocence of evil—what Styron has termed a "vacuous unawareness of evil"—cannot endure in the postwar world, for Stingo must ultimately admit *l'univers concentrationnaire* into America's cultural and historical imagination.

Through Sophie and her gradual revelations to him, Stingo must piece together the primal nightmare of our era and discover how it becomes the "end" of history. In his essay "Hell Reconsidered" (1982) Styron writes: "If slavery was the great historical nightmare of the eighteenth and nineteenth centuries in the Western world, slavery's continuation in the horror we have come to call Auschwitz is the nightmare of our own century" (95). Just as Sophie must reject the vision of some Elysian era in Poland prior to the Second World War, the narrator must learn that "this fresh American experiment with its hint of bucolic beguilements" is simply a national indulgence masking far more somber historical realities. Sophie, Stingo, and the manic Nathan play at urban pastoral during their Brooklyn summer, trying to enact a fable of the world before the Holocaust, indeed before slavery; but the dark, demonic side of Nathan and the flawed dislocation of self that permitted Sophie to assume complicity in the Nazi horror reproduce the madness of the Holocaust. Not even in the exuberant landscape of a triumphant postwar America can people exist beyond the perimeter of the Nazi horror, beyond the "inescapably pervasive charnel-house mist" (154).

Sophie, like her literary muse Emily Dickinson whose poetry echoes through Styron's narrative, is wed to death—to the dominating and destructive forces of history. Her past seems to trail "its horrible smoke— as if from the chimneys of Auschwitz—of anguish, confusion, self-deception and, above all, guilt" (187). She represents a new form of mass society posited in Richard L. Rubenstein's *The Cunning of History*, a study that the mature Stingo, reflecting Styron's extensive reading of Holocaust literature, alludes to in his effort to understand the postmodern condition. Rubenstein, an American professor of religion, suggests a perspective on the Nazi era that implicates the American future: "Regrettably, few ethical theorists or religious thinkers have paid attention to the highly significant political fact that the camps were in reality a new form of human society" (235). Rubenstein terms this new form the "society of total domination," evolving from chattel slavery and receiving "despotic apotheosis" in Auschwitz. Sophie, one of the "favorites" of this slave society, survives through collusion and complicity, including the sacrifice of one of her children—her primal "choice" that reflects the other ambiguous choices in her life. In a sense, Sophie is trapped in a world of male primacy that reflects the society of total domination. She submits to her rabidly anti-Semitic father and husband; to Commandant Hoss, for whom she works as a secretary while at Auschwitz; and to the loving but sadomasochistic Nathan who, phallic and infernal, wraps her in brilliant costumes before enacting his final solution—their suicide—at the end of the novel. Sophie cannot valorize the promise of America when confronted with the manifold forces of total domination that impinge on her life.

Although *Sophie's Choice* is a somber inquiry into the legacy of Auschwitz and American slavery, a study of psychic dislocation and cultural marginality, Styron's novel, like the other works examined in this chapter, also possesses the carnivalizing rhythms characteristic of postwar or postmodern fiction of immigration. In an interview conducted by Philip Rahv, Styron alludes to the "comic awareness so exquisitely poised between hilarity and anguish" that characterizes the Jewish experience (West 152). Similarly, in an interview with Stephen Lewis, he acknowledges the "erotic lunacy" (West 262) that dominates the tragic relationship between Sophie and Nathan and that informs the architecture of the entire novel. What Judith Ruderman astutely terms the "double rhythm" of the novel (129–39) extends to Stingo's obsessively comic quest for sexual experience and to the stylistic juxtapositions that turn Sophie's Auschwitz into a simulacrum of heaven within the infernal landscape of the camps. *Sophie's Choice* is a tragicomic novel of alternating and competing rhythms, with the comic brio serving as release from the horrors of the death camps embedded in the deepest fabric of the novel. Styron's menage of Sophie, Stingo, and Nathan confirms the insane and grotesque contemporary condition and reinforces Singer's assertion that the world after the Holocaust is *meshugah*.

Following the burial of Sophie and Nathan, the narrator retreats from the world of death to Coney Island, where he drinks himself into a bizarre, carnivalesque, hallucinatory state:

> Later in the night's starry hours, chill now with the breath of fall and damp with Atlantic wind, I stood on the beach alone. It was silent here, and save for the blazing stars, enfoldingly dark; bizarre spires and minarets, Gothic roofs, baroque towers in spindly silhouette against the city's afterglow. The tallest of those towers, a spiderlike gantry with cables flowing from its peak, was the parachute jump, and it was from the highest parapet of that dizzying contraption that I heard Sophie's peals of laughter as she sank earthward with Nathan—falling in joy at the summer's beginning, which now seemed eons ago. (514)

Stingo falls asleep on the beach, haunted by dreams out of Edgar Allan Poe, to discover upon awakening in the morning that three children have covered him with a protective blanket of sand. From this comic-pastoral bed, the narrator rises to reaffirm the redemptive power of America to transcend judgment day, to continually reinvoke "morning . . . excellent and fair." The spectacle of life, with all of its terrifying historical dissonance, prevails over the events that have destroyed Sophie and Nathan.

American novelists try to make sense of the world after the Holocaust by inventing immigrant survivors like Sophie, Sammler, and Herman Broder whose experience of the Nazi era confronts the evolving epic of America in the postwar period. From the realm of profound evil, they journey to America as displaced persons who can never again feel comfortably at home in any part of the world. The ruptures in history prevent them from being fully reborn. By turns ironic, tragic, factual, elegiac, American writers challenge with serio-comic ruthlessness notions about the triumph of the spirit for Holocaust survivors and interrogate as well those established myths of the Promised Land.

3

Migrant Souls:
The Chicano Quest
for National Identity

Moving, always moving. From Guadalajara to Monterrey
to Reynosa, then across the border to Laredo.
... Moving, moving, always moving.
—Raymond Barrio, *The Plum Plum Pickers*

Epochal changes in United States immigration policy wrought by the Second World War affected not only those Europeans fortunate enough to escape the ashes of the Holocaust and journey to a new nation as refugees and displaced persons, but also the waves of Mexican immigrants who flowed north across the Rio Grande border as *braceros*—yet another new immigration category—to support the American war effort. Admittedly, the "imaginative geography" of Mexican Americans, to appropriate a phrase from Edward Said's *Orientalism* (59), differs radically from the political and cultural domain of those Holocaust survivors who found refuge in America. Nevertheless, both groups reflect the overarching realities of exile caused by World War II, the psychic dislocations spawned by life in postwar America, and the shifting, dualistic, increasingly oppositional behavior to American culture that becomes the hallmark of the immigrant experience in American fiction.

Basic to the experience of immigrant and migrant groups comprising the canon of contemporary American fiction is a deeply rooted sense of duality. Nowhere is this phenomenon of duality—of the self divided psychically and culturally, of being both a part of the American experience and yet differentiated from it—more apparent than in the lives of those Mexican Americans who appear in the distinctive body of Chicano fiction that started with the publication of José Antonio Villarreal's *Pocho* in 1959. Because of race, caste, family, community, heritage, culture, and demographics, the Mexican migrants who flowed across the border in the turbulence of the twentieth century from the Mexican Revolution of 1910–1920 to World War II—a vast historical tapestry that Villarreal weaves skillfully into *Pocho*—reflect a binational and bicultural pattern of behavior that tends to produce psychic ambivalence and divided national loyalties. Such individuals project a sense of cultural separation that contends with the strong assimiliationist powers of the dominant American nation. Ultimately, the millions of Mexicans crossing the border before and after World War II embark on a quest for reconciliation of these competing tendencies. Moreover, as with all quests, especially in fiction, they seek some numinous object, a transnational or transcultural Grail that will enable them to balance the discords inherent in their two cultural worlds, those separate but interconnected domains that lie south and north of the Mexican-American border and are linked uneasily by colonial mission and imperial ideology.

La Frontera

To approach the border—*la frontera*—as an ideological center in Chicano fiction is to slip through a crack in time and enter an imaginative realm where notions of migrants and natives, "us" and "them," insiders and outsiders, local and national, the periphery and the core seem to coalesce in a concatenation of transcultural forces. Bathed in the granular light of the greater Southwest and California, those Mexican lands that prior to 1845 stretched from the Rio Grande northward as far as lower Oregon and Wyoming, the migrants and immigrants who populate this fictive world are both situated in time and place and voyagers backward through the history of the region in search of their essential genealogies, their mixed origins and identities, their anomalous national culture. In *A New Time for Mexico* (1996), Carlos Fuentes observes that in Mexico, "there is not and never has been one single time, one central tradition, as in the west. In Mexico, all times are living, all pasts are present" (16). The post-1945 epoch reveals large numbers of Mexican-American artists and intellectuals utilizing this fluid sense of time to search for Chicano identity or *chicanismo*; it is a quest to unearth the "roots" of Chicano culture and identity that embraces the multiple myths of the peoples and nations that have contended for space along the border since pre-Columbian times. The Southwest is an integral part of the mythology of nation-building, projecting tensions rooted in the United States' imperial role in its conquest of lands claimed originally by Spain and subsequently by an independent Mexico. Conquest and westward expansion are central to the construction of the national identity of the United States, but in recent years the established version of American history has been subjected to reevaluation by a new generation of Chicano and Chicana novelists and intellectuals, who pose competing versions of national identity based on *mestizo* or mixed origins rather than white, Anglo-Saxon Protestant antecedents.

The Southwest is a principal symbolic landscape of national identity in novels as diverse in aesthetic and cultural intention as *Pocho* and Rudolfo Anaya's *Alburquerque* (1995), which for admittedly arbitrary purposes might serve to frame the boundaries of contemporary Chicano fiction. The Southwest, carved from the northern half of old Mexico, is a region whose modern border was established in 1848 by the ratification of the Treaty of Guadalupe Hidalgo and subsequently by the Gadsden Purchase of 1853 that transferred additional lands in southern New Mexico and Arizona to the United States. As such, the greater Southwest is conquered, colonized territory. Any national identity emerging from this landscape must acknowledge the complex issues of competing histories and cultural mixing that are played out against the historical backdrop of ancient worlds, colonial societies, and emerging civilizations. "Every Mexican," observes Américo Paredes in "The Folk Base of Chicano Literature," "knows that there are two Mexicos—the real one and Mexico de Afuera (Mexico abroad) as Mexicans call it . . . composed of all the persons of Mexican origin in the United States" (4). The Southwest thus is a microcosm that captures the entire Mexican-American experience. This region also adumbrates the relations of power among Mexicans, Americans, Mexican Americans, and Native Americans contending for their own versions of Manifest Destiny.

The very doctrine of Manifest Destiny derives from the war fought by the United States against Mexico from 1846–1848 over Texas. This national myth was created by John O'Sullivan who, writing in the *Democratic Review* in June 1845, asserted that it was "the fulfillment of our manifest destiny to overspread the continent allotted by Providence for the free development of our yearly multiplying millions" (Weinberg 12). That approximately 100,000 Mexicans constituted the host culture of the Southwest and California in 1845 did little to alter the myths of Manifest Destiny and westward expansion that became the pattern of national representation in the nineteenth century. Manifest Destiny and the stream of immigrant history converge at the Rio Grande—known to Mexicans as the Rio Bravo. Flowing some 1,880 miles from southwestern Colorado to the Gulf of Mexico, the river is at once the site of the epic migratory struggle of Mexicans from south to north and the symbol of what Fuentes terms the "territorial mutilation" (201) that ceded the north of Mexico from Texas to California to the United States after the Mexican War. But the border is also the site of psychic fissures: migrants crossing the river carry the mythic knowledge that they are strangers in their own lands. They inherit a traumatic past, for they embody a *historia* (which in Spanish translates as both history and story, or fiction) that has forced a colonizer's identity—first Iberian and then Anglo-American—on them.

In Anaya's *Alburquerque*, which is not strictly a novel of contemporary immigration but rather a fiction of mixed and mysterious final arrivals, a delusional politician named Frank Dominic, who invents a Spanish ancestry traceable to the *conquistadores*, dreams of rechanneling the Rio Grande and turning the city's downtown into the Venice of the Southwest, a romantic isle filled with canals, parks, and corporate palaces. Like Coronado, who in 1540 marched up the Rio Grande, Dominic imagines his own El Dorado. He wants to carve an earthly paradise from the metropolitan center, unaware that he and others are serpents in the Garden. Along with the other main characters in Anaya's novel, he is a traveler in the labyrinth of history. That the outcome of the city's mayoral election, contested by an Anglo male, an incumbent Chicana mayor, and Dominic (who is married to a Latina but whose own origins are actually Italian), hinges on multiple cultural mysteries and unknown identities suggests that the Rio Grande Basin is a realm of deeply hidden and mixed origins. Reed Way Dasenbrock correctly notes of Anaya that "the Hispanic culture of the Southwest is derived from the pre-Columbian world and from Native American culture. And this is why he sees this local identity in global terms, as part of an emerging New World and non-Western identity that can meet the old European world on equal terms" (245). The Southwest offers a fluid perspective on the "nation," which is one reason Anaya in his interview with Feroza Jussawella acknowledges, "I have always been very interested in the migrations of people, especially in the Southwest" (245).

As the twentieth century moves to a close, the city of Albuquerque itself is contested metropolitan or national space, the quintessential imperial city. In the novel, Anaya restores the city to its original spelling prior to 1880 when the railroad reached la Villa de Alburquerque and "legend says the Anglo stationmaster couldn't pronounce the first 'r' in 'Albur,' so he dropped it as he painted the station sign for the city." Albuquerque thus is a complex symbolic terrain, a contemporary transnational crossroads in which migrant souls ranging from new corporate colonizers to Anglo retirees mix with native tribes whose ancestral homes are north of the Rio Grande, Chicanos with their pre-Columbian and Spanish origins, and other New World people actively seeking their true identities. Albuquerque is the postmodern cosmopolitan city. Within this urban landscape, the reader apprehends a unique iconography in which local, national, and international versions of historical destiny intersect. At this intersection of local landscape and epic national destiny—the formation of what Benedict Anderson (1983) terms an "imagined community"—lies the very traditional architecture of race and ethnicity. He notes, "The city was still split. The Anglos lived in the Heights, the Chicanos along the valley. The line between Barelas and the Country Club was a microcosm of the city. One didn't have to go to El Paso and cross to Juarez to understand the idea of border" (37–38). However, the collective consciousness of the city's inhabitants both acknowledges these traditional cleavages *and* negotiates the space between them. Marriages and relationships across these borders blur the lines of origin. The very complication of Chicano mestizo with the accretion of Anglo blood signifies the late twentieth century's search for a new national project acknowledging "difference" but also seeking a unique form of synthesis or cultural hybridity.

Whether the evocation of landscape centers on Albuquerque or the small New Mexican towns and llanos of Anaya's best-known novel *Bless Me, Ultima;* the impoverished Texas terrain of Tomás Rivera's . . .*y no se lo trago la tierra (And the Earth Did Not Devour Him)*; or the mutable

"Golden Land" of California in the migrant odysseys of Villarreal's *Pocho*, Raymond Barrio's *The Plum Plum Pickers*, and other novels, the settings in this fiction suggest a decentering of national identity. These landscapes evoke a world or environment that produces an essential fragmentation and alienation of traditional lives seeking passage into modernity. Typically the migrant souls depicted in this fiction are trapped between traditional rural or campesino culture and the colonizing impulses unleashed by the forces of modernity. For the older generation of Mexican migrants that came to the United States in the years following the Mexican Revolution—those violent decades characterized by the Mexican novelist Martin Luis Guzman as a "fiesta of bullets"—no national synthesis of the warring impulses of tradition and modernity seemed possible. This reality, for example, constitutes an important subtext in Villarreal's *Pocho*, where the father, Juan Mario Rubio, who had fought for more than ten years with Pancho Villa, merely substitutes one form of national chaos for another of cultural and economic subjugation in his passage across the Rio Grande to the United States. However, the children and grandchildren of these original migrant families inherit a mixture of traditions and cultures that prepares them provisionally for the world they enter in the years before, during, and after the Second World War. That Richard Rubio, the son of the Villa loyalist, enlists in the Navy during World War II, which constitutes the conclusion of *Pocho*, suggests a new nationalist mission for the sons and daughters of their original twentieth-century migrant parents.

Villarreal's Immigrant Saga

The immigrant saga of the Rubio family in *Pocho* is typical of the push and pull of those economic and political forces that forced millions of Mexicans to leave their country for *una vida mejor*—a better life—in the United States, first in modest numbers during the 1920s and 1930s (the latter a decade during which many Mexican nationals and Mexican-American citizens were deported because of the hardships of the Depression), and then in increasing waves during and after the Second World War. Yet as William Finnegan has noted aptly in "The New Americans" (1996), the new migrants seem "locked in a struggle as old as serfdom" (53) and indeed as old as their forebears. In the years after 1910, almost one-eighth of Mexico's population, overwhelmingly rural, migrated to the United States, a passage facilitated by their exclusion from the Immigration Act of 1924, which imposed strict quotas on immigration from other parts of the world. According to Rodolfo Acuña in his seminal work *Occupied America: The Chicano's Struggle Toward Liberation* (1972), more than 500,000 Mexicans immigrated to the United States in the 1920s, and perhaps 40,000 in the 1930s (140). Their exclusion from the Immigration Act was the result of powerful lobbying by economic interests throughout the Southwest that required cheap and abundant migrant labor to harvest the fields, work in the mines, and build the railroads, in the process creating the superstructure for the explosive growth that would occur in the Southwest after World War II. The utilization of these early migrants became a model for the harnessing of campesino labor during the war years. The scholar Oscar J. Martinez in *Border People: Life and Society in the U.S.-Mexico Borderlands* (1994) summarizes this twentieth-century phenomenon of border crossing: "Although some Mexican Americans on the border are descended from colonial Spanish-American families, most trace their presence in the region to the waves of immigrants from Mexico that began at the outbreak of the revolution in 1910. Those who arrived after 1940 are particularly numerous because of the much heavier immigration flow during the half-century of extraordinary economic expansion in the U.S. Southwest that was initiated by World War II. Physical proximity to Mexico has assured strong adherence to Mexican cultural norms and the maintenance of the Spanish language" (91). Border culture, as Martinez suggests, facilitates the binational behavior of *fronterizos*—the migrants, commuters, settler migrants, and newcomers who constitute the borderlands milieu.

Villarreal's *Pocho*, which has been derided by some Chicano critics for its assimilationist tendencies, is nevertheless the paradigmatic text illuminating the symbiotic relationship between the Mexican and United States borderland culture that was established in the years leading up to World War II. In his introduction to the 1970 Anchor reprint edition of the novel, Ramon E. Ruiz correctly emphasizes the distinctive strength of *Pocho* in its depiction of the evolution of borderlands or cross-cultural migrant society. He states, "Villarreal writes with gusto and success of the *pochos*, the population born of Mexican parents, who retain some of the characteristics of their Mexican ancestry: the love of Mexican food, the customs of the old country, the acceptance of the patriarchal family pattern, and something of the Spanish language. But *pochos* can no longer be Mexican, if only because they saw the light of day in the United States, but more importantly because their way of life eventually develops into a concoction of Mexican and American customs, traditions, and aspirations" (ix). The very word *pocho* suggests the duality of identity and the difficulty of the quest to resolve this duality for Mexican Americans. As James D. Cockcroft (1986) explains: "This Mexican word—from the Uto-Aztecan (Mexican Indian) *potzi* describing an animal that is short or tailless—here refers to a U.S. reared person who is comically inept and thus 'tailless' in two cultures" (195). At the center of narrative gravity in *Pocho* is this encounter of the self—this "Americanized" Mexican or Chicano—with competing or rival cultures.

In *Pocho*, the central protagonists are Juan Rubio and his son Richard. The father's national identity is defined largely by his affiliation with and remembrance of the Villa legend: the epic stories and heroic deeds he participated in as a colonel during the Mexican Revolution. Rubio is a peon, a product of hallowed Mexican soil. "Our ancestors," he declares as he plans his passage from Ciudad Juarez to El Paso del Norte at the outset of the novel, "were princes in a civilization that was possibly more advanced than this one" (8). Possessing no great love of either Spanish (*gachupines*) or "gringa" civilization, Rubio falls back on the virtues of honor, manliness, and dignity—*machismo*—for whether he is south or north of the border, he apprehends that his wandering life can have no center without the preservation of these virtues.

With one imagined national paradise in ruins, Rubio becomes part of an epic migration to the new Promised Land.

> Thus Juan Rubio became a part of the great exodus that came of the Mexican Revolution. By the hundreds they crossed the Rio Grande, and then by the thousands. They came first to Juarez, where the price of the three-minute tram ride would take them into El Paso del Norte—or a short walk through the open door would deposit them in Utopia. The ever-increasing army of people swarmed across while the border remained open, fleeing from squalor and oppression. But they could not flee reality, and the Texans, who welcomed them as a blessing because there were miles of cotton to be harvested, had never really forgotten the Alamo. . . . It was the ancient

quest for El Dorado, and so they moved onward, west to New Mexico and Arizona and California, and as they moved, they planted their new seed. (15–16)

The cotton growers who offer their mixed blessings to the new arrivals employed tens of thousands Mexican migrants in Texas fields in the 1920s. These growers' associations were the beneficiaries of the "revolving border door" system established and policed by the U.S. Border Patrol that was created in 1924. Along the 2,000–mile border between Mexico and the United States, the U.S. Border Patrol guaranteed a steady flow of Mexican migrants at harvest time, and forced a reverse migration of the same migrants once the crops were in. Later the Bracero Program that started during World War II and lasted well into the 1960s would provide another generation of Mexican migrants for the farms of Texas, California, and other western states.

The "great exodus" following the Mexican Revolution takes Rubio and subsequently his family to California, where they experience the "nomadic" life of migrant workers, settling finally in the Santa Clara valley below San Francisco, but dreaming always of returning to Mexico. Although he lacks formal education, the elder Rubio possesses a strong sense of lived history as well as a cynical perception of the false visions of the colonial world. Mexican nationalism is an assertive part of his personality, but he understands also the savage betrayals that aborted the revolution. Because the informing energies of Rubio's life derive from the revolution, when he moves across the border he suffers historic deprivation: this new geopolitical terrain—the United States—can never nurture his sense of national identity as a Mexican. Migrancy is now his condition, forcing a tenuous diasporic identity on him that results ultimately in the abandonment not only of his dream to return to Mexico but also of his family.

Rubio reads United States history backward through centuries of usurpation and colonialism to pre-Columbian times. Sensitized to the accumulated woes of history, he loathes all forms of political oppression—from the Spanish colonizers and their clerical conspirators to the colonizing institutions of his adoptive land, characterized for example by an educational system that permits Anglo schoolchildren to call their darker peers *cholo* or "dirty Mexican." Considering his new world, Rubio declares, "All the people who are pushed around in the rest of the world

come here, because here they can maybe push someone else around"
(100). Always the militant, he becomes the focus of authority for the
Mexican families settling in the Santa Clara Valley in the 1930s; he sympathizes with the attempts of the communists to organize the migrants,
and helps the new American peons, "the Oakies," who invariably fail to
repay him. But when he becomes a homeowner in Santa Clara, the irreversible process of assimilation begins: "He was unaware that he was fashioning the last link of events that would bind him to America and the
American way of life" (129).

Rubio's son Richard is the filter through which the diaspora consciousness—the customs, values, and language of Mexico and the United
States respectively—is fashioned. Essentially Richard rejects all forms of
cultural hegemony; he is a youthful skeptic who feels he can control his
own destiny. An avid reader of Horatio Alger books who senses early
that he is destined to be a writer, the young Richard is atypical of second-
generation children of immigrants whose classic tendency is to renounce
their parents' origins and fiercely embrace the American Dream. As first
student in his catechism class and the only son among eight sisters, Richard apprehends that he has been chosen to construct an identity from
the family's old and new cultures. He is saddened when he perceives the
irreversible acculturation of the Rubio family: "He was aware that the
family was undergoing a strange metamorphosis. The heretofore gradual
assimilation of this new culture was becoming more pronounced. Along
with a new prosperity the Rubio family was taking on the mores of the
middle class, and he did not like it. It saddened him to see the Mexican
tradition disappear" (132). Yet Richard also assists in the acculturation
process, forging new ties through his school experience and friends in
the neighborhood, moving easily through the interstices of the two cultures, actually enjoying a dialectical connection to traditional and modern societies. Richard understands the class, racial, sexual, and economic
conditions that frame society, and the contradictions between traditional
and urban cultures that produced the flamboyant *pachucos* or "zoot suit-
ors" of the 1940s, that "lost race" whose rebelliousness Richard admires.

By the end of the novel, with its allusions to the Conscription Act
of 1940, the mobilization for the war effort that would see tens of thousands of young Mexican Americans enlist and die in disproportionate
numbers in Europe and the Pacific, and the internment of Japanese
Americans—all telescoped in the concluding pages of *Pocho*—Richard

synthesizes the martial virtues of his father's generation and the acculturating spirit of patriotism or loyalty to his new society by enlisting in his nation's armed forces. Forged by the period stretching from the Great Migration northward to the Great Depression to the Second World War, the young Richard is now a mature settler in the New World. He assuredly does not exist in a paradise, but America also is not an exhausted dream; in fact, the American experience enables him to forge his own identity in the post-modern, post-industrial, and decidedly transnational world that awaits him on his return. As a wanderer on the borderline of these worlds, his task is to construct an identity that frees him from the cycles of campesino economic oppression but also enables him to objectify his existence as a Chicano in Anglo culture. That Richard imagines his future vocation as a writer (the novel has decidedly autobiographical overtones) suggests that he will survive the war and that the task of cultural differentiation—the challenge of imagining a national community—will be a continual psychic process for him.

Braceros

The events of the Second World War and the postwar era signal a critical watershed in the history of Mexican migration to the United States. The vast tide of Mexican immigrants coming to the "border belt" of Texas, the upper Rio Grande Valley of New Mexico and Colorado, the central valley of California, metropolitan Los Angeles, the Salt River Valley of Arizona, the San Francisco Bay basin, and key cities stretching from Denver to Chicago to New York during this epoch would make Mexican Americans the dominant demographic force in the development of Hispanic culture in their adoptive nation. According to Geoffrey Fox (1996), the census report of 1993 "classifies as Mexican 14,628,000 of the 22,750,000 Hispanics here, or 64.3 percent of the total Hispanic population nationwide" (33). World War II reversed the immigration policies of the previous decade, which had witnessed the forced repatriation of Mexicans and the start of undocumented entry of Mexicans into the United States that had started in earnest during the Depression. In August of 1942, after Mexico had declared war on Germany, Japan, and Italy, it entered into a bilateral agreement with the United States to create the "Mexican farm labor program," better known as the Bracero Program. Legalized as Public Law 45 and intended originally as a wartime emergency act to provide cheap agricultural labor for the Southwest, it assured over the quarter century of its existence an ideological basis for the conscription of migrant labor to serve the economic needs of the nation.

Perhaps the most unique agreement in U.S. immigration history, the Bracero Program, which increasingly was coordinated by numerous governmental agencies up to the time of its demise in 1964, institutionalized a colonial situation that throughout the twentieth century had recognized Mexico as a convenient and contiguous source of cheap labor. Kitty Calavita, who in *Inside The State: The Bracero Program, Immigration, and the I.N.S.* (1992) offers the most detailed and documented account of the vagaries of this program, estimates that from the time the first five hundred Mexican farm workers arrived in Stockton, California, on September 4, 1942, to alleviate the wartime labor shortage until 1964, "five million 'braceros' were contracted to ranchers and growers in twenty-four states" (1). The wartime Bracero Program alone provided more than 219,500 workers as contracted labor. When the original program ended officially on December 31, 1947, United States growers lobbied the federal government for extensions and informal annual agreements. The Immigration and Naturalization Service in 1947 also devised a program whereby undocumented Mexican migrant workers could be legalized on the spot—termed in official quarters "drying out the wetbacks." The unintended result, of course, was increased undocumented migration, since Mexicans knew they could be readily legalized if apprehended by authorities. According to Calavita, "between 1947 and 1949, approximately 74,600 braceros were contracted from Mexico, while 142,000 undocumented workers were legalized and contracted directly to growers. In 1950, fewer than 20,000 braceros were imported, and over 76,000 illegal aliens were paroled to local farmers" (28–29). INS enforcement policies therefore provided both legal and illegal immigration from Mexico. Ernesto Galarza correctly describes this phenomenon in his history of the era, *Merchants of Labor: The Mexican Bracero Program* (1964) as a "bonanza" for American farmers.

Although the bracero agreement ostensibly guaranteed Mexican migrant workers transportation, acceptable housing and working conditions, and minimum wages, the increasing flow of cheap undocumented labor provided growers with an attractive alternative to contracted laborers. Thus there never developed any reciprocity in what essentially constituted, as the authors of the study *The Mexican-American People* (1970) maintain, a "caste system" (Grebler and Moore 8–9). This struggle between the owners and the workers, the colonizer and the colonized, ultimately would lead to resistance by the United Farm Workers under Caesar Chavez in the 1970s, resulting in the passage of the California Agricultural Relations Act of 1975 that mandated orderly collective bargaining agreements between growers and farm workers. But during the bracero era, what we might term the nation's project of internal imperialism, consciously sustained and supported by federal policies and local authority, created the conditions of oppression for Chicano farm workers and a new mythos that Chicano (and Anglo) writers would investigate in their fiction.

Just as World War II had provided the justification for the original Bracero Program, the outbreak of the Korean War in 1950 enabled Congress to pass new legislation to continue the program and thereby suppress wages in the agricultural sector of the Southwest. With new legislation such as the Migrant Labor Agreement of 1951, the official parameters of the Bracero Program sanctioned a policy of intervention in the capitalist enterprise that invariably benefited the growers. Even the most bizarre or aggressive changes in immigration policy reinforced the political effort to sustain a culture of internal colonization. During the 1950s, for example, an essentially hands-off era, the INS implemented a policy of rounding up undocumented Mexican immigrants, transporting them to the border, having them step across into Mexico and then back into the United States as legally contracted braceros—a procedure which Calavita notes became known as "a walk around the statute" (41). Thus when "Operation Wetback," sanctioned under Title III of the McCarran-Walter Act of 1952 which permitted the deportation of illegal aliens, was launched in 1954 by the militant head of the INS, General Joseph Swing, the apprehension and deportation of more than one million undocumented Mexican workers in the first year alone was ameliorated by the reinvigoration of the Bracero Program with 398,650 contracted laborers in 1955 and 445,197 in 1956 (55). By the time the Immigration Act of 1965 for the first time in history imposed a quota of 120,000 persons annually to be admitted from the Western Hemisphere, the tide of Mexicans to the United States was so large and irreversible in its momentum as to be largely unstoppable. Thus the revival of a revolving door policy seen in nascent form in the 1920s acquired the power and authority, an ideological component of sorts, that both invited Mexican migrants to a New World and restricted them to rural and urban ghettoization. Immigration policies fostered precisely those cultural dislocations and resentments seen in *Pocho* and the body of subsequent Chicano fiction interpreting the colonial condition of the *mestizo* migrant, this composite immigrant inhabiting a new nation that ironically had belonged in part to Mexico before the Mexican-American War.

Given the imperial history of the Southwest, it is not surprising that Chicano historians, literary critics, and novelists embrace a theory of internal colonialism as the most salient explanation of the Mexican-American condition. The basic outlines of this theory were first enunciated in what is now a classic of Chicano historiography, Rodolfo Acuña's *Occupied America: the Chicano's Struggle Toward Liberation* (1976). Acuña's thesis is that "Chicanos are a colonizer people in the United States . . . the conquest of the Southwest created a colonial situation in the traditional sense—with Mexican land and population being controlled by an imperialist United States" (1–3). The history of Mexican Americans in the United States thus is unusual because of their original presence in the nation even prior to the nation's founding. How then can Mexican Americans possibly imagine their own past except as the products of internal colonialism? And internal colonization resembles the contours of the more conventionally discussed external colonization: "The relationship between Anglos and Chicanos remains the same—that of master-servant. The principal difference is that Mexicans in the traditional colony were indigenous to the conquered land. Now, while some are descendants of Mexicans living in the era before the conquest, large numbers are technically the descendants of immigrants" (4). Subsequent social scientists such as Mario Barrera (1979) and numerous literary critics, notably Manuel de Jesus Hernández-Gutiérrez (1994), have expanded the internal colony paradigm to conceptualize the true situation of the Mexican-American population in the United States. Essentially all theorists assert that you cannot apply traditional Eurocentric models of immigration to the experience of Mexican Americans. As Barrera states in *Race and Class in the Southwest,* the internal colony model "became the means of criticizing a number of academic writings which treated America's racial minorities within the same framework as European ethnic immigrants" (189). Similarly, Gutiérrez, who applies this theory most cogently to Chicano narrative in *El colonialismo interno en la narrativa chicana* (one of the many texts in Spanish published by Bilingual Press, which more than any other publisher has made Chicano literature available to the public in Spanish, English, and bilingual editions), states that the Eurocentric paradigm is specious: "Segun este modelo, los nuevos immigrantes entran primero a los Estados Unidos, luego se asimilan y entonces obtien en la movilidad social" (3). This process of arrival, gradual assimilation, and social mobility ignores the fact that the native element of Mexican-American identity, defined at its core in terms its *mestizo* composite and its caste attributes, requires an adjustment of contemporary immigration theory to accommodate the reality of subjugated communities. If imperialism, as Edward Said asserts in *Culture and Imperialism*, "means thinking about, settling on controlling land that you do not possess, that is distant, that is lived on but owned by others" (7), we can see the relevance of "distant" imperialism to the internal models offered by Chicano critics.

Migratory labor from both Mexico and the borderland communities is at the center of the theory of internal colonization as well the narrative discourses of identity unfolding in *Pocho*, Rivera's *Tierra,* and Barrio's *The Plum Plum Pickers.* The fictive territory of these three novels maps the internal condition; the debate about assimilation and the resistance emerging from this cultural situation; and the prospect for a postcolonial future as the migrant experience interrogates the myths of the New World. In this fiction, Mexican and Chicano migrants are conditioned by the forces of internal colonialism, which thrives on racial discrimination linked organically to the subjugating pressures of labor-intensive capitalism. Race and caste create the colonized identity of migrants who move continuously through Anglo-American capitalist society, coming into an unequal relationship with economic and social forces but also remaining culturally desirous of metropolitan society. As Barrera suggests in *Race and Class in the Southwest*: "Internal colonialism is a form of colonialism in which the dominant and subordinate populations are intermingled, so that there is no geographically distinct 'metropolis' separate from the 'colony'" (189). The process of asserting an identity or acceptable state of existence within this hybrid nation is a daunting enterprise, involving both the positing of an authentic self and the reimagining of one's own past.

Tierra: *The Quest for Chicano Identity*

Tomás Rivera centers the ideological debate over the need to reconstitute personal, communal, and historical identity in his introduction to the first edition of Chicano novelist Ron Aria's *The Road to Tamazunchale* (1975): "I think it is imperative that those Chicanos who need it, immerse themselves in the profound and satisfying intent of finding their identity. . . . Chicanismo to me represents the rebirth of a spirit. . . . I believe that the most important thing for art and literature is to liberate itself from dogmas and to express freely not only the suffering, the injustices, but rather the totality of the Chicano. Our intent in literature, then, has to be totally human" (9). Rivera's point is that while colonized peoples carry humiliating wounds, they cannot permit themselves to be submerged in the realities of economic subjugation, but rather must make a broader effort to achieve a basic cultural identity fundamentally different from that which the colonial world imposes on them. In an essay titled "Chicano Literature: The Establishment of Community" (1982), Rivera asserts that the urge to reclaim a viable place (*lugar*) in the New World reveals "a colonized mind and a deprived, powerless class. The Chicano had to begin decolonizing the mind" (10).

Rivera's own stunning effort to re-imagine the national community, . . . *y no se lo trago la tierra* (1971), is an example of how the Chicano migrant is the emblematic figure representing the attempt to establish a post-colonial consciousness. On the jacket of Evangelina Vigil-Penon's English translation of his novel, Rivera places the individual quest for identity within the larger search for a communal and national identity: "I wanted to document the spiritual strength, the concept of justice so important for the American continents. With these migrants I saw that strength. They may be economically deprived, but they kept moving, never staying in one place to suffer or be subdued, but always searching for work; that's why they were 'migrant' workers. I see that same sense of movement in the Europeans who came here and that concept of spiritual justice. It was there. And the migrant workers still have that role: to be searchers. That's an important metaphor for the Americas." Rivera's *Tierra* traces the lives and peregrinations of Mexican workers in the post–World War II era and early 1950s, with the Korean War serving as an immediate backdrop. Consisting of two framing vignettes, twelve brief stories or *estempas* that are common to Spanish and Latin American fiction, interspersed with thirteen related sketches, the novel offers a harshly ironic portrayal of the meager existence of Chicano migrants in the Southwest. However, the novel also asserts their ability to sustain their own imagined community despite their economic vicissitudes. With its unique structural technique, the novel resembles the short story cycles typified, for example, by *Dubliners, Go Down Moses,* and *Winesburg, Ohio.* But the cycle that Rivera's novel most closely resembles is Hemingway's *In Our Time.* In both cycles, stories are interspersed with brief related sketches. In both texts, a central character—an unnamed boy and Nick Adams respectively—appears intermittently as a dramatic persona hounded by national events. In both, war serves as a backdrop, although World War I is far more of an overt presence in Hemingway's cycle than later wars are in Rivera's book. Nevertheless, both cycles reveal a national landscape of incipient violence, even as national "reality" for Hemingway differs ultimately from Rivera's depiction of history, politics, and the national estate in *Tierra.*

Although Rivera might have appropriated both Anglo-American and Spanish antecedents (including *Don Quixote*) in his short story cycle, his highly experimental formal and stylistic depiction of national identity in *Tierra* reflects postcolonial and postmodern assumptions. Ramon Saldívar is correct when he asserts in *Chicano Narrative: The Dialectics of Difference* (1990) that Rivera's novel "does not give us historical depiction in the mode of more traditional realism so much as a complex narrative of subjective impressions where strict chronological presentation, orderly compositional development, and linear plot development have broken down" (75). From the very first frame where the nameless narrator establishes as his mission the reclamation of a year that "was lost to him" (1992:8) to the closing frame in which, like Ellison's Invisible Man he has retreated (under the house rather than underground) to ponder his individual and collective destiny, the young migrant narrator searches for a language that will permit him to reassess national society while reaffirming collective Chicano community. Chicano identity is posited on this dialectical tension between the imagined community that is the essence of the modern state and the perception of one's *difference* from the modular forms of the postcolonial nation. For example, in the first story in *Tierra,* "The Children Couldn't Wait," a group of migrant children, oppressed by the stifling April heat in the fields of South Texas (where Rivera himself was born to migrant parents in 1935), approach a forbidden water hole to quench their thirst. The Anglo cattle rancher who enjoys hegemony over the fields, the water, and his migrant souls, shouts at one child who keeps returning to drink: "What he set out to do and what he did were two different things. He shot at him once to scare him but when he pulled the trigger he saw the boy with a hole in his head. And the child didn't even jump like a deer does. He just stayed in the water like a dirty rag and the water began to turn bloody" (86–87). The rancher's rifle is virtually synonymous with national power, with the absolutism of Manifest Destiny that insists on political and economic control over its subjects. Children, of course, do not understand the contours of national power and national identity. Yet the face of the murdered child registers in the consciousness of the central figure in *Tierra*, as the thematic link between "The Children Couldn't Wait" and the brief sketch preceding it suggests: "What his mother never knew was that every night he would drink the glass of water that she left under the bed for spirits. She always believed that they drank the water so she continued doing her duty. Once he was going to tell her but then he thought that he'd wait and tell her when he was grown up" (85). It is the task of the central figure to become aware of the fundamental lines connecting his thirst (and his conscious rejection of traditional beliefs) and the thirst of the sorely oppressed child who is killed in the first tale. This project of discovering his essential post-colonial or decolonized self through a series of seasonal migratory revelations (the twelve main stories function as a complete year *and* an allegorical decade in the lives of these migrants) will force him to mediate between his Mexican past and the neocolonial present. Only by apprehending his national situation will he be able to construct an identity that enables him to transcend his imperialized world. Thus the fragmentary nature of *Tierra* reads like a national jigsaw puzzle, serving at one level as a reflection of the migratory segments in the Chicano farmworkers' annual odyssey from the fields of south Texas, northward into the heart of mainland America, and back to the border region; and at another interconnected level as a search through the fragments of family and ethnic tradition for a creative and vibrant rather than inert and "colonized" cultural identity.

That Chicano identity must be fashioned from the materials of two cultures, both with their respective demands and constraints, requires a viewpoint or perspective that constantly interrogates *and* sustains cultural memory. For example, just as the major character in *Tierra* apprehends the bigotry, violence, and oppression of the Anglo world in "The

Children Couldn't Wait," he also develops an inner perspective on the *curanderia* and Catholicism of his migrant community. (Rivera's critique of Catholicism as a subjugating or colonizing force is an ideological tendency seen also in *Pocho* and other novels of the Chicano experience.) In the sketch that follows "The Children Couldn't Wait," a sleeping mother has an exchange with a "spirit ... present in her body" (89) over the fate of her son Julianito who has been officially declared missing in action in the Korean theater. Similarly, in the next story, "A Prayer," another mother invokes a host of Catholic deities to bring her son back alive from Korea. The migrant mothers do not understand the historical situation or the competing imperial ideologies that have claimed their sons. Conversely, the boy's growing apostasy, revealed in the signature story "And The Earth Did Not Devour Him," where he questions the viability of God to solve the problems of a subjugated community, suggests that Rivera believes that both nationalism and indigenous culture contain elements that diminish and potentially imprison the individual who seeks an authentic identity. Although *Tierra* has been treated most typically as the canonical Chicano text that rejects assimilation (as *Pocho* does not) and reaffirms ethnic identity, it is more useful to perceive the nameless narrator, the anonymous bearer of his race, as a contemporary voyager constantly being formed and transformed by the influences of his environment *and* the struggle between the old and the new.

Within the cycles of Mexican immigration history, the young consciousness at the center of *Tierra* is formed by the rigors of the migrant experience, the structures of the larger society, and the primary associations and continuities within his immediate community. It is through what Rivera in an essay titled "Fiesta of the Living" (1975) terms "the ritual of remembering" that the young boy is able to establish a living relationship with his culture. The struggle (*la lucha*) between cultures thus is one involving an effort to maintain a vital base in one's culture even as the individual confronts the "other" Anglo universe. The boy's ritual of remembering typically forces him to recall events that reflect violence and deprivation: the sickness and deaths of parents and relatives; the communal rivalries and betrayals; the intermittent schooling of migrant children and omnipresence of numerous forms of institutional racism; the seasonal rituals tied to the Catholic church that are persistently critiqued by Rivera. This ritual unfolds through the constant movement of migrant peoples across a strange and unforgiving national landscape. In one sketch, a campesino doubts there is a state called Utah where a contractor wants to send them for work; his companion surmises that it might be near Japan. In another sketch, a drunken Anglo woman precipitates a crash that kills sixteen spinach pickers. In a third, a priest blesses the cars of campesinos for five dollars each and uses the proceeds to visit his parents in Barcelona, Spain. And in one of the longer and more technically unique stories near the end of the novel, "When We Arrive," a series of interior monologues captures the thoughts of more than a dozen migrant workers being transported in a truck from the fields of Texas to Minnesota. The truck has broken down at four in the morning, and in this bizarre nocturnal world, one migrant wonders if they will ever arrive: "When we arrive, when we arrive, the real truth is that I'm tired of arriving. Arriving and leaving, it's the same thing because we no longer arrive and . . . the real truth of the matter . . . I'm tired of arriving. I really should say when we don't arrive because that's the real truth. We never arrive" (145).

These arrivals and departures that frame the migrant community's history are the essence of the Chicano universe that the unnamed central consciousness must actively "remember" if he is to establish his own social identity. From the Texas winter of the cotton pickers depicted in the first story of *Tierra,* through the spring and summer months in Utah, Iowa, Michigan, and finally Minnesota, the boy must discover the consciousness of his race. With the introductory or frame unit, "The Lost Year," he had been in danger of forgetting his own culture. With the end frame, "Under the House," he reconstructs a usable past out of the tapestry of family lore and Mexican history stretching from the defeat of Napoleon's troops in 1872 through the Revolution to the present. Instead of erasing all memory of one's origins—what Friere alludes to in *The Pedagogy of the Oppressed* as being submerged in reality and Fanon in *The Wretched of the Earth* likens to being "without an anchor, without a horizon, colorless, stateless" (218)—he reconceives or re-imagines an authentic culture that grows out of the unique narrative pieces of the text. By retreating under the house, reconstructing the cultural contradictions contained in the sketches and seemingly anomalous stories constituting *Tierra,* and then emerging into the world at the very end, he completes a cycle of self-discovery that liberates him from marginalized history and propels him into the Chicano ethos—an awareness of his distinctive cultural identity.

Imagined Communities

The collective experience of the migrant community in *Tierra, Pocho* and other texts forces a refinement and modification of Benedict Anderson's seminal definition of the modern nation in *Imagined Communities: Reflections on the Origin and Spread of Nationalism* (1983): "In an anthropological spirit . . . I propose the following definition of the nation: it is an imagined political community . . . and imagined as both inherently limited and sovereign. It is *imagined* because the members of even the smallest nation will never know most of their fellow members, meet them, or even hear them, yet in the minds of each lives the image of their communion" (15). Such a concept of nation is foreign to the migrant community in *Tierra*, whose members cannot "imagine" Utah, travel across America in the dark, experience only racism in their dealings with Anglo society, and remain an oppressed group in a system of virtual *apartheid* within the modern American state. The question for the migrant "nation" in *Tierra* is how to sustain private lives within the community while existing in a public domain where Anglo farm owners, police, school teachers, and shop owners are alien forces reminding them of the disparities between the two cultures.

The very fact that *Tierra* was written originally in a vernacular Spanish that captures the folk rhythms of the borderlands milieu suggests the deep differences separating migrant and Anglo society, keeping the former on the periphery of the nation. Virtually all fiction by Chicano writers (notably that by Rivera and Rolando Hinojosa, whose seven novels constituting the borderland epic *Klail City Death Trip* series were first written in Spanish before translation into English) contends with the issue of language as it relates to the national project and the project of modernity. Chicano fiction in its variegated Spanishness and binguality violates those modular norms preferred by the modern canon and the modern state. It exists outside of that "homogenous time" (of which English is a homogenizing component) that Anderson sees as an attribute of the modern nation (17–49). The migrants seemingly possess the rudimentary bilingual equipment that permits them passage through American society, but their rootedness in vernacular borderlands Spanish creates an identity that is recognizably Mexican and thus clearly distinct from Anglo-American forms of narrative. Combined with folklore, communal memory and cultural traditions, and religious beliefs, rituals and practices, the bilinguality of Chicano fiction suggests a postmodern tension between traditional and modern national projects.

With the Chicano migrant fiction written by Mexican Americans (and also Anglo-Americans), a new set of historical claims is advanced that confronts the national project and asserts a rival agency in its implicit critique of North American history. These rival claims amount to a rediscovery of a New World consciousness which, as John Lynch shows in *The Spanish American Revolutions, 1808–1826* (1973), is rooted in the early idea common among Mexicans that *they* were the true Americans ("nosotros los Americanos") and that America belonged to them ("nuestra America"). Within such a field of rival discourse, the national mission or project becomes a subject for revision as the very assumptions of national power, identity, and hegemony are interrogated. From the perspective of contemporary Chicano history, we see the impact of internal colonialism—especially the arrayed forces of commodity capitalism and agricultural production—on indigenous cultures, but also the resilience of dispriviledged migrant groups in their construction of the means of survival and the preservation of ways of life. Even in novels like *Tierra* where we sense a complete dominance of national power over economic lives, it is the enduring characteristics of Mexican culture—its relative imperviousness to the most egregious forms of national intrusion—that establish the limits of colonial rule. Thus, while acknowledging the inevitable interdependence of Mexican and Anglo culture, we can understand that Chicano fiction advances a historiography whose agenda demands cultural self-representation.

The ethnic, religious, and communal sense of self-representation in *Tierra* confirms the powerful insights of the Subaltern commentator Partha Chatterjee who in *The Nation and Its Fragments: Colonial and Postcolonial Societies* (1993) elucidates an "anti-colonial nationalism" (5) that has transformed the postcolonial societies of Asia and Africa. Of all the immigrant groups in the contemporary United States, it is the Mexican-American community, and notably its migrants, that best supports Chatterjee's effort to deconstruct Anderson's thesis of imagined community to accommodate postcolonial and postmodern realities: "If the nation is an imagined community and if nations must also take the forms of states, then our theoretical language must allow us to talk about community and state at the same time" (11). Chatterjee advances a theoretical framework in which anticolonial nationalism, typified by his case

study of India, divides social institutions into two domains—the material and the spiritual, or the outside and the inside. The outside world is
the domain of the colonial nation, typified by its control of the economy
and technology; while the inside world or indigenous community—of
language, race, family, ritual, and religion—contains "the essential marks
of cultural identity" (6). Consequently the entire issue of the *identity* of
colonized peoples is not posited on nationalist assumptions but rather
on a sense of *difference* from national society. Chatterjee writes, "This
domain of sovereignty, which nationalism thought of as the 'spiritual' or
'inner' aspects of culture, such as language or religion or the elements of
personal and family life, was of course premised upon a difference between the cultures of the colonizer and the colonized. The more nationalism engaged in its contest with the colonial power in the other domain
of politics, the more it insisted on displaying the marks of 'essential' cultural differences so as to keep out the colonizer from that inner domain
of national life and proclaim its sovereignty over it" (26). Thus the hegemonic and normalizing mission of the modern nation—and, in the context of the United States, the postmodern nation—confronts the
impermeable "alienness" or otherness of cultural groups whose inner
domains challenge the intrusive powers of the dominant state, offering
rival historicities that differ from the history of the nation.

Barrio's Dystopian Satire

We see this agenda for cultural self-representation operating in *Pocho*,
whose narrative takes readers from the Mexican Revolution up to World
War II; in *Tierra,* spanning the decade after the Second World War; and
in a third novel, Raymond Barrio's *The Plum Plum Pickers* (1969), whose
narrative sweep completes three decades of history by bringing it into
the tumultuous decade of the 1960s. Like Villarreal's *Pocho*, Barrio's novel
is set in the Santa Clara Valley of California, and, just as the economic
disruptions of the depression serve as the essential historical backdrop
for *Pocho, The Plum Plum Pickers* focuses on the era of agribusiness and
concentrated commodity capitalism as migrant workers struggle to create a new political history and ideology of resistance in more contemporary times. Highly experimental in method and tone, combining satiric
fantasy, political allegory, and documentary realism, *The Plum Plum Pick-*

ers invokes the clash of ideologies typifying the 1960s as rival cultures struggle to assert their mutually conditioned historicities. From the moment readers confront the main protagonists, the migrant couple Manuel and Lupe Gutierrez, in their shack within the Western Grande Compound, set in the imaginary Santa Clara town of Drawbridge, they are in a realm of postmodern political allegory in which imprisoned migrant souls, trapped on a latter-day imperial plantation, must struggle to fashion a destiny within the apparently hopeless domain of Anglo power—of total colonial rule.

The seemingly omnipotent owner of the Western Grande Compound, a feudal kingdom whose thousands of acres were appropriated slowly from previous owners of Spanish ancestry—the Californiaos—through legal subterfuge, is Mr. Frederick Y. Turner, who delegates to his supervisor, the grotesque Morton J. Quill, the task of managing the lives of his overexploited Mexican peasants. The very name of the owner, linked to the name of his feudal domain, suggests an ironic play by Barrio—typical of his overall method in the novel—on the concept of the frontier and westward expansion popularized by Frederick Jackson Turner in *The Frontier in American History* (1893). It is clear that Turner's frontier thesis, which Barrio parodies and subjects to scathing satire and cultural critique, espouses a Eurocentric theory of society whereby immigrants, composed largely of northern Europeans, are molded by the wilderness environment to produce a stipulative new species, the "American." Turner in the collection of essays comprising his seminal work acknowledges ethnic heterogeneity while implying that his immigrant prototype was the northern European: the essence of his new American. Turner's later work betrays a disdain and condescension toward the new immigrant groups from southern and western Europe. In the final paragraph of *The Frontier in American History*, he declares: "This then is the heritage of the pioneer experience,—a passionate belief that a democracy was possible which should leave the individual a part to play in free society and not make him a cog in a machine operated from above; which trusted in the common man, in his tolerance, his ability to adjust to differences with good humor, and to work out an American type from the contribution of all nations . . ." (359). However, these Old World immigrants, of northern European stock, differ from the "tides of alien immigrants surging into the country to replace the Old American stock in the labor market, to lower the standards of living and to increase the pressure of population upon the land" (271). Turner's crucible of the frontier in which a mixed race of immigrants fuses to become the prototypical American thus reveals precisely those hegemonic biases and conflicts that Barrio satirizes in *The Plum Plum Pickers*.

That one of the oldest ethnic groups in the United States escapes Turner's formulations is not surprising, but Barrio gleefully reinserts the Mexican-American component into the frontier thesis as an elemental force confronting "the old American stock." One of the unique aspects of *The Plum Plum Pickers* is the manner in which Barrio subjects Turner's utopian thesis to a dystopian analysis. Francisco Lomeli in his useful introduction to the Bilingual Press edition of the novel (1984) is quite correct in detecting this dystopian strain. And although Lomeli does not connect the dystopian world of *The Plum Plum Pickers* to Frederick Jackson Turner's frontier thesis, he does elucidate quite nicely the process whereby the California dream is turned into a nightmare of longing for the migrant families victimized on the Western Grande Compound by "agents of dystopia" (18). The Western Grande Compound, shaped by the forces of neocolonialism and molded by the political climate of California in the 1960s, quite literally traps economic immigrants in a terrain which, once the "drawbridge" is raised, exposes them to random, mercurial, and continual oppression by such dystopian agents of the community as the Dickensian Mr. Quill; his agent in the enterprise, the Mexican labor recruiter Roberto Morales (who as the word play suggests lacks all morals); and a supporting cast of political caricatures like Governor Howlin Mad Nolan (Ronald Reagan) and a certain "tap-dancing senator" (George Murphy). Because of inequalities of power, the diasporic world of the oppressor and the oppressed in Drawbridge can never be "bridged"; instead, Barrio argues from an ideological position that advances his novel beyond *Pocho* and *Tierra*, the system must be destroyed.

The political and economic framework of total control that Barrio satirizes in *The Plum Plum Pickers* removes the Mexican and Mexican-American farmworkers from both the nation's mythic past and any intrinsic sense of *mestizo* or cultural identity. "This permanent disease called California, the newest of most modern tortures" (43), is a hegemonic nightmare that fosters in Lupe Gutierrez an alternately romanticized nostalgia for her parents' home in Salpinango, near Guadalajara, and a longing for the artifacts of commodity capitalism—a nice home, a refrigerator, a dependable car—from which she is equally removed. At the outset she has a colonized mind, as does her docile, hardworking husband, who toils ceaselessly in "the pickers' paradise, the migrants' home away from home, his own proven domain" (32). Yet Lupe and Manuel also possess an incipient understanding of the system of oppression, of their forced wanderings not as the frontier heroes of Frederick Jackson Turner's scenario, but rather as conquered peoples subjected to an odyssey of oppression: "Moving, always moving. From Guadalajara to Monterrey to Reynosa, then across the border to Laredo and then that hijo de a malcrido hijo de la gran puta Texas Ranger in Rio Grande City—and now here, Santa Clara. Moving, moving, always moving." (38). Lupe, as Barrio indicates, could build half a cathedral with her dreams, but the reality is that they don't have a brick to call their own.

The legacy of dispossession shared by the Chicano migrants actually fuels the hegemonic California dream of the latter twentieth century. California itself is an imagined community whose economic and political rituals seem rooted in its Edenesque origins. Its totalizing claim to the national experience is conditioned by a sense of itself as a "chosen" state of almost biblical proportions—pretensions that Barrio persistently deflates through his parodic editorializing style:

> This was California.
>
> This, the richest, the greatest, the most productive chunk of rich earth in the world, this munificent cornucopian state pouring forth an unbelievable glut of gorgeous peaches, a blizzard of plums, a plethora of apricots, pears, and tiger lilies, a bloat of tomatoes and ravishing radishes and cool cucumbers and bugproof lettuce, carloads of magnificent vermin-free vegetables a mile long, was only just getting started.... Quite a remarkable, sophisticated invention, as the U.S. headed toward its glorious 21st century, combining big land combines with perpetual migrant slavism. (80–81)

Barrio equates California's "lush paradise" (174) with an ideology of nation building that is predicated on the robust exploitation of Chicano migrant labor. California in its excessive ripeness is bizarre and grotesque, a postmodern parody of the Garden of Eden whose imperial assumptions Barrio challenges as he attempts to shift the locus of power in his narrative of resistance.

In the attempt to forge a new sense of self-representation and also a rival cultural consciousness, Barrio asserts in *The Plum Plum Pickers* that Mexican Americans must align themselves with the radical movements of the 1960s. At the beginning and conclusion of the narrative, Barrio frames this ideology of resistance against internal colonization around the pathetic figure of Mr. Quill, who in the first chapter awakens from a nightmare of anti-colonial rebellion and at the end is found hooded and hanged from a tree looming over the migrant shacks. Although Barrio does not ascribe Quill's death to any one person, it is reasonable to infer that the only character possessing the political consciousness capable of organizing and committing such an act is the twenty-four-year-old migrant worker Ramiro Sanchez, "born in South Texas Morellan campesinos from Michoacan" (43), a *fronterizo* with a critical consciousness, a dissident clearly at war with the dominant culture. Ramiro, who has moved from the periphery to the center of the alien nation, understands the system of labor that indentures him to the Western Grande Compound. In chapter 21, Barrio offers a rendition in prose poetry of Ramiro's epic struggle to escape this contemporary feudalism:

> From predawn blackness Ramiro picked ripe his fruit.
> He picked to dusk.
> He picked from prehistory into glassbright civilization.
> From precolumbian artifacts to freeways to the future.
> From Aztec elegance to the latest word in slums. . . .
> He would find a way, some way out.

In this visionary riff, consistent with the other Brechtean methods the author utilizes in the novel, Ramiro becomes the conscience of his race— *La Raza*—the embodiment of the culture, history and traditions of his people. His "dream" by the end of the novel is to marry Margarita, the daughter of another migrant couple on the Western Grande Compound; and produce children who will one day become the lawyers, teachers, and judges required to fight the system of colonial oppression, reassert the Mexican-American legacy, and recapture a share of the California dream.

Barrio in *The Plum Plum Pickers* elaborates an agenda for the nation that acknowledges and incorporates "the return of the natives, redskins turned south, Aztec to Tenochtitlan, and now coming back north again to Santa Clara" (48). The task is to recapture and reconstruct an indigenous history based on both authentic and archetypal Mexican sources rather than Anglo-American accounts—to create a new historical consciousness and identity capable of contesting national knowledge. The Mexican and Mexican-American migrants who flow back and forth across the border are the embodiment of this history. They represent the struggle for identity and power, reminding readers that Mexican history is coextensive with the history of the nation. This struggle or conflict is inherent in the life of the border, where two cultures and two political systems confront each other. And for the *pocho-pachuco*, as Américo Paredes observes laconically in his essay "The Problem of Identity in a Changing Culture: Popular Expressions of Culture Conflict Along the Lower Rio Grande Border," cultural conflict spawns a crisis in identity for the "poor soul wedged between the pyramid and the skyscraper" (Ross 93). Paredes observes that the Chicano's awakened sense of identity is also a challenge to that same identity, for one's emerging national consciousness provokes the primal question, "Who are we?" Thus the problem of self-representation can seem resistant to solution as the individual contends with colliding cultural spheres. Lupe in *The Plum Plum Pickers* typifies this problematic relationship:

> Where did she come from? Why was she here? Lupe often talked about Mexico and Guadalajara, but Mexico was nowhere for her. It was as foreign to her as Belgium. Did that mean she had no home? In Mexico she had seen that, except for the very rich, just about everybody was very poor. At least here in her country, in the U.S., everyone that wanted to could work and not be ashamed of being poor, or poor in the sense of not starving but perhaps not having everything you saw in sight in all the shop windows or TV ads or big discount houses. (102)

Lupe is "California born ... which was once Mexico," and her postcolonial travail, shared by so many other characters in contemporary Mexican-American fiction, is to extrapolate a meaningful identity from the cultural contradictions and conundrums she confronts.

Even as the migrants in *The Plum Plum Pickers* seek a usable form of self-reference, their identity problem is compounded by the racist stereotyping of Anglo culture and immigration categories. Barrio offers a

Whitmanesque catalogue of the migrant stereotype: "Nationals. Wetbacks. Alambristas. Descamisados. Braceros. Migrants. Commuters. Greencarders. Seasoners. River crossers. Night riders. They all met and they all fulfilled the same conditions: Cheap traveling rotating convenient exploitative farm labor" (82). Mexican immigrants and migrants, reduced to official and popular categories of representation, have an acute perception of their position within an imperial setting. For them to imagine another identity or even a double identity in the manner suggested by W.E.B. Du Bois in *The Souls of Black Folk* is to engage in a political effort to seek a cultural horizon above that of economic domination. Thus Lupe's husband Manuel feels "a thrill of power" (94) when he confronts the labor contractor Morales, thereby altering the imperial contest that formerly had inhibited him from asserting an authentic identity. And when the Drawbridge *Courier* announces a spreading strike among the migrant farmworkers, the full political context of the struggle for power as a means of self-representation becomes clear.

Migrant Souls

Ultimately it is the total social structure of American society and its history of discrimination against Mexican Americans, combined with the capitalist forces of production, notably the demand for cheap labor, that threatens constantly to reduce the Mexican immigrant's and Chicano migrant's sense of identity to that of a commodity. Awareness of oneself as a commodity-migrant within American culture becomes a timeless curse as this pattern of commodity exchange repeats itself from generation to generation. In Richard Vasquez's *Chicano*, a chronicle of the Sandoval family over several generations, from their passage through revolution-torn Mexico to the barrio of East Los Angeles, the first two generations work the orange groves of southern California; while two daughters representing the second generation, Hortensia and Jilda, become prostitutes. "You don't know what the hell this country's about" (54) declares Hortensia, who understands that she too is part of the prevailing social relations of production. Subsequent Sandoval generations will see the traditional Mexican family disrupted forever by World War II; by the postwar drift of Mexican-Americans to East Los Angeles, which Vasquez depicts as a Hogarthian underworld of thieves, tramps, and al-

coholics—a realm of "deviants" spawned by the dominant social structure; and by the fruitless attempts of the last generation in the 1960s to
assimilate into Anglo society. By the end of *Chicano*, the young woman
who represents the family's most promising possibility for assimilating
into the dominant group in society dies of an abortion forced upon her
by her Anglo boyfriend, the scabrous scion of a prominent Midwestern
family who aptly enough is a sociology major at U.C.L.A. While *Chicano*
is a fairly simplistic textual model of the relations of power in American
society, the perpetual fate of Americans of Mexican descent as a native
labor force subjected to discriminating practices captures the continuing struggle to unravel the entanglements of power defining social relations in the United States.

Even when the institutionalized exploitation of successive generations of Mexican Americans is transcended, an ambiguous identity remains for individuals who are deeply rooted in the borderlands ethos of
duality. It is as if the "push and pull" of traditional immigration theory
carries over to the bipolar psychic movement of attraction and repulsion
characteristic of border society. In Arturo Islas's *Migrant Souls* (1990), a
sequel to his first novel *Rain God* (1984) chronicling three generations of
the Angel family (and clearly semi-autobiographical), the sense of being
pulled in two linguistic and cultural directions is acute. The matriarch of
the Angel family, Mama Chona, had crossed into the United States from
bloody Juarez in the second decade of the twentieth century to escape
the Mexican civil war, but she does not encounter an Edenesque cultural
sphere: "The Rio Grande . . . shallow, muddy, ugly in places where the
bridges spanned it . . . was a constant disappointment and hardly a symbol of the promised land to families like Mama Chona's. They had not
sailed across an ocean or ridden in wagons and trains across half a continent in search of a new life. They were migrant, not immigrant, souls.
They simply and naturally went from one bloody side of the river to the
other and into a land that just a few decades earlier had been Mexico.
They became border Mexicans with American citizenship" (41–42). The
central protagonist in the narrative, Josie Salazar, grows up in the late
1940s and early 1950s close to the Rio Grande in the Texas town of Del
Sapio. Her spirit is with her father, Sancho Salazar, who likes to fish and
hunt in the mountains of northern Chihuahua, and not with her mother's
pseudo-Hispanic (in actuality *mestizo*) Angel side of the family. The
Salazar-Angel family is not disadvantaged but nevertheless is subject to

cultural antipathies. This conflict in family identities is made clear at Thanksgiving in 1947, when the mother, Eduviges, an Angel, cooks a turkey in a symbolic act of acculturation. But Sancho Salazar is more the Mexican nationalist: "Eating turkey is going to turn my girls into little *gringas*. Is that what you want?" (22). Despite her psychic bond with her father, Josie crosses cultures as a schoolgirl in the 1950s, ultimately marrying a man, Harold Newman, who is half Mexican and half Anglo. Yet she divorces him ten years later, acknowledging a dangerous falsification inherent in her drift from the traditions of her father and her movement toward assimilation into American culture. She too at a metaphorical level is a "migrant soul," entering the new world of freedom and mobility forged in the postmodern crucible, but returning finally to her family and to her hybrid cultural identity.

Consciousness of Mexican identity or *mexicanidad* is ultimately the source of strength for the Mexican-American protagonists of contemporary Chicano fiction. Mexicans and Mexican Americans come and go across a common border, often torn between two cultures and two national lifestyles. These migrant souls manage the bipolar nature of the border as well as the national or metropolitan sphere precisely when their roots (*raices*)and spiritual values (*esencias*) are sufficiently strong to assert a countervailing cultural nationalism. Their rootedness in Mexican culture is precisely what enables them to mediate between the two spheres and resist the totalizing claims and legitimizing power of the United States, even as the nation asserts such claims on all Americans. Rudolpho Anaya's *Bless Me, Ultima* (1972) is of course the classic statement of *mexicanidad*, the quintessential response to the radical conjuncture of cultures in the Second World War and postwar eras. Set against the backdrop of the war, with the explosion of the atomic bomb at Los Alamos looming over the New Mexican landscape like the harbinger of a new age, Anaya's novel, filtered through the consciousness of the young narrator Antonio, traces the movement of his family from the llano to the town of Guadeloupe, from a vaquero tradition "as ancient as the coming of the Spaniard to Nuevo Mejico" (2) to the newer metropolitan world. Historical time and geographical movement are the twin forces threatening the family's collective identity. As Antonio's father, Gabriel, observes, "The war sucks everything dry . . . it takes the young boys overseas, and their families move to California where there is work" (3). The father is unhappy with both their movement to the metropolitan center and the national imperatives of the war: "My father's dream was to gather his sons around him and move westward to the land of the setting sun. But the war had taken his three sons and made him bitter" (13). Rejecting the migrant imperative of constant movement across the national landscape, Anaya instead turns his narrative inward, finding in the process a more authentic promised land in the very soil that Mexican Americans and their Mexican ancestors have always inhabited.

As Anaya himself has observed, his central character Antonio is the paradigmatic New World person, a cultural composite who "incorporates the Espanol and the Indio, the old world and the new" (Jussawalla 247). His mother is a Luna, a descendent of villagers and priests; his father a Marez, the descendent of seamen and vaqueros. Moreover, younger than his three brothers who enlist during World War II and return with the "war sickness" (61) inside them and subsequently embark on fragmented migrations into the postwar nation, Antonio turns instead to the tutelage of Ultima, "a curandera, a woman who knew the herbs and remedies of the ancients, a miracle worker" (4) who comes to live with the family in her old age. With Ultima, the narrator embarks on an epic interior journey, "lost in a labyrinth of time and history" he did not know (37). Through her, he learns of the cultures of the Indians of the Rio del Norte, the Aztecs, Mayas, and Moors. This indigenous education in his cultural origins is deeper than that offered by the public school system (where the teacher calls him Tony) or his church schooling, both of which try to mold identity to preconceived norms; or by the involuted "Wild West" settings and violent action that seems to parody Anglo-American claims to the frontier. Through Ultima, Antonio moves in an enchanted realm where he can imagine a community; this community contains inherent dangers but always delivers him to a promised land of safety in which he can explore the never-ending task of cultural self-representation.

Antonio inherits the power of Ultima, a force at once spiritual and political, for he has the ability to discover who he is. Anaya states in his interview with Jussawalla: "I would hope that he would be a shaman, but, you know, a shaman is another kind of priest. The point is not so much what he becomes. We can't dictate what people become, but what we can hope to do is to liberate people by having them become their most true selves, to find their deepest potential. Then you will recognize the models of colonialism that are set over you, and you'll know how to accomplish your goals in life. So to me the most important aspect of *Bless Me, Ultima* is that process of liberation" (49). Antonio, this New World person, is assuredly *mestizo,* a person who stands at the end of a corridor of migration that captures the essence of southwestern culture. He is an amalgam of Indio, Espanol, Mexicano, and Anglo-American. As an indigenous person, he transcends all colonization models, discovering instead an ability to struggle constantly—like the mythical Golden Carp that appears as a leitmotif in the novel—to liberate himself from all forms of servitude. His historical sense ultimately embraces many empires and an abiding, almost mystical awareness of his conflated destiny as a privileged traveler among cultures. Of all the migrant souls in Chicano fiction, Antonio moves nearest to the Promised Land.

As Anaya and other Chicano novelists insist, the Mexican-American search for the Promised Land involves an effort to redefine personal and national consciousness in a revolutionary manner: to reclaim Aztlán, the ancestral homeland of the Aztecs that lay somewhere north of the ancient capitol of Tenochtitlan in what is today Mexico City. Thus the protagonists in Chicano fiction seek identities predicated on continual movement across territorial borders and a common quest for a sense of national origin rooted in the oldest myths of the continent. These migrants cross borders redolent with these earlier myths. Border crossing, the back-and-forth mosaic of motion, is coterminous with the Chicano sense of national identity formation. Even in Chicano fiction rooted in urban environments, the borderlands trope of territorial movement permeates the destinies of the characters. In Sandra Cisneros's *The House on Mango Street* (1991), the young narrator states: "We didn't always live on Mango Street. Before that we lived on Loomis on the third floor, and before that we lived on Keeler. Before Keeler it was Pauline, and before that I can't remember. But what I remember is moving a lot" (3). Reminders of Mexico—linguistic, familial, cultural—form Esperanza's consciousness, making her an imaginary traveler floating across national borders and imagined geographies even as she contends with the rigors of her urban existence.

The quest for myths or origins can also take protagonists back into Mexico. In Ana Castillo's *The Mixquiahuala Letters* (1986), for example, the narrator's blueprint for feminist liberation requires persistent returns to Mexico: "Mexico City, revisited time and again since childhood, over and over again as a woman. I sometimes saw the ancient Tenochtitlan, home of my mother, grandmothers, and great grandmother, as an embracing bosom, to welcome me back and rock my weary body and mind to sleep in its tumultuous, over-populated, throbbing, even pulsating heart" (92). Castillo's allusion to the ancient Aztec capitol in this epistolary novel involving forty letters from Teresa to Alicia that deal with Chicana and Latina lives in America is at the heart of a reverse migratory passage into Mexico, a motif first seen in Josephina Niggli's *Mexican Village* (1945) and a persistent dream of leave-taking and passage back to origins that influences a considerable body of Chicano fiction.

In the final analysis, border culture is a liminal space where mythic and historical contestations can be fought out, where visions of Paradise can be negotiated. This is the vision that Carey McWilliams ends his classic *North of Mexico* with: "Here in the heart of the old Spanish borderlands, the oldest settled portion of the United States, a new world has been born and the isolation of the region has been forever destroyed. Like the peoples of the world, the peoples of the borderlands will either face the future one and together or they are likely to find themselves siftings on siftings in oblivion" (304). McWilliams's musings embrace both ancient lives and the dawning of the nuclear age. With Los Alamos hovering over the borderlands landscape that McWilliams invokes, the Chicano presence reminds us that Paradise can indeed be lost and humanity extinguished, or regained through life-sustaining myths and leave-takings for more promised lands.

4

Metropolitan Dreams: Latino Voyagers from the Caribbean

I followed Desi Arnaz down the hallway. On the walls, framed
photographs of Arnaz with just about every movie star and musician,
from John Wayne to Xavier Cugat. And then there was a nice hand-
colored glamour-girl photograph of Lucille Ball when she was a model
in the 1930s. Above a cabinet filled with old books,
a framed map of Cuba, circa 1932. . . .
—Oscar Hijuelos, *The Mambo Kings Play Songs of Love*

The American drive for empire that functions as the ideological and geopolitical backdrop of much Chicano fiction also serves as a postcolonial
motif in contemporary novels and short stories exploring Latino emigration from the Caribbean to the United States. Numerous writers—
Julia Alvarez, Oscar Hijuelos, Christina García, and Judith Ortiz Cofer
among them—share a vision of migration to American shores that is
rooted in the imperial history of the hemisphere—the tradition of conquest and colonization experienced by the islands of the Caribbean. The
postwar arrival of these Hispanic voyagers from the Caribbean at the
metropolitan centers of America, notably New York and Miami, is the
contrapuntal counterpart to the more typically rural settings seen in that
strain of Chicano fiction tracing the present-day consequences of the
forces of internal colonialism. However, the dark current of economic

exploitation prevalent in Chicano fiction gives way in the narratives mapping the movement of Hispanic groups from the Caribbean to the mainland metropolis to a more ambiguous exploration of the myth of American opportunity.

Colonial Legacies

The Caribbean Basin and each of its island constituents has its own unique history of colonialism, one that is entwined in the rivalry among the Great Powers—Great Britain, Spain, France, and most recently the United States—for dominion over these Third World colonies or what Lloyd George once termed "the slums of the Empire." With Cuba, the Dominican Republic, and Puerto Rico, the tradition of imperial intervention by the United States is, of course, a strong aspect of twentieth-century power politics. The history of American involvement in the affairs of these islands is not a transitory or random series of events but rather crucial markers illuminating the ways in which the production of contemporary immigrant fiction is tied to specific transnational processes that capture the ongoing course and consequences of the quest for empire. The aging Desi Arnaz portrayed at the end of *The Mambo Kings Play Songs of Love* (1989) by Oscar Hijuelos is thus both the real and fictive embodiment of this colonial legacy. Named Desiderio Alberto Arnaz y de Acha by his distinguished and dispossessed Cuban parents, whose extensive properties were appropriated by the Batista regime, and the first Latin performer to have his own television show as the thick-tongued, volatile Cuban counterpart to America's comic goddess, Lucille Ball, he spends his last days in America in luxurious isolation in the hills of Belmont, California, a lonely exile in his adoptive paradise. Desi Arnaz, the New World immigrant success story whose cinematic life frames and suffuses Hijuelos's novel, defines the character of the Latino immigrant from the Caribbean who is obliged to confront the question of nationality from the dual perspective of one's original cultural derivation—in the case of the characters in *The Mambo Kings Play Songs of Love* a fixed sense of *Cubanidad*—and the ascendant and more hegemonic penetration that the United States experience achieves over the immigrant mind. For such immigrants, national identity can only be provisional, for in linguistic, cultural, and spiritual terms those Americans who trace their origins to

Cuba, the Dominican Republic, and Puerto Rico—the islands constituting the Spanish Caribbean—negotiate lives between two contending worlds.

Even though Cuban Americans, Dominican Americans, and Puerto Ricans look at themselves and other Latinos and Latinas in distinct and often oppositional ways, they share a mutual heritage as dual inheritors of colonial history, first under Spain and subsequently as clients of the United States. They also share a common heritage deriving from exploitative plantation economies, the legacy of slavery and indenture, and the unique kinship patterns of mixed-race societies. By 1898, Spain had lost virtually all of its former possessions in Latin America and was on the verge of losing Cuba to indigenous nationalist forces. Faced with the prospect of a free and independent Cuba—*Cuba Libre*—the United States, which had coveted the island for the better part of the nineteenth century, declared war on Spain in 1898, using the sinking of the U.S battleship *Maine* as a pretext. The Spanish-American War was not an altruistic response by the United States to Cuban aspirations for independence, but rather a robust attempt to deprive Cuba (and also Puerto Rico, which in 1897 had been granted a liberal charter of autonomy by Spain) of its desired status as an independent nation. As Louis A. Pérez, Jr. asserts in *Cuba: Between Reform and Revolution* (1988), "A Cuban war of liberation was transformed into a U.S war of conquest. It was a victory to which the United States first laid claim, and from which so much else would flow" (178). Not a single Cuban or Puerto Rican representative attended the December 1898 Treaty of Paris negotiations, which released Cuba from Spain and legitimized the United States' claim over the island; ceded Puerto Rico and Guam to the United States; and, for $20 million, surrendered the Philippines as well. Thus the United States, which began military occupation of Cuba on January 1, 1899, and which legitimized its control over Cuban sovereignty through the Platt Amendment of 1901, was poised at the start of a new century to exercise its role as an imperial power, the colonial successor or replacement for the old Spanish regime.

Although today Cuba and the Dominican Republic are independent nations and Puerto Rico a commonwealth "freely associated" with the United States and whose people are American citizens, all three islands have endured a twentieth-century legacy of intervention by their imperial neighbor. President Theodore Roosevelt's speech to Congress in 1904 in which he reaffirmed the Monroe Doctrine and also asserted the right of the United States to intervene in the Caribbean and Central America—the Roosevelt Corollary—had noticeable impact on the Spanish-speaking Caribbean. In 1905, Roosevelt used the threat of intervention to force the Dominican Republic to accept an American customs collector to straighten out the island's tangled foreign debt, and in 1916, American marines occupied the island to suppress an insurrection and prevent German penetration, an occupation that would last until 1924. Similarly, three times in the first two decades of the twentieth century—in 1906, 1917, and 1921—troops were sent to Cuba to protect American interests. Despite President Hoover's vow to promote a "retreat from imperialism" and President Franklin Delano Roosevelt's Good Neighbor policy of the 1930s, the lingering reality of exploitative American economic power and support for repressive and corrupt island governments (combined with the continuing presence of U.S. troops in Puerto Rico) affirmed the United States' role in the Hispanic Caribbean as the dominant colonial power. As Eric Williams documents meticulously in *From Columbus to Castro: The History of the Caribbean 1492–1969* (1970), the "American Sugar Kingdom," characterized by the domination of island economies by American capital investment and backed by political presence and military assertions of power, became the new colonial reality of the twentieth century. By 1940, for example, the Cuban American Sugar Company controlled half a million acres of cane land, while four large American companies controlled an equal amount of acreage in Puerto Rico, comprising two-thirds of the total in sugar-cane farms on the island. Similarly, two American companies—South Puerto Rico Company and the West Indies Sugar Corporation—dominated the Dominican economy. Antonio Benitez-Rojo observes in *The Repeating Island: The Caribbean and the Postmodern Perspective* (1992) that sugar is the overarching unifier in the Caribbean's experience of domination. American control of railways, banks, refining mills, wharves, and cargo lines— a massive plantation economy, transnational in character and termed by Dr. Williams, the former prime minister of Trinidad and Tobago, an "American juggernaut" (431)—reduced Cuba, Puerto Rico, and the Dominican Republic to island dependencies. Moreover, the massive sugar monoculture had a pernicious effect on other island economies, with Cuba experiencing a precipitous decline in tobacco exports—from 40 percent of total exports in 1902 to 10 percent in 1939—while Puerto

Rico, whose staple export crop during Spanish rule had been coffee, actually had to import it by 1940. Shaped by American intervention and control, Puerto Rico, Cuba, and the Dominican Republic experienced the harsh realities of colonial dependency that ultimately would create the diasporic movement of their populations to the United States after World War II.

Prior to World War II, there had been little hint of the massive exodus of Spanish-speaking peoples of the Caribbean to the United States that would characterize the postwar era. The passage of the Johnson-Reed Act in 1924, also known as the National Origins Quota Act, which assigned quotas based on a percentage of each ancestry group in the United States, favoring northwestern European nations and extending the ban on Chinese to virtually all Asians, had exempted the independent nations of the Western Hemisphere from the system. The 1924 Act permitted colonial possessions such as Barbados and Jamaica to apply for immigration through England's unfilled quotas, while Cuba and the Dominican Republic, as well as Mexico and other Latin American nations, enjoyed protected status largely because of the demands—as seen in the previous chapter—for cheap migrant labor. The discriminatory features of the National Origins Quota Act, combined with the effects of the Great Depression, effectively reduced immigration rates in the 1920s and 1930s. Moreover, the restrictive state policies of the Trujillo dictatorship in the Dominican Republic and his Batista counterpart in Cuba also kept outward migration from these islands in check during this period. Consequently as late as 1950, according to Robert Daniels, citing census data in *Coming to America* (1990), there were "only thirty thousand foreign-born Cubans in the whole country: thirteen thousand in New York, eight thousand in Florida, and a little over a thousand in California" (373). Nevertheless, there was steady immigration from the Caribbean during the prewar and postwar years—approximately 188,000 from 1931–1960 based on calculations derived from the 1993 *Statistical Yearbook*. The number of immigrants from the Caribbean was small, but these individuals were precursors of the great "fourth wave" of Hispanic Caribbean and African-Caribbean immigration that would transform the demographic face of the United States in the contemporary period. Creating indigenous immigrant networks and communities in the northeast, most typically in the quintessential city of immigrants, New York, these early groups served as links in the growing pattern of movement back and forth from the islands to the United States mainland. According to the 1960 census, for example, which converges in a demographic sense with the diasporic watershed caused by the overthrow of the Batista regime, there were 124,416 Cubans in the United States, of whom 75,156 were Cuban nationals and the rest Cuban Americans born in the United States. As pre-revolutionary Cubans, they had entered the country as immigrants; subsequently, after Fidel Castro assumed power on January 1, 1959, they would be admitted in three successive waves as refugees (Reimers 159).

Hijuelos and the Cuban Odyssey

One can see the historical course of Hispanic and specifically Cuban immigration from the Caribbean to the United States in the first novel of the Cuban-American writer, Oscar Hijuelos. This neglected but distinguished work of fiction, *Our House in the Last World* (1983), is a parable of the twentieth-century Cuban immigrant experience tracing the intertwined lives of the Santino family from the 1920s to 1975. Hijuelos designs each chapter around watersheds in history that capture the phases and stages of the Cuban migratory experience: *Cuba, 1929–1943; America, 1944–1947;* and so on through thirteen chapters ending with *Ghosts, 1969–1975* and a brief epilogue. Told retrospectively by Hector, the younger son of Alejo and Mercedes Santino, the narrative explores the relationship of historical dependence between Cuba and the United States in the twentieth century from the early decades when life in the city of Holguin, in Cuba's Oriente Province, seemed a self-contained colonial world, to the disruptions—familial and national—triggered by the Cuban revolution. As a subject for cultural inquiry, Hijuelos perceives Cuban-American immigration history as a continuation of colonialist practice that raises pointedly political questions about power, dependence, and subordination. Unlike the dispossessed immigrant families who serve as paradigms of internal colonialism in Chicano fiction, the Santinos and their extended kinship group do not arrive in America penniless. Alejo and Mercedes leave for America in 1943 with a legacy of five thousand dollars—the early prototype of Cubans who are viewed as *los ricos* or "rich kids" among Latino groups. However, as soon as they embark for America, they begin to decline in status. Aboard ship the gregarious Alejo manages to squander some of their inheritance by entertaining other rich Cubans, gambling, and loaning money to a Havana con artist who promises him a partnership in a shoe store in the Bronx. They still have the resources to fuel their dreams of the Promised Land, but their arrival in the port of New York suggests the ambiguous power and danger of the immigrant dream: "In the morning all passengers rushed to the railing because the ship's whistle had sounded entry into New York harbor. New York, America. *Los Estados Unidos.* "De Junidad Stays?" They saw warships, tugboats, and American flags everywhere. They saw the Statue of Liberty, startling as the moon. . . . Mercedes and Alejo were happy and excited, checking through customs like a couple of rich Cuban tourists in New York for a visit" (34–35). They arrive in wartime but seem blithely ignorant of it. They are "startled" but not mesmerized by the Statue of Liberty. They pretend they are rich, but are not. From this ironic perspective, which includes a linguistic play on the meaning of America, Hijuelos constructs an immigrant vision of the United States predicated on misconceptions. Their "new home" in America is destined on their arrival to be a room in the upper West Side apartment of Alejo's sister, who had immigrated to the United States in 1934. This first "house in the last world," to invoke the title's conceit, will be filled with acrimony and recriminations. America will assuredly become the last world for Alejo, who quickly squanders all of their remaining money and is forced into the immigrant world of restaurant employees, destined to never rise above the rank of sous-chef; while for the sensitive, poetic, spiritual, and deeply dissatisfied Mercedes, the last world—her vision of Paradise— increasingly will become the romantic memories of her childhood in Oriente Province and her delusional (or mystical) visions of a previous reincarnation in the time of Columbus.

In *Our House in the Last World,* as well as his next novel *The Mambo Kings Play Songs of Love,* Hijuelos focuses on the discrepancies in the American Dream for Cuban immigrants and their children and on the bizarre ways in which *el exilio* produces paradoxical representations of identity. Cuba and America are persistently overlapping realms of experience. Just as the Santinos seem to inhabit a warren of rooms, first in the apartment they share with kinfolk and subsequently in their own decrepit apartment, their lives in New York City, the symbol of America for "old" immigrants and "new," are also labyrinthine, as phantasmagoric as the drunken revelries of Alejo and his innumerable drinking companions who litter the rooms, hallways, and, on occasion, closets of their home during endless years of all-night parties. The ever-affable Alejo, who did not want to be a farmer like his brother in San Pedro, finds companionship among the polyglot immigrant coworkers constituting the hotel restaurant staff, drinking with them in "kinship . . . Greek, Italian, Jew, Haitian, Latin, Negro, having a few laughs, talking about women, and teaching each other phrases in their own languages, in a long run entangling English with French and Italian and Spanish and Greek and Yiddish and jive" (59). During his quarter of a century of life in America, he grows corpulent on food and drink, a 300–pound parody of the well-fed immigrant at the American banquet who in actuality is left behind economically even as other Cubans whom he befriends and loans money to prosper. He is the atavistic essence of *Cubanidad*, working hard in a "kitchen staff of refugees" (103), ruling the family dictatorially, surmounting heart attacks and operations, until one fine evening, while working a second job at Columbia's University Club, an aneurysm in his brain explodes, his immigrant odyssey ends, and his life becomes a ceremonial memory for family and friends.

Just as Juan Rubio and his son occupy the narrative center of Villarreal's inquiry into the migrant Chicano experience in *Pocho*, the relationship between Alejo and his second son, Hector, is implicated in the widening spiral of exile and identity—the investigation of what it means to be Cuban American—in Hijuelos's novel. Whereas the older son, Horacio, develops into a profane, pragmatic, and mildly cynical "American" who moves away from the family and marries an Irish-American woman, Hector remains the distinct focus of his father's attention, even though the boy is estranged from his parents and the Latino universe of New York City, uneasy in Anglo society, and ambivalent about his dusty memories of Cuba, which he had visited once with his mother and older brother. That one visit triggered his passive, inconsolable behavior, for during the trip he contracted an infection—later magnified to a mysterious and metaphorical "Cuban disease"—that hospitalized him for more than a year after he returned to the United States. During and after that year, Hector draws a linguistic and psychic cordon around himself by refusing to speak Spanish and stumbling and stuttering into the English-speaking world, where his behavior is a simulation of powerlessness. In his imagination, Cuba becomes a pernicious component of his personal and cultural nightmare: "Cuba gave the bad disease. Cuba gave the drunken father. Cuba gave the crazy mother. Years later all these would entwine to make Hector think that Cuba had something against him. That it made him sick and pale . . . and excluded from the life that happy Cubans were supposed to have" (94). Later, following the Cuban revolution, the tales of relatives and refugees who stay with the Santinos before moving to better, more upscale lives in New Jersey and Miami convince Hector that Cuba is "a house of horrors" (156). As the cynical Horatio observes of his younger brother, "He's just dumb when it comes to being Cuban" (165).

Prone to melancholy and solitude and uncertain of the means of psychic survival, Hector cannot create any form of cultural performance that might center his personality. The only "truth" he can extrapolate from the anomalies of the immigrant experience is that the construction of a coherent identity is an exhausting process:

> Hector was tired, tired of being a Cuban cook's son and hearing people say, "Oh you look just like Alejo!" Look like Alejo? It made him cringe. He felt like a freak, a hunchback, a man with a deformed face. Like Alejo? At least Alejo had his people, the Cubans, his brothers, but Hector was out in the twilight zone, trying to crawl out of his skin and go somewhere else, be someone else. But he would do nothing to change himself to his own satisfaction. Anything he did, like growing his hair long or dressing like a hippy, was an affectation, layered over his true skin like hospital tape. Hector always felt as if he were in costume, his true nature unknown to others and perhaps even himself. He was part "Pop," part Mercedes; part Cuban, part American—all wrapped tightly inside a skin in which he sometimes could not move. (175)

Unlike those middle class and professional Cuban exiles who are the legacy of Castro's overthrow of the Batista regime, an era treated by Hijuelos in later sections of the novel, Hector does not remember Cuba as an imagined Eden; nor can he embrace the American Dream as many of these exiles were able to do. Arriving in infancy by boat from Cuba, flying back and returning by plane in childhood, he experiences in young adulthood the fragmentation of postmodernity that is the new terrain of postcolonial immigrants. Hector is caught inextricably between worlds and cultures, "in the twilight zone" as Hijuelos writes. But Hector's very rootlessness underscores his membership in the contemporary community; and his editorial detachment (for it is his voice that maps the new terrain of postwar immigrants) provides him with the capacity to see in the interstices between cultures a "few spots" (226) in his new "house" in America that are beautiful. Hector graduates from college, reconciles with his mother, and travels America to the Grand Canyon, Disneyland, and Niagara Falls, the monumental terrain of the New World paradise. He becomes a copywriter *and* a writer, objectifying his condition by recomposing it—and even seeing the warm, heavy hands of his dead father, the Cuban, in his final dreams.

For Hijuelos, America and more pointedly New York City is a grand stage upon which migrants and exiles from Cuba can compose and reconstitute a cultural vision. Indeed, Hector, the emergent writer in *Our House in the Last World*, and the two Castillo brothers who are musicians in Hijuelos's second novel, *The Mambo Kings Play Songs of Love*, struggle as artists to compose "songs of love" about their adoptive land. As with his first novel, Hijuelos in *The Mambo Kings* offers a retrospective of the postwar Cuban experience in America through the eyes of Cesar Castillo, who is drinking himself to death in the Hotel Splendour in 1980; and Eugenio Castillo, the son of Nestor and nephew of Cesar and the ultimate recorder of his family's immigrant odyssey. The task of remembrance for Eugenio is to imagine the Cuba that produced his parents and relatives, for as he acknowledges to Desi Arnaz during his visit—a pilgrimage of sorts—to the famous star's home in California in the early 1980s, he has never been to Cuba; consequently he can only inscribe his cultural heritage through an artistic effort to reconceive or reinvent that world through the panorama of his family's immigrant life in America. This "record" of remembrance (the bulk of the novel is structured like the two sides of a phonograph record) involves an effort to understand the tyranny of movement and time, for time runs out first for his father and then for his uncle. Time from the arrival of Nestor and Cesar Castillo in New York in 1949 to 1980 begins gloriously and turns bad. But their immigrant world—of lush, romantic nights in New York's dance halls and days of harsher realities—is the text that Eugenio must read, the record he must play, if he is to come to terms with the human and cultural interactions that have formed him. And Cesar and Nestor themselves, the Mambo Kings, must also try to construct hybrid identities that will permit them to negotiate a place in the postwar national culture.

The two brothers, the Mambo Kings, arrive in New York City at a moment in history when Latin music and dance was at such a height of popularity that it could support an extended community of immigrant artists—Tito Puente, Xavier Cugat, Pérez Prado, Machito, Beny More, Tito Rodriguez, and dozens of others who constitute a "lost epoch" (339). With the dance halls, cabarets, and clubs proliferating from Brooklyn to the Bronx—the Imperial Ballroom, the Palladium, the Biltmore Ballroom, Havana Madrid, the Hotel Manhattan Towers, the Savoy—nightlife seemed a constant carnival of Latin rhythms as bands battled for popularity and fame. Cesar Castillo and his younger brother Nestor, sponsored by a cousin living in New York City, are "part of the wave of musicians who had been pouring out of Havana" (31) as periodic tango, rumba, and mambo crazes swept the United States. With Havana casinos during the Batista era dominated by big American brass bands led by Artie Shaw, Fletcher Henderson, and Benny Goodman, even the best Cuban musicians experienced a form of artistic colonialism as their music was relegated to the lesser clubs. In their own native land, they were deprived of cultural power. For Cuban artists and musicians, America beckoned from the dance halls of Manhattan to the hills of Hollywood. Greater and lesser success stories abounded: Cesar Romero, Gilbert Roland, and other Cuban immigrant artists who had found in America a Golden Land. "But the most famous success story would be that of a fellow crooner whom the brothers knew from Santiago de Cuba, where they sometimes performed in dance halls and in the *placitas*, sitting out under the moonlight, strumming guitars. Desi Arnaz" (33). For Cesar and Nestor, the lure of America is the lure of celebrity like that enjoyed by Arnaz: the possibility that they might reverse the relations of power that marginalized them in Havana but might make them more desirable in New York.

The odyssey the brothers embark on from their parents' farm in Oriente Province to Havana to New York City both reproduces traditional immigration theory and provides a critique of their passage from the margins of the colonial world to the metropolitan center. Hijuelos's second novel is a major cultural text precisely because of its unique invocation of a brief Golden Age in the artistic life of the city when it was possible for Latino and Latina musicians to embrace the myth or dream of American success. In January of 1949, Cesar and Nestor fly out of

Havana on a Pan Am clipper to Miami and then northward by train to New York City, which is blanketed in two feet of snow. Their immigrant agenda is success, but in their "thin-soled shoes and cheap Sears, Roebuck overcoats" (34) they are not dressed for it or for a northern winter. Hollywood's penetration of Cuban culture, including Bing Crosby's angelic film rendition of *I'm Dreaming of a White Christmas*, is a heartwarming vision antithetical to the frozen upper West Side landscape at 500 La Salle, west of 124th Street and Broadway, that becomes the locus of their lives in America. They are also shocked by the "malevolent prejudice in the air" (36), the suspicion of older immigrant groups in the neighborhood of people speaking Spanish, the eggs thrown at them from rooftops, the dangerous streets. Nevertheless, the privileging power of Cuban immigrant culture serves to sustain them. Cuban culture valorizes their passage to urban America, predisposing them to center their lives in that world and carefully negotiate assimilation into the more dominating realm of American culture: "That was the way it happened with most Cubans coming to the States then, when every Cuban knew every Cuban. Apartments filled with travelers or cousins or friends from Cuba—just the way it always happened on the *I Love Lucy* show when Cubans came to visit Ricky in New York, *de visita*, turning up at the door, hat in hand, heads bowed demurely, with expressions of gratitude and friendliness" (36). A functioning Cuban community serves as the Castillo brothers' anchor as they develop new linguistic facility in English, find menial jobs, and learn to read the iconography of American urban culture.

Music enables the Castillo brothers to make sense of their new world and to bridge the distinct territories of Cuban and American culture. The love-drenched music they write and play with their band, the Mambo Kings, has the transformative power to bring heterogeneous peoples from the margins and center of New York's society together in a matrix of communal emotion. Their songs—"Solitude of My Heart," "A Woman's Tears," "Twilight in Havana," their famous "Beautiful Maria of My Soul" that lands them on an *I Love Lucy* segment—are a universal map of love, desire, memory, and longing. The imagery and rituals of love are the ordering principles of their art as well as their personal and professional lives. For the handsome and hypersexual Cesar, who deserts his wife and daughter for life in America and who represents the essence of "macho temperament" (31), love (and lovemaking) is the deepest pattern of psychic functioning. For Nestor, who is "plagued by memory" (44) of a doomed affair in Cuba with "beautiful Maria" and who moves through immigrant America and his marriage like a "somnambulist" (108), love is the symbol of loss and the limitations of his life in the United States. Only through their music can the brothers achieve a mystical confluence of artistic harmony that neutralizes a sense that more than love is required to structure American reality. Moreover, the paradoxical nature of fame in America is striking when their success in the 1950s is juxtaposed against their doomed fates: Nestor's death in a car accident as they are returning from a band engagement and Cesar's subsequent drifting in and out of music and increasing immersion in the subterranean reaches (he becomes his building's superintendent, burrowing into the boiler room) of immigrant life.

In reading *The Mambo Kings*, which won a 1990 Pulitzer Prize, we can appreciate the ingenuity of Hijuelos's framing of the novel around the Castillo brothers' penultimate moment of success in America—their appearance on the *I Love Lucy Show*. One night in 1955, Desi Arnaz catches the brothers' act at the Mambo Nine Club on 58th Street and Eighth Avenue and likes what he hears. Their music, filled with the "sadness and torment of love" (125), reminds Arnaz of his own past and his family in Cuba. Moreover, in conversation with them, he learns they are all from Oriente—the brothers from Las Pinas and Arnaz from Santiago de Cuba. Arnaz decides to have them on his show, and their appearance and subsequent fame represents the apex of their crossover success as musicians in America. One of Hijuelos's major achievements is the way in which the flexible narrative lines of the novel converge and capture two iconic aspects of the Cuban-American experience: Desi Arnaz and the mambo. Gustavo Pérez Firmat observes: "If Ricky Ricardo is one of the great icons of Cuban-American culture, the mambo is the other. Like Ricky, the mambo is no less American than Cuban . . . as a bicultural creation with divided roots and multiple allegiances, the mambo has always been Cuban American" (80). Anointed by Ricky Ricardo, the Mambo Kings luxuriate in the cultural vagaries of their music, their adoptive nation, and the promise of success that Hijuelos keeps resolutely at the center of his novel. Yet the distinctive Latin-Caribbean rhythms of their music—at once a happy celebration and an evocation of profound sadness—capture the fragility of the dream. Even musical success is rooted in the historical moment, and by 1960 the mambo tunes that had been popular during the decade of the 1950s were being supplanted by Latin jazz; by their absorption into rhythm and blues; and by the different Latin sounds of Tito Puente and Celia Cruz, the latter the most famous singer to emerge from the exodus of musicians following the Cuban revolution.

Imagined Edens

Castro's revolution—what Cesar considers "a new kind of sadness" (259) distinct from the nostalgia that affects older Cuban immigrants—is the watershed that inevitably impinges on the fiction of Hijuelos, Christina García, Christine Bell, Virgil Suarez, and other novelists who are preoccupied by the disruptions caused by this historical encounter. As Hijuelos acknowledges in *The Mambo Kings*, Castro kicked out the Mafia and closed down the Havana nightclubs, usurping the power and authority of the worst manifestations of American imperialism and creating in a broader sense a new postcolonial framework for imagining this island nation. Cesar, the "ex-Mambo King" who starts playing music again in order to help relatives in Castro's Cuba, is a sort of ethnographic witness to the emergent tide of Cuban refugees streaming toward America after 1959:

> Sometimes he found himself hanging around the bars and cantinas of Washington Heights and, on occasion, Union City, where in the early sixties many of the feverish Cubans had settled. Sipping his *tacita* of *café negro*, he would listen quietly to the political chitchat. The newly arrived Cubans, bitter and forlorn; the old established Cubans trying to figure out what was going on in Cuba: a man with a shaking right hand whose older brother, a jeweler, had committed suicide in Havana; a man who had lost a good job as a gardener on the DuPont estate; a man whose cousin had been sent to prison for walking down the street with a pound of sugar hidden in his shirt, a man who had lost his farm. . . . (262)

The leveling effect of the Cuban revolution, suggested by the catalog of sad fates enumerated by Hijuelos in this passage, would end the American colonial enterprise in Cuba but also substitute Soviet hegemony in terms of ideological results. Castro is the ruling passion for the "feverish Cubans" who were expelled by the revolution and who land on a vast continent as the outcasts of empire.

The Batista years, preceded by the cruel era of the dictator Gerardo Machado, known as "The Butcher," had created, of course, its own immigrant stream, including Desi Arnaz, whose parents had supported Machado and had owned thousands of acres of land prior to their appropriation. Batista, a former cane cutter, had assumed power in 1933 and initially had presided by popular mandate over a rapidly democratizing nation that by 1940 was the most open in the Caribbean. However, following his stunning decision to relinquish power and emigrate to Florida, and Cuba's disastrous experiment with democratic elections, Batista returned in 1952 to establish a totalitarian regime. He was supported by American business interests that "dominated the Cuban economy, owning over 90 percent of the telephone and electricity services, 50 percent of public transport and railways, and 40 percent of raw sugar production" (Carroll 58). Perceived as brutal and corrupt, and the captive of American economic interests and crime syndicates, Fulgencio Batista created the conditions that led to his overthrow, the triumph of Castro, and the subsequent flood of exiles to America.

The dynamics of Cuban migration to the United States in the wake of the revolution—an exodus of close to a million people—is markedly unique within the panorama of contemporary American immigration. As Ilan Stevens observes in *The Hispanic Condition: Reflections on Culture and Identity in America* (1995), Cuban exiles "are torn between an imagined Eden left behind and their present status as secure Americans" (51). They experience a profound nostalgia for Cuba that seems a part of their spiritual identity: even the real/imaginary Desi Arnaz invoked by Hijuelos remains Cuban to the core of his being, resurrecting the Cuban landscape in his home and gardens overlooking the Pacific. "I chose this climate here because it reminds me of Cuba. Here grow many of the same plants and flowers . . . I haven't been back there in over twenty years" (402). What Christina García terms "dreaming in Cuban," the title of her lyrical first novel, is a metaphor for the Cuban condition in America. On the one hand, Cuban Americans are the most privileged group of Latinos in the United States. They have the lowest unemployment rate among Hispanics, and the highest per capita income; according to Stevens, they learn English faster than Chicanos and Puerto Ricans, and they are more politically active. At the same time, they display a disproportionate nostalgia and extreme melancholy for Cuba—as if they are, in Hijuelos's words, "on the verge of falling through an eternal abyss of longing and solitude" (405) in their memories of a lost land.

Dreaming, of course, compensates for a geopolitical reality that deprives post-revolutionary Cuban exiles of any immediate opportunity to return to what they imagine as a vanished paradise. After 1960, Cubans came to America not like traditional Cuban immigrants who preceded them but rather on "parole" as displaced persons, as refugees or exiles who under the authority of the executive branch granted by the Refugee Relief Act of 1953, could be admitted beyond any strict quota limits. Eisenhower had used his parole power to admit Hungarian refugees following the Hungarian Revolution of 1956; before him, Truman had established the precedent of admitting refugees through his 1945 directive and subsequently the Displaced Persons Act of 1948. It was only after 1959, however, that a global exodus of exiles would move toward America, propelled by Third World instability from Salvador to Southeast Asia to Eastern Europe. The Cuban exodus was the first mass movement of refugees signaling this historic change in United States immigration history.

Between 1959 and the Mariel boatlift of 1980, more than three-quarters of a million Cubans were paroled to the United States, an influx of refugees that would result in significant permutations in immigration policy. David Reimers in *Still the Golden Door*, basing his analysis on the work of the social scientists Antonio Jorge and Raul Moncraz, divides this exodus of Cuban exiles into three stages or "waves": the first from 1959 to 1965, during which approximately 209,000 Cubans entered the United States; the second from 1965 until 1972, when 368,000 additional refugees arrived; and the third wave of nearly 130,000 Mariel refugees in 1980 (159–65). Prior to the Cuban missile crisis of October 1962, 3,000 people, largely upper and middle class, were arriving weekly from Cuba, with most settling in Miami and, to a lesser extent, in New York, Newark, and Union City. To assist in resettling these exiles, Congress passed the Migration and Refugee Act of 1962. It also had to deal with the parolee status of Cuban refugees, for under existing immigration provisions they could not apply for permanent resident status; consequently, in 1966 Congress passed the Cuban Adjustment Act allowing Cuban refugees to adjust to permanent resident status after two years in the United States.

The Immigration Act of 1965 eliminated national origins quotas and substituted overall hemispheric caps of 170,000 visas for immigrants from the Old World and 120,000 visas for those from the New. Circumventing Congressional intent, President Johnson invoked his parole power to admit additional Cuban refugees on the very day he signed the act into law at the base of the Statue of Liberty. Similarly, although the 1980 Refugee Act raised annual ceilings, President Carter exercised his parole authority to admit both Marielitos and Haitian boat people under yet another new category, "Cuban-Haitian Entrants (Status Pending)." Thus for two decades Cuban refugees as a distinctive group had a significant impact on evolving immigration policy.

Dreaming in Cuban

The Cuban community that emerged in the United States in the wake of Castro's revolution did more than merely augment their earlier immigrant counterparts. They shared the same distinctive Cuban cultural identity but were unique in their political bearings; in terms of sheer numbers, they would become a dominant political force in the Miami area and, to a lesser extent, in the greater New York metropolitan area. Moreover, new fault lines would develop between family members who stayed behind to either support or be subjugated by the revolution and those who risked everything as refugees in a new nation. Christina García's *Dreaming in Cuban* (1992) has at its narrative core this archetypal conflict between the old and the new: oscillating between Havana and Brooklyn (and touching down also in Prague), the story of the del Pino family and the four women who dominate it captures the fractured territory created by the Cuban revolution. In her first novel, filled with the magical realism that has become the post-revolutionary signature of contemporary Latin American narrative, García shows how Cubans are forced to experiment with national identity, reinventing the old and new countries of their dreams after decades of twentieth century colonialism.

It has been said that exile is the nursery of nationality, and in *Dreaming in Cuban*, the *idea* of Cuba is a shifting and ambiguous dream for the four del Pino women whose destinies shape García's novel. Each character embodies variant strands of national culture. The mother Celia transfers an unrequited personal passion for a lost love to "*El Líder*," spending nights on the porch of her seaside home scanning the horizon for Yankee intruders. Her daughter, Felicia, homicidally insane, is the sort of "social malcontent" destined for a tragic fate in postrevolutionary Cuba. Another daughter, Lourdes, an exile in Brooklyn, is a Cuban-American success story with her "Yankee Doodle Bakery" chain. And Lourdes's daughter Pilar, the true cultural hybrid in the novel, is a prematurely cynical and disillusioned young artist whose major dream is to return to Cuba before she loses any capacity at all to imagine her Cuban origins. Pilar in her punk rebelliousness protests the assimilative tendencies of American culture but is very much embedded in its artistic subculture. She is a sort of double exile from both America and Cuba, caught in the interstices of cultures and seeking an approved route through the postmodern universe. Toward the end of the novel when she has returned to Cuba to visit her grandmother, she states, "Cuba is a peculiar exile, I think, an island-colony. We can reach it by a thirty-minute charter flight from Miami, but never reach it at all" (219). The implication, and here García's fondness for Wallace Stevens manifests itself, is that the world is a "tropic of resemblances" from which the exiled imagination, constantly engaged in a dream-like movement of exile and return, must ultimately construct an authentic reality. And this reality will necessarily affirm the continuities between the Cuban past and present for those who stayed behind and those who make their home in another world.

The revolutionary moment that García investigates in her novel suggests worlds in collision. In a geological metaphor reminiscent of the same powerful trope governing Russell Banks's *Continental Drift*, García posits a moment in history—the revolution of 1959—that is cataclysmic: "The continents strain to unloose themselves, to drift reckless and heavy in the seas. Explosions tear and scar the land, spitting out black oaks and coalmines, street lamps and scorpions. Men lose the power of speech. The clocks stop. Lourdes Puentes awakes" (17). This surreal instant in which Lourdes's subconscious animus awakens to reality is "revolutionary" in its continental subversions, its playful juxtaposition of elements, and most significantly its reversal of the male-female hierarchy. García herself is the polar opposite of a writer like Hijuelos who revels in his first two novels in the imperialism of *machismo* (although in his third novel, *The Fourteen Sisters of Emilio Montez O'Brien* he constructs a homage to women). Lourdes, who has grown exceedingly fat and concupiscent in America, awakens next to her exhausted husband

Rufino, whom she has devoured like a succubus throughout the night, in a sexual extension of her voracious consumption of the pastries in her bakery. A hardened outcast of one political revolution, she comically suppresses all traces of the "feminine," the conventionally exotic and pliant image of Cuban women, and in a radical act of transmutation becomes "manly" in her behavior. Convinced that she has clairvoyant powers, Lourdes can imagine or "dream" of an androgynous utopia in which women possess the power to transform both colonial and gendered history. This is the unintended consequence of the Cuban revolution, as profound as the movement of continents or the uprooting of societies and cultures. García, by seriocomically pushing males to the periphery of her cultural universe, imagines an all-female revolution that will eliminate multiple forms of gendered tyranny.

How the Cuban revolution created "nomads" (5) of family members but also forced a new orientation of identity is a theme that García deals with explicitly in *Dreaming in Cuban*. Imperialism, synonymous with the Batista years, created its own forms of misrepresentation for both sexes. Celia's husband Jorge, for example, embraces the American dream of success on Cuban soil, spending his life "selling electric brooms and portable fans for an American firm. He wanted to be a model Cuban, to prove to his gringo boss that they were cut from the same cloth" (6). Devoted to Celia but not her true love, a salesman but not his own master, he is deeply symptomatic of the cultural afflictions inherent in colonial society. A shadowy figure who, dying of cancer in a New York hospital, ultimately "ascends" in "a nimbus of holiness" (19) to mythical status, Jorge suggests the ruptures in society and identity caused by the subordinating tendencies of colonial culture. Dead in America, his soul drifts south to appear before his wife, ever vigilant beside the ocean, to say good-bye. Only as spirit can he reunite with the family left behind in Cuba, for the one gesture left to separated family members, as Celia tells her granddaughter Pilar near the end of the novel, is to "wave from opposite shores" (240).

Unlike her father and her husband, and her sister and mother, Lourdes welcomes the "possibilities for reinvention" (73) offered by immigrant America. Passing through the polyglot streets of Brooklyn, she "ponders the transmigrations from the southern latitudes, the millions moving north," and finds it good. Dispossessed and literally raped by the revolution, she wants no part of Cuba, hurling herself instead with patriotic fervor into the American experience. She sells tricolor cupcakes and Uncle Sam marzipan, relishes the July 4th extravaganzas, patrols the streets as a uniformed auxiliary policewoman in a menacing rage against any criminal who might violate the sanctity of life in America. She rejects the "tropic of resemblances" for the colder latitudes. As Pablo Medina suggests in his memoir, *Exiled Memories: A Cuban Childhood*, warmth is forever associated by Cubans with their island nation; snow and ice with America. Lourdes, leaving Cuba for Miami, cannot stand the heat there. "I want to go where it's cold," she declares (69), and begins her odyssey northward until, arriving in New York City, she finds the world cold enough. She moves to the other side of the immigrant equation, replacing her Cubanness with a decidedly adversarial Americanness that celebrates her embrace of a new national empire.

García paints Lourdes, assuredly the most striking character in the novel, with parodic goodwill, but is careful to demonstrate how her resistant nationalism receives antiphonal orchestration in the lives of the other del Pino family members. The battle to make sense of several contending legacies falls to Lourdes's daughter Pilar who is skeptical of her mother's born-again American patriotism but equally bewildered by her visions of Cuba, in which her *abuela*, her grandmother Celia, appears in hazy dreams. Pilar is the second-generation hybrid, an uneasy amalgam of alien traits, separated from mainstream American life but ignorant also of Cuba: a figure in quest of a usable legacy. "I think migration scrambles the appetite," she muses. "I may move back to Cuba someday and decide to eat nothing but codfish and chocolate" (173). Inheriting the conflicting resistance cultures of her family, she must discover some form of unity within her inescapably mixed heritage. Poised between two worlds, feeling displaced by yet another diasporic postwar exodus, she must recover her mixed legacy by returning to Cuba. Writing of her own displaced Egyptian heritage, the English writer Penelope Lively observes: "Displaced persons are displaced not just in space but in time; they have been cut off from their own pasts. If you cannot revisit your own origins—reach out and touch them from time to time— you are forever in some crucial sense untethered" (175). Fueled by diasporic dreams, Pilar runs away abortively to relatives in Miami, thinking they will aid in her passage to Cuba, but she gets only a taste of home before they return her to Brooklyn. But after the death of her aunt Felicia, she and her mother return out of respect during a brief

period of thaw in Cuban-American relations in 1980 that permitted exiles to return.

In Cuba, Pilar moves from a nostalgic dream to an understanding
of the traumas of exile and return. For Pilar, "dreaming in Cuban" involves a search for her Cubanidad. Her fantasy of return might be what
V.S. Naipaul has called the immigrant's obsessive defect in vision, but
she nevertheless feels the wounds of exile far more acutely than her parents. She must experience for herself the reality that *la Cuba de ayer* simply no longer exists. And so, taking advantage of a brief period of amity
existing between the Carter administration and Castro that permitted
the return of exiles, she accompanies her mother to Cuba, only to be
caught up in the one-week crisis at the Peruvian embassy in Havana that
would precipitate the Mariel boatlift. Yet even confronting the hard realities of revolutionary Cuba cannot eliminate the sense of nostalgic con-
nectedness Pilar feels for Cuban culture and the world of her grandmother,
both of whom share the same birthdates and the same lyrical vision of
Cuba as a blue, tropical paradise: "I've started dreaming in Spanish, which
has never happened before. I wake up feeling different, like something
inside me is changing, something chemical and irreversible. There's a
magic here working its way through my veins. There's something about
the vegetation, too, that I respond to instinctually—the stunning bouga-
invillea, the flamboyants and jacarandas, the orchids growing from the
trunks of the mysterious celba trees" (235). In the same paragraph, however, Pilar acknowledges that she belongs more to the United States than
Cuba, that she must go back to New York, enacting what David Rieff in
his penetrating study of the Cuban community in Miami, *The Exile*
(1993), calls "this modern-day version of the Fall" (149). Pilar, who paints
obsessively, records everything, and becomes the custodian of her
grandmother's unmailed love letters, returns with a knowledge of the
"compacted light of the tropics" (7) and her electric, spiritual, clairvoyant kinship with her Abuela Celia that will keep her *cubanía* alive.

Pilar left Cuba at the age of two and returns as a young adult at
another moment of revolutionary crisis—the Mariel boatlift that serves
as the precipitating force of exile in other novels including *Latin Jazz*
(1989) and *The Cutter* (1991) by Virgil Suarez; the surreal, futuristic fantasy *The Doorman* (1991) by Reinaldo Arenas, and Christine Bell's *The
Pérez Family*. Unlike the characters in the novels by Arenas and Bell, Pilar
belongs to what Gustavo Pérez Firmat in *Life on the Hyphen: The Cuban-*

American Way (1994) terms an "intermediate immigrant generation," a group that "falls somewhere between the first and second generations." Quoting the Cuban sociologist Rubén Rumbaut, Firmat labels these exiles the "1.5" or "one-and-a-half generations." Such individuals, observes Rumbaut, "are marginal to both the old and new worlds, and are fully part of neither of them" (4). Pilar must negotiate the old world and the new, destined to exist in the interstices of the two cultures, using her linguistic and artistic resources as tools of transculturation as she moves between these cultures. Firmat makes the point that this hybrid or bicultural state of existence is actually a positive feature of the exiled personality because one-and-a-halfers, while never feeling entirely comfortable in either culture, can make subtle choices as they constantly construct and reconstruct their identities. "One-and-a-halfers gain in translation," declares Firmat. "One-and-a-halfers feed on what they lack. Their position as equilibrists gives them due freedom to mix and match pieces from each culture: they are 'equi-libre'" (7).

Whereas Pilar elects life on the margin as her bicultural destiny, the souls who are displaced by the Mariel crisis and who represent the third wave of Cuban exiles in Christine Bell's *The Pérez Family* do not seek to amplify their *cubanía* but rather, especially in the case of Dorita/Dottie, the picaresque heroine at the center of the novel, suppress it in their effort to become exemplary Americans. A pre-Mariel exile like Pilar can dream of return, but Marielitos have a different understanding of the truth about Cuba. When a group of dissidents drove a truck into the grounds of the Peruvian embassy in the Miramar section of Havana in the spring of 1980, they precipitated the unleashing of events that would result in 125,000 new Cuban refugees being exiled to Miami. After Castro on April 4, 1980, withdrew the troops that had surrounded the Peruvian embassy, almost 10,000 refugees seeking asylum flooded the grounds in a single day. Following prolonged negotiations, the Castro regime announced that any *escoria* or "scum" wanting to leave Cuba could do so from the single port of Mariel on the island's north coast. And Castro, in a brilliant display of political theatre, decided to augment the refugee flow by including significant numbers of criminals, mental patients, and homosexuals in this new immigrant stream. (Arenas, himself exiled in 1980 as an undesirable, deals with the homophobia of the Castro regime in *Old Rosa*, 1981; *Farewell to the Sea*, 1986; and other novels.) Bell alludes to this "boatlift exodus, as suspected criminals, homosexuals and madmen emptied from Castro's jails" (29) in *The Pérez Family*. For Marielitos in the aftershock of the boatlift, the nostalgia and lyricism seen as the essence of Cubanity in *The Mambo Kings* and *Dreaming in Cuban* would be replaced by different versions of identity in exile.

Marielitos

The new wave of Cuban exiles captured with comic gusto by Bell in *The Pérez Family* arrived in a largely penniless condition. Representing a stratum of Cuban society unseen in the earlier waves of Cuban immigration, they experienced a far greater sense of refugee dislocation than their predecessors. Some Marielitos indeed were criminals: during the 1980s, a few hundred were incarcerated for crimes committed in the United States. Bell creates a soap opera out of this Mariel milieu, with four of the principal characters reflecting the composition of the group. Juan Raul Pérez, a twenty-year political victim of Castro's prisons, arrives in America emotionally spent and deracinated. The enterprising Dorita, a "Cuban madonna hip" with a record that includes "suspicion of prostitution," is a survivor of multiple attempts by patriarchy, aristocracy, military dictatorship, capitalism, communism, and ordinary men to "screw" her. Her "son" Felipe is an eighteen-year-old former Marielito street punk who is wanted by the Miami police for drug trafficking. And the senile "father" whom Dottie also finds in order to complete her makeshift Pérez family and thereby gain priority for sponsorship is a clinically insane Marielito with a penchant for aimless wandering and tree climbing. The bizarre concatenation of events that brings the Pérez "family" together in the Miami refugee camp and, later, in Little Havana, presents immigrant life as a comedy of errors in which the American Dream is not so much a delusion as it is a parodic puzzle that only the most resilient souls can solve.

The seriocomic quartet comprising the Pérez family (Felipe and Papa will perish in their new paradise by the end of the novel) enter the New World in almost primal form. Led from the start by Dottie, the dynamic Mother Courage of the novel, they must begin life in America at the basic level of survival: they battle for food, clothing, work. The refugee camps depicted by Bell are poorly organized, resembling asylums for the displaced and disinherited. Dottie, perceiving the flaws in this system of dislocation rather than relocation, learns to manipulate it to attain freedom. She has the capacity to constantly reinvent herself: "She was going to have a second chance to live the way she dreamed life should be and not the way it turned out" (20). With her dreams of John Wayne and Elvis Presley, of nail polish and rock and roll, she is the innocent abroad: "the second I stepped into the United States, I am a new woman" (27). And Miami offers her the perfect urban dreamscape: "Miami in the afternoon sun is crayola and bright. Like a child's drawing, the city is imaginatively colored and unimaginatively out of proportion. Slender palms stand in disbelief against giant lego constructions. Soft clouds float by garish concrete. Rows of aqua and pink houses insult the shimmering sea and sky they frame. The streets themselves parallel and intersect with the simple logic of a child's board game. Miami fit Dottie's idea of freedom perfectly—it was simple, gaudy, and close at hand" (40). Whereas some—notably her makeshift husband Juan—might find confusion or banality in the explosive proliferation of the vegetative and architectural elements constituting contemporary Miami, Dottie embraces this landscape. She is favorably disposed to Miami's trajectory of postmodern culture as well as to the traditional verities of the immigrant dream. Selling flowers on a Miami street corner after her "family" has received shelter in a local church habitat, she is a commercial hit with her sexy walk and *joie de vivre* approach to commodity culture. "People who never rolled down their windows for faces on the corner rolled down their windows for Dottie. This wasn't the sad-eyed face of a heavy-hearted refugee. This wasn't the face of poverty, danger, or pleading. This was a smiling face, with polka dots flying and hips swaying. Her eyes were full of flowers and her feet caught the rhythms of salsa and rock" (168). Carrying on her own internal and overt discourse with culture, she knows how to redraw the boundaries and negotiate the terrain of postmodernity.

Dottie's gleeful immersion in the contradictory and inchoate realm of the postmodern stands in contrast to the confusion of her companion Juan who, beset by nightmares, bald, toothless, and confused, wanders the streets of Miami in search of his former wife and daughter, who have entered into the sequestered middle class comfort and the banality of Miami's commodity culture. Juan's dreams of drowning are the reverse of Dottie's dreams of freedom. "Dottie knew exactly where she was—in the land of plenty. Sparkling golden beauty" (61). By contrast, Juan muses that he needs a map to orient himself geographically, politically, and psychically. He is "outside those perimeters" (57) that encapsulated his married life prior to the revolution, wondering why the light in Miami is like the light in Cuba and why everyone in Miami speaks Spanish with a Cuban accent. Perhaps he is just in another prison. He is dazed by "the awful freedom" of his new world, overwhelmed by the pace of urban life "moving by him at futuristic speed" (100). Slowly, however, nurtured by Dottie, he learns to control "this madness" of his exiled life. He emancipates himself from political nightmares and personal dreams of reunion with his actual wife Carmela, knowing that his emerging path into postmodernity—his new map of desire—must be shared with his surrogate wife Dottie.

When Juan Pérez muses, "I need a map" (57), he expresses figuratively the historical and psychic condition that the Cuban exiles in *The Pérez Family*—indeed all exiles—confront, especially in urban environments. Fredric Jameson in *Postmodernism, or The Cultural Logic of Late Capitalism* observes that "the alienated city is above all a space in which people are unable to map (in their minds) either their own positions or the urban totality in which they find themselves" (90). Jameson, of course, theorizes that an ability to engage in "cognitive mapping," understood not so much as a cartographic or geographic skill as a dialectic through which one understands one's social relationships in the postmodernist moment, is an existential imperative for those inhabiting post-industrial space. Dottie and Juan learn how to mediate their passage into the world of late capitalism. By contrast, certain texts by Cuban-American writers that convey a postmodern aesthetics as well as ideology—novels like the surreal futuristic fable of exile life in New York City *The Doorman* (1987) by Reinaldo Arenas and the absurdist narrative of the exiled condition in Miami in *Raining Backwards* (1988) by Roberto Fernández—affirm the alienating tendencies of the contemporary urban totality. For the protagonist Juan, a Marielito, in *The Doorman*, New York resembles "an immense underwater city. And the people . . . rushing in all directions, disappearing through subway openings—didn't they look like fish seeking temporary refuge?" (18). The doorman finds his own refuge among the pets who are kept in various states of servitude by the gallery of grotesques inhabiting the apartment complex where Juan works. Ultimately he joins the animals in an odyssey across America, exiles seeking a natural paradise beyond dehumanizing urban boundaries. Similarly, Fernández in *Raining Backwards* reconstructs Miami as a fragmented metropolis (the novel itself is composed of a montage of aesthetic forms and styles) in which Cuban exiles seem to lead imaginary rather than "real" lives. *Raining Backwards* is a surreal satire on the Rodriguez family and their immediate neighbors, all of whom coexist in urban realms beyond the strictly rational. In fact, the intent of Fernández's satire is to suggest that there is no inner logic or rational organization to the life of the exile. The contradictions of exile and urban life in the postmodern texts by Arenas and Fernández are mystifying—beyond the realm of reason—but curiously they admit romantic and mystical visions of paradise in the New World.

The encroachments of exile and memory, of politics and everyday life, of urbanization and mass culture prevalent in the fiction of Cuban emigration to the American metropolis reflect precisely the same complexities and ambiguities of the Dominican experience in *How the García Girls Lost Their Accents* (1991) by Julia Alvarez. Raised in the Dominican Republic and emigrating to the United States in 1960 for her college education, Alvarez in her first novel offers the same deft, lyrical, and comically capricious rendition of the contours of immigration seen in García's *Dreaming in Cuban*. The episodic and recursive narrative structure of both novels centers on political cataclysm and flight—in Alvarez's novel, the last turbulent years of the dictator Rafael Trujillo. Both novels, mediating between two cultures, center on the lives of women: Carla, Sandra, Yolanda, and Sophía in *How the García Girls Lost Their Accents*, who arrive in New York City in 1960 dispossessed of their genteel upper-class lifestyle. Operating from their own unique cultural perspectives, both novels validate a sense of the past and the triumph of New World popular culture. García and Alvarez attempt to reunite cultural spheres through the lives of women who can operate on the frontiers of the postmodern.

If Castro's triumph might be viewed as a break with the modern tradition of American imperialism in the Caribbean, the history of the Dominican Republic in the twentieth century might also be seen as an *aborted* severance and reconstitution of imperial tradition, for the years after Trujillo's assassination in May 1961 led to instability, renewed American intervention, and, until recently, the frustration of Dominican aspirations for genuine autonomy. The dominant influence of the United States over Dominican politics—and the consequent surge of emigration from the Dominican Republic to New York City in the period after 1960—is part of the tapestry of imperialism typical of the American

Century's role in the life of the Hispanic Caribbean. Sharing (often un-comfortably) the island of Hispaniola with Haiti, the Dominican Re-public was almost annexed at the initiative of President Ulysses S. Grant in 1870 until public and Congressional opposition killed the initiative. However, by 1880 American bankers had taken control of the Domini-can Republic's troubled customs service, ultimately paying off the Republic's foreign debt and becoming, in the process, the protector of the island nation. By 1929, following the eight-year military occupation of the Dominican Republic by U.S. Marines, President Hoover could safely proclaim a "retreat from imperialism" in the Caribbean, fully confident that American business interests now controlled the sugar and banking economies of such islands. Moreover, Trujillo had come to power in 1930, and for three brutal decades controlled with American complicity al-most three-fourths of all economic activity in his nation.

The dilemmas of exile and arrival treated by Alvarez in *How the García Girls Lost Their Accents* are geared to the distinct historical and political situation of the Dominican Republic during the last years of the Trujillo regime. In terms of aesthetic practice, Alvarez devises a tripartite narrative structure moving backward in time, with part one of the novel covering 1989–1972; part two 1970–1960; and part three 1960–1956. Each section projects the nature of exile on a spatial or geopolitical grid that is far broader than the enclosed world of the aristocratic García clan dur-ing their years in Santo Domingo or the reconstruction of their immi-grant lives in metropolitan New York. The structural trajectories of the novel result in an interesting convergence of family and imperial his-tory at the specific moment in 1960 when Dr. Carlos García, his broth-ers, and their families, are implicated in a failed CIA plot to overthrow Trujillo and must flee with few possessions and an uncertain immi-grant itinerary, propelled into new national space by a failure in Ameri-can foreign policy.

"Dominican-York"

The Garcías flee to the quintessential American city of immigrants and exiles—New York—an urban enclave where they must confront radi-cally new forms of family and social life. Their passage into exile and arrival in New York is symptomatic of a new historical epoch in which

Dominicans would join other groups—Jamaicans, Chinese, Haitians, Indians, Russians—in an immigrant transformation of the city. The García family actually arrives somewhat in advance of the surge in Dominican immigration that started after Trujillo's death, for during the long Trujillo era it had been exceedingly difficult for Dominicans to emigrate to the United States. The Garcías' essential motive for immigration—political persecution—would send a larger wave of Dominicans to New York when the Dominican Republic's president, Juan Bosch, was overthrown in the military coup of 1963 and subsequent U.S. occupation of the island fostered significant migration outflow in order to diffuse political tensions. The adult Garcías are political refugees, but they slowly lose their Dominican identities and embrace traditional immigrant verities, obtaining green cards and ultimately becoming naturalized citizens. Unlike their Cuban-American contemporaries, the Garcías reconstitute themselves as a transnational household, emulating the constant movement between the Dominican Republic and New York initiated by the girls' grandfather who, as a diplomat in the United Nations, would often return to the island bearing gifts.

Dominican settlement in New York constitutes the most significant arrival of any specific immigrant group in the city in recent times. According to data compiled by New York City's planning department and released in a 298–page report, *The Newest New Yorkers* (1997), the Dominican Republic has been the largest source of immigrants for several decades, accounting in the 1990s for one out of every five immigrants to the city. The 1980 census had identified 127,700 Dominicans living in the New York metropolitan area, with most in Washington Heights and the lower East Side in Manhattan, the South Bronx, the Greenpoint section of Brooklyn, and the Jackson Heights section of Queens. This demographic base was augmented by an average annual arrival of 14,470 Dominicans from 1982–1989, and by an average of 22,028 from 1990–1994. Although political repression continued to be a factor in the outward flow from the island to New York throughout the 1960s and 1970s, the far larger impetus was economic motivation as a migration stream that was largely urban and precariously middle class sought greater opportunities in the United States. The García family, of course, is not strictly part of this movement of labor from the "periphery" to the "core" that governs the historical structuralist approach to international immigration movement laid out in most cogent form by

Alejandro Portes and Robert Bach in *Latin Journey: Cuban and Mexican Immigrants in the United States* (1985). Whereas the demand for cheap migrant labor is the animating force in several of the seminal works of Chicano fiction discussed in the previous chapter, explaining also the recent movement of hundreds of thousands of Dominicans into New York's service economy, the essential contours of the Garcías' immigrant experience are molded by their political displacement—much like many of their Cuban contemporaries—from their formerly lofty position within the hierarchically organized society of the Dominican Republic.

Most Dominicans arriving in New York City move from the relative scarcity of commodity culture in their native country to one of abundance in the United States. One of the subtle ironies of *How the García Girls Lost Their Accents* is the effort by Alvarez to dispossess her fictive family so completely that, stripped of class privilege, they too arrive in a condition of "abrupt exile" (116) that leaves them more dependent than many other Dominican immigrants. New York City is a shock to the exiled Garcías: "At home there had always been a chauffeur opening a car door or a gardener tipping his hat and a half dozen maids and nursemaids acting as if the health and well-being of the de la Torre-García children were of wide public concern" (179). The Garcías live in a rented apartment, dependent on a fellowship and on the generosity of American physicians who offer Dr. García what is tantamount to economic piece-work or subcontracting on the periphery of the medical establishment as he struggles to pass American medical exams and start a practice in the Bronx. Dr. García, of all members of his family, never loses his accent or his strong sense of patriarchal authority. Nor does he affiliate with other members of the Dominican community. But he is a realist: he knows that he is no longer part of *alta sociedad* or the oligarchy that had dominated economic and political life under Trujillo. "The revolution in the old country had failed. Most of his comrades had been killed or bought off. He had escaped to this country" (25). Dr. García sustains the cultural referents and relations that make him the center of family life, but his embrace of the American work ethic and social mobility reveals a significant adaptation to the economic and political realities of his new nation. Dr. García prospers, moving his family around the city and ultimately to the Long Island suburbs after his clinic in the Bronx restores him to a stable level of prosperity that is more middle class than lavish in its contours. When he has the opportunity to return in 1970 after several additional minor revolutions make the Dominican Republic more hospitable to former exiles, he rejects the lure of the indigenous culture, announces that he is *un dominican-york!* and subsequently obtains American citizenship for the entire family.

Even as Dr. García becomes *un dominican-york,* the women in the family effect their own more profound cultural negotiations. The doctor's wife, Laura, assumes the powerful image of a model mother who reinvents herself culturally (and often comically) before her daughters' eyes. Educated in the United States, Laura was among the early members of the oligarchy to sense that the Dominican Republic had become "a crazy hellhole" (202) under Trujillo. Her abrupt exile momentarily forces her to see her island nation "through the lens of loss" (212), but her more significant ability to transform nostalgia into American inventiveness tends to legitimate her identity before her girls *and* her husband. She becomes the "daughter of invention" that one chapter appropriates as its title. Laura bubbles with inventiveness: to her daughters she is "their Thomas Edison Mami, their Benjamin Franklin Mom" (137), breaching the patriarchal script laid down as canonical Dominican family lore. With her propensity for malapropisms ("it takes two to tangle") and her tendency to violate family norms, she becomes, at a critical time early in the family's exile, the inheritor of her ancestors'—the original conquistadors—conquering spirit. Rejecting the opportunity to return to the island, she declares: "Better an independent nobody than a high-class houseslave" (144). Devoted to her husband and usually deferential, she nevertheless develops the capacity to confront him: "This is America, Papi, America! You are not in a savage country anymore!" (146). Laura García negotiates family, community, and national life in idiosyncratic ways that nevertheless validate her identity and legitimize a very special relationship with her four daughters.

Whereas Dr. García attends to the economic survival of his household in America, his wife enacts representations of New World arrival that often perplex her daughters but prepare them paradoxically for the cultural counterpoints in their lives as women in America. Christine Downing in *Women's Mysteries: Toward a Poetics of Gender* (1992) argues that "women are hungry for images through which we might see *ourselves*" (7), and for the García girls it is their "Thomas Edison Mami" who illuminates the matrix of their lives. Laura's formative power over her daughters is decidedly inventive. Confronted, for example, with the prospect of looking after four young girls in a new urban environment, she dresses the girls by color: Carla, the oldest, in yellow and, in descending chronological order, Sandi in blue; Yolanda or Yoyo in pink; Sofía or Fifi in green. Laura is an immigrant epistemologist, inventing ways of knowing for her daughters that the girls often cannot initially construe. During the phase when their mother is obsessed with inventing a household product that will transform them into millionaires, the daughters feel bereft of guidance: "Here they were trying to fit in America among Americans; they needed help figuring out who they were, why the Irish kids whose grandparents had been micks were calling them spics" (138). Yet in the course of their lives, the daughters learn from their mother of invention, organizing personal and social experience in an "invisible sisterhood" (121) that is the lasting tapestry of their lives.

As the García girls mature into women in America, they do not lose their sense of Dominican culture (they spend summers in the island) even as they order their reality to the concatenation of American culture. They acculturate rapidly, rejecting Dominican images and symbols of patriarchy and female subordination: "Island was the hair-and-nails crowd, chaperones and icky boys with their macho strutting and unbuttoned shirts and hairy chests with gold chains and teensy gold crucifixes. By the end of a couple of years away from home, we had *more* than adjusted" (108–9). Despite their parents' strictness, the García girls whether in private schools, college, marriage, divorce, or sexual relationships, are rebellious, constantly seeking their own signature identities. Although Papi is a coercive force in their lives, they manage to love him without surrendering the ordering principles of their personal and professional lives: psychoanalysis for Carla; schoolteaching for Sandi; writing for Yolanda; and outright domestic revolution for Fifi, "the other great power" (31) in the house, who runs off to Michigan with her German-American husband Otto and conducts silent warfare with her father. Even as they reject their father's hegemony over their lives, the García girls gather as *familia* for his seventieth birthday at Fifi's house. "They were passionate women, but their devotions were like roots; they were sunk into the past towards the old man" (24). Yet it is precisely during a party game on her father's birthday that Fifi asserts her own dominant position in the hierarchy of family power by kissing her blindfolded father fully on the lips, a pivotal moment in which the ideology of the dominant male in Dominican culture is turned upside down.

It is Yolanda, of all the Garcías, for whom the alchemy of immigration seems the most troublesome. Aptly nicknamed "Yoyo," and the character who both launches the novel and ends it, she oscillates between two cultures in a way that her other family members do not. In the most thorough study of Dominican international migration, *Between Two Islands* (1991), the sociologist Sherri Grasmuck and anthropologist Patricia Pessar stress the "psychic dependency" Dominicans express toward Manhattan Island and the island of Hispaniola. This psychic oscillation is possible because "these two islands are bridged by a binational market for labor and commodities, by social networks, and by transnational households" (16). All of the García girls shuttle between two islands for their childhood summer vacations, thereby keeping their Dominican cultural referents even as they assimilate into American society. Yet only Yolanda seems susceptible to an ideology of return or reverse migration to Hispaniola. In the opening section of the novel, "Antojos," which can be translated roughly as a "craving" for something, Yolanda is "home" in the Dominican Republic for her birthday, after an absence of five years. Because the narrative moves backward in time, this is the most contemporary period in the García chronology, and in the year 1989 "Yolanda is not so sure she'll be going back" (7). Despite her rusty Spanish and the pressures of reintegrating herself into the García "clan" with its hierarchical and patriarchal imperatives and its retinue of dark-skinned servants, Yoyo the writer seeks the verbal, emotional, and cultural structures that will enable her to find a center to her turbulent life. Her "craving" (expressed physically in her passion for *guayabas* or guavas) is for a cultural context or a socially constructed reality that might reduce the yoyoing pattern of her existence. She seeks *real* experience by driving into the interior region of the island, where the action and imagery of the journey suggest both re-initiation into the concrete experiences of a relatively primitive world *and* the dangers inherent in such a quest. Her birthday cake had been shaped like a map of the Dominican Republic, and in her solitary journey into the interior of the island she too is a cartographer seeking to plot a new stage in her existence. She is "caught in the mighty wave of tradition" (9), and, embedded in a landscape suggesting an entirely different domain from the one offered in Manhattan, "she believes she has never felt at home in the United States, never" (12).

At the end of the novel, however, in the last section, titled "The

Drum" and situated both in actual (1956) and retrospective time, we sense the dominant and determinant force of American culture in the lives of the Garcías, confirming the imperial design that will always project family members, including Yolanda, into the realm of American experience. In this concluding section, Yolanda's grandmother brings her a magnificent drum from F.A.O. Schwarz, the epicenter of commodity culture for children and, within the taxonomy of relations among nations, suggestive of the decidedly loud penetration of the Dominican Republic by the United States. Poised between the patriotic beat of her American drum and the powerful island forces signified by the voodoo practices of the Garcías' Haitian maid Pila, Yolanda as a ruminative adult understands she must always reconstruct a self out of two cultures. A cat from whom she stole a kitten and named Schwarz, hiding it in her drum before the kitten escaped, becomes part of the map of her unconscious. In America, "there are still times I wake up at three o'clock in the morning and peer into the darkness. At that hour and in that loneliness, I hear her, a black furred thing lurking in the corners of my life, her magenta mouth opening, wailing over some violation that lies at the center of my art" (290). In dreams, in life, and in the stimulus of art, Yolanda emerges as the most central consciousness of the novel (and also the signature voice in Alvarez's much less successful 1997 sequel, *Yo*), a figure through whom we perceive the "violation" or trauma visited on those immigrants from the Caribbean who have difficulty reconciling fully the power lines of two cultures.

Puerto Ricans and the Promised Land

Although the power lines and postcolonial struggles of each island nation in the Caribbean are discrete, it nevertheless can be argued—even in the case of Puerto Rico, which because of its unique status as an American commonwealth sends migrants to the United States rather than immigrants—that postwar immigration patterns from the Hispanic Caribbean periphery to the metropolitan center reflect common and continuing forms of neocolonial experience. Cubans, Dominicans, Puerto Ricans: all are part of the "master narrative" of postcolonial immigration to the United States. Each has an essential piece of the postwar immigration process, different and distinct from the others but implicated also in the mythic symmetry of island movement to the Promised Land. Puerto Rico, however, is an especially unique example of this hybrid transnational migratory process, cursed and blessed by a metahistory that places it squarely in the interstices of the nation: not quite the "fifty-first state," not quite independent and free. Despite its anomalous identity, Puerto Rico is part of that bloc of colonial territory the United States appropriated from Spain following the Spanish-American War. Puerto Ricans were granted American citizenship and the freedom to travel to the mainland under the Jones Act of 1917, but throughout the twentieth century Puerto Rico remained, up to 1952 when a plebiscite approved self-government and Commonwealth status, an island dependency subject to the control of American corporations and the U.S. Congress. Whether or not the condition of Puerto Rico as an *estado libre asociado* intensifies the sense of colonialism among island residents or is the final solution to colonialism, as G.K. Lewis poses the question in *The Growth of the Modern West Indies* (1968), is an issue that lingers in the collective consciousness of Puerto Ricans today. Their constant movement back and forth from Puerto Rico to the mainland is a result largely of island unemployment but also perhaps an emblem of the fragmentation of Puerto Rican identity as it collides with American realities.

Migration by Puerto Ricans to the mainland prior to World War II was modest, rising from 53,000 to 70,000 between 1930 and 1940, with most migrants living in New York City. During these years, passage to America by boat was expensive, the equivalent of a laborer's average annual wages. The war, with German submarines patrolling the Caribbean and making voyages to the mainland hazardous, halted migration, but after the Second World War, the Puerto Rican exodus became a part of the emerging narrative of movement resonating through postwar American fiction. Overpopulation, underemployment, and poverty, despite the impact of Operation Bootstrap, which had started in 1940 and had been designed to strengthen and diversify the island's economy, were the factors precipitating the Puerto Rican migration boom. Combined with the surplus of unskilled jobs on the mainland in the aftermath of the war and the opening of the skies to relatively inexpensive travel by air (with some airlines advertising one-way fares of $50), Puerto Rican migration exploded, rising steadily through the decade following the end of World War II to a point where 675,000 Puerto Ricans lived in the United States by 1955, with 500,000 of them concentrated in the New York area.

Nicholasa Mohr, who was born in New York City's El Barrio, captures this migratory stream in the preface to the cycle of short fiction, *El Bronx Remembered* (1975): "There have been Puerto Ricans living in the mainland U.S.A. since the middle of the last century. But it was after the Second World War, when traveling became cheaper and easier, that the greatest influx began. In 1946, Puerto Ricans could purchase, for a small amount of money, a one-way ticket to the mainland. As citizens they did not face immigration laws or quotas . . . and so they arrived by the tens of thousands, first by freighter and later by airplane" (ix). Mohr in her preface offers a brief but subtly subversive critique of the neocolonial forces influencing this vast migratory tide: Puerto Ricans forming their own neighborhoods throughout New York City from Brooklyn to the Bronx, but conscious of their common destiny as "strangers in their own country . . . with a different language, culture, and racial mixture. Like so many before them, they hoped for a better life, a new future for their children, and a piece of that good life known as the 'American dream.'" As in her award-winning first novel *Nilda* (1973), which has erroneously been pigeonholed as a book for adolescents, Mohr in *El Bronx Remembered* constructs twelve stories around the lives of children and adults consigned by the discriminatory spatial practices of the new nation to the South Bronx barrio. Covering the years from 1946 through 1955, this short fiction cycle presents migrant lives involved in an attempt to invent a new sense of self and culture within the larger context of recent neocolonial history.

Mohr characterizes the postwar decade in American history as an era susceptible to power relations of dominance and subordination—involving race, class, and gender—as new immigrant groups embrace the American Dream but are pushed to the boundaries of this national vision of plentitude, or excluded from it by such historical and social practices as ghettoization. From Mohr's perspective, the barrio is simultaneously a refuge from the assimilative power of the hegemonic nation and a station in the road to a better life. It is also a realm where personal and group identity can be worked out within the fluid boundaries of competing cultures. The barrio, in short, is the arena in which national relations can be contested. In the first tale in the collection, "A Very Special Pet," the Fernández family, having sold their rural farm in Puerto Rico to finance their movement to the mainland, are travelers from the periphery to the metropolitan center. The narrative reads like a discourse on the geographic and psychic displacement of postmodernity: "city life was foreign to them, and they had to learn everything, even how to get on a subway and travel. Graciela Fernández had been terribly frightened at first of the underground trains, traffic and large crowds of people. Although she finally adjusted, she confined herself to the apartment and seldom went out" (2). Graciela, the focus of the tale, exists in that social space that Mary Louise Pratt has popularized as the "contact zone," the arena "where cultures meet, clash, and grapple with each other" (34). Phrased differently, Graciela "adjusts" but clings fiercely to a postcolonial identity rooted in its "otherness." Her husband might work hard as a porter, her children might go to school—all signs of the causality by which immigrants and migrants are molded by national forces. At the same time, however, Graciela cannot be absorbed totally into this new national culture, even when economic imperatives threaten to engulf her. When her husband Eugenio falls ill, she plans to slaughter the family's pet chicken, Joncrofo (named after her favorite Hollywood star, Joan Crawford), in order to prepare a strong broth for him. Yet Joncrofo "la gallina," living in the kitchen and tied to a long piece of twine attached to her box under the sink, is the tangible link for the Fernández family to Puerto Rico, the visible incarnation of their dream of reverse migration back to the island to purchase an even larger farm. Thus the battle in which Graciela engages the militant hen in a kitchen struggle of epic dimensions constitutes a psychic crossroads in the family's existence in the contact zone. Mrs. Fernández *almost* kills the hen, but is prevented by her screaming children, whereupon she revives Joncrofo with an eye-dropper filled with rum. To have slaughtered Joncrofo for practical— that is, American—reasons would have destroyed the family's vision of return. At the end of the tale, Graciela returns to her bicultural life, sweeping up hen's feathers in her American apartment while singing a familiar song in Spanish. "It was about a beautiful island where the tall green palm trees swayed under a golden sky and the flowers were always in bloom" (12). Graciela escapes cultural hegemony—the melting pot— even as the family's pet hen escapes the cooking pot.

It is characteristic of the stories in *El Bronx Remembered* that Mohr develops perspectives on "Othering," to apply Gayatri Spivak's term, that permit her Puerto Rican migrants and their children to interpret their place within two overlapping cultural domains. In one story, titled ironically "A New Window Display," a boy named Little Ray arrives from the island, becomes popular with the children, but contracts a respiratory illness and dies before he can enjoy his first snowfall in America. He becomes, in keeping with Puerto Rican burial traditions, the subject of a new window display of photographs of the deceased at Funeria Ortiz. In another tale, "The Wrong Lunch Line," a Puerto Rican girl, Yvette, whose best friend is the Jewish girl Mildred, learns about racial and religious parameters as she tries to transgress America's racist conventions in the spring of 1946, and is punished by school authorities, persisting in her friendship and rebelliousness nevertheless. And in "Uncle Claudio," the children in one family apprehend the allure of reverse migration as their aunt and uncle, scarcely in the mainland for a few months, rapidly retreat to Puerto Rico, disoriented by the dissolution of identity in New York City. As young Jaime says of his Uncle Claudio: "'First he says there are too many people all living together with no place to go. In his own home, in Humacao, people take it easy and know how to live. They got respect for each other, and know their place. At home, when he walks down the street, he is Don Claudio. But here, in New York City, he is Don Nobody'" (92). Sensing a lack of authority, identity, and voice, Uncle Claudio talks back to the Empire, validating his otherness by activating the cultural alternative of return.

A similar destiny awaits the male protagonist in Mohr's rich and subtle novella "Herman and Alice," when Herman, who is gay and has married the pregnant teenager Alice out of friendship, only to be deserted by her, decides his heterosexual masquerade in America should end and he should return to Puerto Rico and his family. Herman fuses the radical otherness of ethnicity and gender into an identity that is actually fluid and in many ways authentic. He is hardworking and respected by everyone in the building, including the brash high school dropout he tries to nurture and save from random existence. Thus his "return" is not so much a surrender as a carefully planned decision not to be circumscribed by the categories and codes of mainland culture. A truly hybrid soul, Herman looks forward to the freedom of return: "His family would meet him at the airport, and then they would all drive to Arecibo. He had planned everything carefully, and was pleased as always that things were going on schedule" (158). Herman in his hybridity is a triumphant figure, a postmodern New World person who is open to alternative forms of life and opportunity. He can function in the barrio but also in the supple interstices of the global system.

Mohr's chronicle of barrio life in *El Bronx Remembered* might very well have served as a model for a similar collection of short stories, Judith Ortiz Cofer's *An Island Like You* (1995). Cofer, who was born in Puerto Rico and moved to Paterson, New Jersey, as a child, moves her barrio across the Hudson River but sustains the same sense of an urban realm as both an island of comfort and conflict in a sea of national culture that typifies the fiction of Mohr. The American-born teenagers who form the continuous and recursive spine of the stories in *An Island Like You* conduct lives in two cultures: the household and public rituals of the Puerto Rican neighborhood competing with the school-yard realities and jukebox sounds of their American lives. Typically, the boys and girls in Cofer's short fiction cycle must confront their Puerto Rican heritage. In "Bad Influence," Rita spends a summer in Puerto Rico with her grandparents, safe from a dangerous high school Lothario; sullen at first, she sinks slowly into the safety and joy of her grandparents' world, enjoying a summer that turns out to be "one of the best" (25) of her life. In "An Hour with Abuelo," the teenager Arthur is forced to spend an hour with his grandfather in an American nursing home. Depressed initially like Rita in the earlier story, the boy gradually becomes mesmerized by his grandfather's tale of life in Puerto Rico and passage to America until, forgetful of time, his Abuelo tells him his hour is up and he must leave. Cofer examines this generational conflict from a different perspective in one of the more accomplished comic pieces in the collection, "Don José of La Mancha," where a daughter, Yolanda, observes in anger and fascination as Don José, fresh from the Puerto Rican *campo* or countryside, transports her widowed mother into romance and a new life. At the outset, Yolanda thinks Don José acts like a *jibaro*, or country hick. However, she witnesses the transformation of her mother because of his courtly manners and formal devotion to her. What is transferred to Yolanda is a version of love considerably at variance from the lusty rituals she and her friends anticipate. What the children in *An Island Like You* learn from their parents and grandparents is that their Puerto Rican heritage is not "un ciro, nada," to invoke a motif from "Abuela Invents the Zero." Instead, there are requirements and expectations rooted in blood and cultural tradition that are perilous to reject. The generation born of the parents and grandparents from Puerto Rico might be part of the fatalistic logic of urban youth culture in America. At the same time, they apprehend the two languages and two cultures that constitute the competing and potentially unifying forces as they construct lives in the era—as some critics term it—of late American imperialism.

New World Adam and Eve

Cofer locates the migrant lives of the characters in her novel *The Line of the Sun* (1989) in this same historical period extending from the 1950s into the 1970s. She elevates cultural politics to the realm of myth in the novel, creating in the wildly grotesque but exceedingly engaging figure of Guzmán a New World "savage" or *nino del diablo* who in his passage from the rural Puerto Rican town of Salud, to his subway life in New York, to his brief, dangerous sojourn in the Paterson barrio, and finally to his return to the island embodies the center-periphery anomalies of postcolonial life. Allowed to flourish in the wildness of his youth in Salud, Guzmán is the prototype of the postcolonial soul who defies all hegemonic practices. He is the demon child of Western imperialism, the "native," sleeping naked with pigs, running amok through the town and the sugar plantation. Taken by his mother to a spiritist, La Cabra, the teenager winds up living with her until she is exiled by the town. Cared for by the community as its wayward and prodigal son, Guzmán escapes the plantation economy of Salud only to find himself indentured in the fields of upper New York state. Escaping again, he enters the subterranean world of New York City, living underground and serving as an errand boy for the subway's employees, sleeping in subway cars and the corners of this postmodern hell. After ten years' absence, he reappears in his sister's apartment in "El Building," the archetypal center of barrio life in Paterson, New Jersey, in time to offer guidance like "a wise harlequin" (190) to his family and to save his nephew, trapped in a fire that consumes the tenement.

This bizarre biography, reconstructed by Guzmán's niece Marisol, who pieces together the "puzzle" of her uncle's life in order to better understand her own, amounts to a mythic narrative of exile and return. At each stage in his exile, Guzmán both interrogates and dismantles the historical moment. For example, his brother Carmelo volunteers for service in 1951 only to be "blasted into a thousand pieces over the soil of Korea" (61); Guzmán by contrast goes underground in America to escape imperial authority. His grotesque life is an extended critique of the norms of Western imperialism *and* American culture. Instead of American existence or Western space, this innocent abroad longs for pure existence and pure space, finding it by returning to Salud, improbably (but possibly in the realm of fiction) marrying the daughter of La Cabra and retreating to the sorceress's beautiful valley, a hidden Eden beyond all boundaries—plantation or metropolitan—of Western civilization.

The circuitous life of Guzmán and his extended family embodies the orientation, the recursive migratory rhythm of people deeply immersed in the myths of exile. Cofer in her novel incorporates the metaphor of Eden as an expression of the paradoxical vision of "paradise" that characterizes the Puerto Rican condition. Often in the novel the divided loyalties of Puerto Ricans are expressed in paradisiacal terms, as when the narrator's mother Ramona, who walks the streets of Paterson like "an alien and a refugee," serves to remind the family of their "illusory Eden" (174) on the island. At the same time, the United States also signifies a spiritual or mythic center of Edenic illusion. For example, the men caught up in the frenzy of the lottery for migrant work on the mainland see this New World opportunity in archetypal terms: "The men must have felt like the sailors who accompanied Columbus on his first voyage" (149). For many people in Salud, "la tierra de nieve sounded like paradise" (152). These binary notions of Paradise fuse in "the ethnic beehive of El Building. It was a microcosm of Island life" (170), a transplanted Eden within the more uncertain and provisional paradise of urban America. El Building is a simulacrum of Eden, a psychic and spiritual urban oasis where its residents can conduct "their lives in two worlds in blithe acceptance of cultural schizophrenia" (171). Yet when El Building is destroyed by fire, Ramona's own dream of Paradise is dismantled; the "destruction of El Building had been her initiation, her rite of passage, and she was slowly accepting that life would never be the same" (280). The family then moves to the suburbs of Paterson, but Ramona's initiation into this American version of Paradise, which lacks any spiritual or communal center, is so dispiriting a *rite de passage* that when her husband is killed in an automobile accident (he had never fully mastered this necessity of suburban life), she too returns to her island center, continuing the narrative of cultural revision that Cofer constructs in *The Line of the Sun.*

Ultimately it is Guzmán who is the New World Adam, a provocative parody of Western efforts to "center" the Edenic myth in a recognizably white world. With his deep bronze features, long ebony hair, and Taino Indian blood, Guzmán decenters conventional perspectives on Paradise, engaging in a persistent effort at cultural revision of national myths. His individual consciousness or identity is rooted in practices and beliefs that constantly interrogate traditional boundaries of myth and national culture. For Guzmán, the vital center is not New York or Paterson or even Salud: it is a pristine world prior to the first Conquistadors. As he retreats to a thickly vegetated area prior to his departure as a teenager for America, he recreates and imagines this prelapsarian world.

> In the shade of the fruit trees Guzmán felt totally free. This land was so abundant. In a few acres grew mangoes, bananas, plantains, breadfruit, avocados, tamarinds, and roots such as yucca that could be cooked and eaten like potatoes. He could easily imagine how the original inhabitants of the Island, the Taino Indians, had led an easy life in an earthly paradise, subsisting on what the earth produced without too much effort, and on what the sea gave them. Even their dwellings were constructed from the trees and palm fronds that were so abundant. Of course, the Spaniards with their gold lust, their fire weapons, and their diseases had changed the Indians' ideal life within a couple of generations. (133–34)

One can conclude that Guzmán's quest is for a world prior to the European conquest, the liquidation of native peoples, the ascent of plantation economies (a motif in Cofer's novel), and twentieth-century colonial domination by the United States. Guzmán spreads himself across time and space before he retreats from both the colonial and metropolitan world to the frontiers of civilization itself, finding freedom *beyond* society and submitting only to his newfound Eve, the beautiful and devout daughter of the "witch" of Salud, as they travel back in time and space to their reimagined Eden, the original plantation.

Unlike most protagonists, Guzmán both reflects and transcends the historical moment in which immigration narratives are situated. His retreat from both Puerto Rican and urban civilization at the end of the novel, as well as the inversion of patriarchal perspectives inherent in his submissive surrender to the devout daughter of La Cabra, is atypical of those immigrant lives articulated within the context of transnational relations. Thus Guzmán's dream of a transcendent prelapsarian Paradise contrasts with the more secular and provisional yearnings of the heroine in Esmeralda Santiago's *América's Dream* (1996), a novel of Puerto Rican migration whose very title suggests a text designed to explore the construction of personal and national identity. While lacking some of the surreal and enigmatic appeal of *The Line of the Sun*, Santiago's novel is a significant contribution to that variety of immigrant fiction that equates sexual subjugation with various forms of neocolonial oppression experienced by immigrants to America.

Santiago, whose memoir *When I Was Puerto Rican* is a notable contribution to the autobiography of immigration, constructs in her novel a figure named América Gonzalez whose identity and very body are controlled by two systems: the system of masculine oppression that the author asserts is inherent in Puerto Rican culture and the transnational system of labor that sends immigrants to the United States for employment in the service economy. As a hotel maid on the island of Vieques off the Puerto Rican coast, América seems trapped in a complex system of power. On the one hand, she is the servant of tourists, whose rooms she cleans; on the other, she is controlled violently by her married boyfriend Correa, the father of her teenage daughter and a man prone to murderous jealousy. Santiago handles the intersections of colonial and sexual subjugation quite deftly in the novel, enabling readers to understand the ways in which ethnic origins and gender are key determinants in the contemporary immigrant experience. As maid and mistress, América is the "other woman" of so much Western fiction and discourse. As an immigrant escaping provisionally from her oppressive island life to a "new" life as nanny and live-in housekeeper for an American family in Westchester County, an affluent suburb north of New York City, she is also the archetypal Other within the social division of power in the United States. Thus sexual and ethnic differentiation are the twin constituents— a sort of epistemological system—that determine América's identity and her relation to the world.

As a victim of both masculine and colonial enterprises, América is an object of definition by a matrix of forces that place her within a specific position in human society. Essentially she is a construction of patriarchal systems that name her as an object of exploitation. Consequently, she is "rapable," a condition that defines her actual life in Vieques and her perception of life and relations in the United States. Katherine

MacKinnon in her seminal essay "Feminism, Theory, Marxism and the State: Toward a Feminist Jurisprudence" notes that "to be *rapable*, a position which is social, not biological, defines what a woman *is*" (651). América internalizes this socially constructed definition of herself, succumbing fearfully to the image imposed on her by her violent lover, whose male perspective on her sexuality seems omnipotent. América submits to rape by Correa just as she submits to her role as housekeeper in the United States, enjoying a temporary escape from one form of violation only to understand gradually that she has merely substituted one type of power relationship for another. From an island of tropical passions, she moves in winter to a world of household machines and icy social relations. She is treated well by her American family, the Leveretts, but in a subordinate position nevertheless, readily terminated after in self-defense she kills Correa, who has followed her obsessively to the United States.

From her submerged state of consciousness and identity, América evolves slowly into an individual who sheds her role as subordinate and learns to assert herself—to be "firm" in her own words—in her social relationships. Along with other immigrant women who serve as suburban housekeepers, she slowly apprehends the reductive nature of their lives but also the paradoxical power they wield over the families they serve. The immigrant women who take América into their society discuss the material conditions of their lives as well as the even more difficult immigrant passages experienced by those men from the islands and Latin America who look for day work every morning and are dropped off like so much expendable cargo at the end of the day "to drag themselves home to the rundown houses on the periphery of the village" (250). América opens her own bank account, sends money to her mother and troublesome daughter, visits relatives in New York City on days off. Associating with the other suburban *empleadas*, she becomes gradually politically conscious: "They describe how, in the places they come from, everyone dreams of coming to the United States. When she tells them that where she comes from people are fighting to win independence from the United States, they seem amazed. 'But you have it so good!' they assure her" (253). Instructed by Correa during her Vieques existence that women should stay out of politics, that she should endure a sort of political aphasia or silence, she learns not to be as "docile as faithful dogs" (253) but rather to construct her own identity—one that is subordinate to no one. By the end of the novel, recovered from her last violent encounter with Correa, she moves to an apartment in the Puerto Rican section of the Bronx, reclaims her daughter, slowly begins an equitable relationship with another man and goes to work as a maid in a large midtown hotel. The symmetry of her movement from her status in a hotel in Vieques to one in Manhattan should not be construed as a mere repetition of social and class relations. América now sustains herself within a challenging field of power relations. Her "dream" is not that of the silent woman imagining an elusive freedom but rather a freedom that she articulates and objectifies. Esmeralda Santiago in her novel works a deft variation on the American Dream, constructing an immigrant narrative in which her heroine slowly rejects *machismo* and neocolonial cultural norms for a sort of personal independence that is a corollary to the myth of freedom and self-reliance inherent in the American national myth.

When the American flag came to Cuba, Puerto Rico, and the Dominican Republic, these islands were transformed, especially after 1940, into what José Marti in one of his poems calls "the shores of exile." Whether island dependencies or postcolonial extensions and instrumentalities of American power, these islands produced a flow of Hispanic immigrants to the urban mainland—and a concomitant body of fiction reflecting the experience—that increasingly has changed both the Union and the literary canon. Although the Caribbean exiles encountered in contemporary fiction tend to Americanize themselves in distinctly urban or metropolitan contexts, they also enact patterns of ethnic separatism—in customs, language, and family life—that suggest an accretion rather than pure assimilation into America's ongoing utopian experiment in pluralism. The *barrio* is, after all, an island refuge within the larger urban scene that reflects the tensions and anomalies inherent in being or becoming *norteamericáno*. The barrio or immigrant neighborhood is the strategic intersection where island folkways and the "American way" seek reconciliation in the construction of identity.

The scenarios of exile and arrival enacted in the fiction of Hijuelos, Bell, García, Alvarez, Cofer, and other writers offer, in the final analysis, a striking panorama of postwar immigrant life in the American metropolis. The fiction of postwar Hispanic immigration can capture the dark, deracinative, underside of American urban life that is central to earlier naturalistic fiction, the grotesque landscapes of Nathanael West, and the animating impulses of film noir. The quasi-autobiographical narrative

Down These Mean Streets (1991) by Piri Thomas and Pedro Juan Soto's short story collection *Spiks* (1973) typify the genre, and assuredly Hijuelos holds a dark mirror to urban life in his fiction. Yet Latino writers offer another vision of the American city in which the stress of urban life is balanced against the city's effervescence and legitimate allure. Cesar Castillo in *The Mambo Kings* might end his days in hotel-faded "splendor," but his postwar journey through New York City is also one of musical, sexual, and human celebration.

The postwar city of immigrants thus is re-mythologized in images of the overarching American Dream: the neighborliness of the barrio, the sunshine of the Miami streets (never quite as brilliant as the sun in Havana but sustaining nevertheless for Cuban exiles), the exotic avenues of opportunity contending with the city's more labyrinthine dangers. The city is not an unredeeming Golgotha for Hispanic immigrants from the Caribbean but rather a scene of metropolitan quest. It is a stage on which postwar immigrants can enact their own versions of arrival, adjustment, and provisional acculturation. For postwar Hispanic immigrants, the city is a doubly appealing arena of opportunity, a place where island culture can be preserved and a port of entry into the American national experience achieved. They arrive as voyagers from what Antonio Benitez-Rojo calls an archipelago of islands into an archipelago of cities, negotiating cultures, rechecking the points on their compasses, and attempting to locate themselves on a new national shore.

5

Middle Passage:
The African-Caribbean
Diaspora

Sometimes the white children on their way to school laughed at their blackness and shouted "nigger," but the Barbadian women sucked their teeth, dismissing them. Their only thought was of the "few raw-mout' pennies" at the end of the day which would eventually "buy house."
—Paule Marshall, *Brown Girl, Brownstones*

Even as contemporary conditions precipitated a flood of peoples from the Spanish-speaking islands of the Caribbean to the American mainland, a stream of English-speaking immigrants from the West Indies—a parallel diasporic movement—flowed to both Great Britain and the United States. These Hispanic and Commonwealth migratory streams are linked by the legacies of colonial history or what the historian Gordon Lewis (1983) describes as an "agrosocial system of slavery developed in its fullest and most harsh form" (2). Yet the formation of an African-Caribbean immigrant identity rooted in the history of slavery is a subject largely absent from or registered in a low key in novels and short fiction by writers tracing the migratory odysseys of Cubans, Dominicans, and Puerto Ricans, although these societies are characterized by high degrees of creolized or *mestizo* culture. Only in the fiction of West Indian immigration is the experience of race and race prejudice linked to the older and newer forms of colonialism.

The West Indian immigrants depicted in the fiction of Paule Marshall, Jamaica Kincaid, Michelle Cliff, and other writers confront a range of vexing questions about their identities and their racial and cultural inheritances. Their polyglot linguistic and cultural practices—so evident in Paule Marshall's novel *Brown Girl, Brownstones* (1959), for example—reflect identities that are filtered through a complex historical consciousness. Within contending historical modalities, the legacies of British imperialism and West Indian slavery embroil African-Caribbean immigrants inevitably in a search for origins or a postcolonial inheritance that spans several continents: Europe, Africa, the Caribbean Basin, and North America. Thus resistance to several forms of traditional and contemporary imperialism, typically centered in African-Caribbean female protagonists in novels like *Brown Girl, Brownstones*, Jamaica Kincaid's *Lucy* (1990), and Michelle Cliff's *No Telephone to Heaven* (1987), begins with the assertion of race as the key determinant in the otherness at the core of postwar African-Caribbean immigrant life.

Postcolonial Middle Passages

Like its Spanish, Dutch, and French counterparts, Great Britain participated for more than two centuries in the transplantation of roughly ten million Africans to the New World—the dreaded Middle Passage that becomes a trope in a significant body of contemporary American fiction: Marshall's *Praisesong for the Widow* (1983), Charles Johnson's *Middle Passage* (1980), Banks's *Continental Drift*, Toni Morrison's *Tar Baby* (1981) suggest the range of this archetypal element. The legacy of Caribbean slave society was one regional manifestation of a global imperial design that subjugated native and exiled populations well into the twentieth century. When the daughter of the main character Avey Johnson in *Praisesong for the Widow*, embarking on a cruise *back* in time, place, and culture to the Caribbean, notes that they are standing in the cruise liner's Versailles Room, she connects their presence to these broader historical realities: "Do you know how many treaties were signed there, in that infamous Hall of Mirrors, divvying up India, the West Indies, the world?" (46). Similarly, with the outbreak of World War II, the father Deighton Boyce in *Brown Girl, Brownstones* is thankful he has two daughters and no sons: "Nineteen fourteen again. Thank God I ain got neither one to send to die in another white-man war" (65). In both instances, the contemporary experiences of these characters, whose lives are culturally constituted by their African-Caribbean background, are historicized and signified by worldwide disruptions caused by the clash of white empires. In their new Middle Passages as cosmopolitan voyagers, they are products of this imperial history, but they also perceive themselves as separate from it: whether in Europe or America, their specific cultural world is captured in the typically ironic stance revealed in the comments by Avey's daughter and Deighton Boyce. Such individuals are both part of the imperial design and distanced from it—slightly off-center as the prevailing cultural nomenclature puts it—always cognizant of their relation to colonial society as they cope with their most recent dispersal to foreign shores.

This off-centeredness of African-Caribbean immigrant identity is reflected in the frenetic pattern of perpetual departures and arrivals as individuals attempt to find cultural space for themselves in the postcolonial or metropolitan world. Descendants of Africans who arrived in the Caribbean in chains, they experience a postcolonial Middle Passage that is the physical and psychic correlative of their original cultural disinheritance. African by descent but Anglophile by colonial cultural conditioning, they emigrate to New York or London only to face issues that had been buried in consciousness, ameliorated by their numerical majority in most West Indian societies, subverted by patterns of class and caste, sanitized by language, education, and ties to England, the motherland. The writer George Lamming, whose *In the Castle of My Skin* (1970) is arguably the finest West Indian novel of the contemporary period, explicitly equates the alienation of the West Indian from his or her cultural roots with the primal horror and disorientation of the Middle Passage and the colonial ascendancy of England over its enslaved masses. In his 1973 essay "The West Indian People," he observes:

> This human diversity encountered itself in a state of original isolation; isolated, that is, by the lack of a common idiom and imprisoned by orders which were absolute. And most important of all, these were orders given in a language the people could not understand. . . . Isolated by a lack of idiom, this humanity made a bid for possession of the language, exposed utterly and naked to the process of being possessed by all the

conceptual and poetic possibilities of the language that would
become their new possession. Supervising this complexity of
learning to be a new man, in a new place, was an authority
whose home was elsewhere. (10)

For Lamming, a superimposed language and culture suppressed African
survival forms, while the British educational system, satirized by Lamming in the figure of the school teacher Mr. Slime in *In the Castle of My
Skin*, substituted the glorious history of England for the brutal history of
West Indian slavery, which receded into the realm of mythic invisibility.
Yet this "borrowed culture," as V.S. Naipaul terms it trenchantly in his
critique of Caribbean culture, *The Middle Passage* (1962), is not sufficiently sustaining for West Indian immigrants to the metropolitan centers, for unavoidably the reality of race emerges from the mythic mist
because of its persistent presence in American life. Migration thus becomes the vehicle whereby West Indians rediscover kinship with their
origins. The African-Caribbean immigrants in *Brown Girl, Brownstones*,
Lucy, and *No Telephone to Heaven* articulate identities in the New World
by apprehending the fact that they are colonial and historical subjects. At
specific points in their new Middle Passages, they encounter permutations of the old enslavement—as when Lucy, for example, senses in her
role as an *au pair* for a white family in New York the contours of the old
slave society, or when a white society matron patronizes Selina in *Brown
Girl, Brownstones*, also invoking the manifold virtues of their African-
Caribbean maid.

West Indian slave culture, which developed in the Caribbean between 1640, when England first colonized some of the islands and conquered others that had been part of the older Spanish empire, and 1838
with the advent of Emancipation, resulted in societies in which black
West Indians were the majority. Thus although experiencing the legacy
of domination, black West Indians never constituted a minority community. The black West Indians of Jamaica, Barbados, Trinidad, Antigua,
the Bahamas—and other islands that for centuries were British colonies
and today are members of the British Commonwealth of Nations—assuredly had to contend with inequalities of power and the colonial stratification of their world, but as a majority culture they negotiated these
differences as much from the perspective of class as from that of racial
division.

Following emancipation, one of the clearest manifestations of class resistance to local economic conditions was the impulse of West Indians to emigrate in search of work or education elsewhere. With the decline of the plantation economy based on sugar production in the second half of the nineteenth century, coupled with the growing abhorrence of West Indians to take low-status jobs as cane cutters (a problem planters solved by importing Asian Indian and Chinese workers), an emigrant odyssey began in search of promised lands. Initially much of the migration was internal with West Indians moving from island to island, but with the construction of the Panama Canal between 1904 and 1914, a surge of Barbadians—perhaps as many as 60,000— signaled the first twentieth-century exodus of West Indians to regions of the New World where their job skills and English-language abilities would provide access to the economic culture. In the first two decades of the twentieth century, a similar exodus of more than 10,000 Bahamians to Florida would help lay the foundation for the emerging metropolis of Miami. From Miami to Brooklyn to Harlem to Boston, West Indian communities—230,000 strong— were entrenched in America by 1920.

Emigration thus is one of the recurrent figures of the African-Caribbean collective imagination. Through this diasporic movement, individuals and communities become aware of their relationship to several national histories and the possibility of constructing new personal and national identities. Formed concurrently by English colonial models and African traditions, West Indian voyagers to the North American mainland enter a new world where their efforts at self-definition require the incorporation of yet another metahistory within their consciousness. They enter the United States as polyglot souls, scarcely parochial in their world views, oriented instead toward metropolitan possibilities. With the first wave of West Indian immigrants (including the parents of Paule Marshall) already entrenched in the United States by 1920, the migratory circuit of movement from the islands to the American mainland was buffeted by the restrictive and essentially racist U.S. immigration policies of the 1920s. The Quota Act of 1921 and the Immigration Act of 1924 had ostensibly exempted West Indians from discriminatory policies, but when immigration from the West Indies jumped to 10,630 in 1924, Congress immediately assigned quotas from the British colonies in the Caribbean to the mother country. By 1925, the number of West Indian immigrants dropped to 304 (Pastor 245–47), an annual figure that prevailed through the 1920s and the decade of the Great Depression. Thus West Indians joined those restricted eastern and southern Europeans, Chinese, Japanese, and other Asians whose otherness was perceived by the national origins system as an impediment to assimilation and a threat to the ethnic composition of the United States.

Marshall's Black Atlantic

In her afterword to the 1981 Feminist Press edition of Paule Marshall's *Brown Girl, Brownstones* (published originally in 1959), Mary Helen Washington alludes to that "small fierce band of Barbadians who emigrated to the United States between 1900 and 1940 . . . to escape the brutal colonial exploitation of blacks in the West Indies" (311). In a sense they arrive as exiles from a colonial system, but as Lamming observes in *The Pleasures of Exile* (1960) they had already been alienated from any sense of national identity because of their history: "To be colonial," Lamming observes, "is to be in a state of exile. And the exile is always colonial by circumstances" (229), of which the color of one's skin is the most readily perceived sign of disenfranchisement. Escaping one realm of cultural and psychic disenfranchisement but finding themselves as immigrants in a new urban space composed of even more sharply articulated racial categories, the Barbadians or "Bajans" in *Brown Girl, Brownstones* must fashion selves from discrepant national histories—those of the United States, the Caribbean, England, and Africa. Marshall's novel, which opens in Brooklyn in 1939 just as World War II was becoming visible to the American mind, captures this sense of cultural uncertainty and displacement—what Paul Gilroy aptly terms "the web of diaspora identities and concerns that I have labeled the black Atlantic" (218). Powerful images of displacement control the narrative movement of *Brown Girl, Brownstones* from the outset, as Marshall invokes a street in Brooklyn whose Dutch-English and Scotch-Irish origins are in the throes of a new form of cosmopolitanism. As the white families move out, West Indians inaugurate an emergent immigrant process that gradually would contribute to the transformation of New York City into a multicultural microcosm of the United States in the twentieth century. Marshall suggests a radical reorienting process as the white population departs and the West Indians arrive:

But now in 1939 the last of them were discreetly dying behind those shades or selling the houses and moving away. And as they left, the West Indians slowly edged their way in. Like a dark sea nudging its way onto a white beach and staining the sand, they came. The West Indians, especially the Barbadians who had never owned anything perhaps but a few poor acres in a poor land, loved the houses with the same fierce idolatry as they had the land on their obscure islands. But with their coming, there was no longer tea in the afternoon, and their odd speech clashed in the hushed rooms, while underneath the ivy the old houses remained as indifferent to them as to the whites, as aloof.(4)

The brownstones, presented as personae, constitute the anchor in Marshall's sea of racial change; indeed her cultural description of the Bajan community focuses on the considerable desire on the part of its members to acquire property or "buy land." Their "dark" arrival on American shores signifies their racial predicament, but their "fierce idolatry" suggests an affinity with their new nation's worship of property rights. In the United States, the ownership of property permits entry into the social structure; it is a confirmation of bourgeois values, and desperately sought by the Bajan women who occupy the domestic and cultural center of the novel.

The Bajan women who situate their families at the materialistic heart of American culture engage in a process of self-fashioning or reconstitution of identity, interacting with their new urban environment while never abandoning their sense of a community whose historical links to the West Indian world temper their values. As Marshall demonstrates in *Brown Girl, Brownstones* and virtually all of her subsequent fiction, one national culture never entirely supplants another, but results instead in a hybridization of culture and identity for immigrants who confront the changing forces of national histories. For the women in Marshall's first novel, the contingencies of gender, power, race, and history raise subtle and problematic issues of belonging or national identification. Silla Boyce, the mother whose forceful personality molds the lives of her husband, Deighton, and her two daughters, Selina and Ina, tries to create existential space for her family so that they can ultimately enjoy a place within American metropolitan life. She is grounded in her new world, uninhibited by multiple forms of discrimination, fiercely attuned to the conjuncture of the Bajan and United States ethos extolling the sacredness of property. To be Barbadian-American might require the adoption of certain new forms of cultural representation, but the process of being both Barbadian and American is facilitated by a common devotion to property. The language and other expressive modes Brooklyn's Bajan community employs to articulate its conception of America might be grounded in the rhetoric and rhythms of the West Indies, but an allegiance to property and the Protestant work ethic promises the community a place on the stage of American civilization. Marshall, of course, does not legitimatize the African-Caribbean quest for material salvation; instead she subjects this quest to careful critique as the various members of the Boyce family and the Bajan community struggle to find their own piece of paradise on Brooklyn's changing streets.

Marshall in *Brown Girl, Brownstones* is quite adept at portraying divergent forms of cultural representation that are grounded in a specific historical movement—the movement of the United States out of the Depression and into the cauldron of the Second World War. Indeed, as World War II dominates the historical horizon, new forms of cultural interaction, accelerating trends in emigration from Mexico and the Caribbean, and economic possibilities for immigrants spawned by wartime requirements of production created a complex order of local and national realities for immigrant groups. Just as World War II opened the southwestern boundary of the United States to Mexican immigration under the terms of the Bracero Program, West Indians received similar dispensations—what Iris Hurley in *Brown Girl, Brownstones* alludes to as "the immigration scheme" (73)—to support the war effort. Ransford W. Palmer in his study *Pilgrims from the Sun: West Indian Migration to America* (1995), observes: "World War II brought a new role for the United States in the Caribbean as a protector of the region from possible German attack. Through lend-lease arrangements with Britain, the United States acquired 90–year base rights in Jamaica and in other islands in 1940. Under the aegis of the Anglo-American Caribbean Commission established in 1942, West Indian workers were recruited to replace American workers in agriculture and nondefense industries" (8). In fact, British West Indians made up 17 percent of the more than 400,000 workers imported between 1942 and 1945 (Palmer 25). For members of the older West Indian community, the war offered new contexts for economic improvement. Silla, for example, in the third and longest of the four "books" of the novel, appropriately titled "The War," obtains employment in a Brooklyn defense factory. And in one of the most striking scenes in the novel, Marshall creates a discourse on American power and possibility as the young Selina (who is ten when the narrative begins) makes a dark, wintry journey through Brooklyn streets to visit the factory where her mother works as a lathe operator, fashioning shells for the war effort. The scene Selina encounters in the factory—"a controlled, mechanical hysteria, welling up like a seething volcano to the point of eruption, only to veer off at the climax and start again" (98–99)—is Marshall's ambiguous invocation of national power. Marshall acknowledges the power of this "new creative force" inherent in the "colossal machine" of the wartime factory, but she also reads (as does Selina) the "machine-mass" as an alienating and dehumanizing force: "The workers, white and colored, clustered and scurried around the machine-mass, trying, it seemed to stave off the description it threatened. They had built it but, ironically, it had overreached them, so that now they were only small insignificant shapes against its overwhelming complexity. They pulled levers, turned wheels, scooped up the metal droppings of the machines as if somewhere in that huge building someone controlled their every motion by pushing a button" (99). The workers, black and white (and also overwhelmingly female as Marshall emphasizes in another passage), are engaged in a necessary but ambivalent enterprise. These women, especially the West Indians, contest for new social and economic space even as the power of the machines to which they are yoked makes them automata in this wartime factory system of labor.

Silla, however, translates her factory world differently, and although "The War" is a title that also captures her troubled relationship with Selina and her husband throughout the novel, her ability to contest dominant forces and adjust to national realities is a strength her young daughter apprehends. Silla is not intimidated by this "machine-force"; if anything, she harnesses it and derives strength from her industrial situation. Fiercely doctrinal in her drive for place and property in the national scene, she treats this wartime opportunity to do more than clean houses for white families as a Golden Age, an almost redemptive moment in the history of urban culture and capitalism. She positions herself as a very powerful human subject within an equally powerful impersonal system of labor. Her daughter's perception of this reciprocal force turns out to be a revelation: "watching her, Selina felt the familiar grudging affection seep under her amazement. Only the mother's own formidable force could match that of the machines; only the mother could remain indifferent to the brutal noise" (100). Selina's journey to the factory, and the discipline she receives from her mother subsequently, represents a major step in her emerging feminist consciousness, for she learns from her mother that difference, conflict, and struggle are the historical conditions whereby she can gain knowledge and identity. Annoyed and remonstrating with Selina during the trolley ride home, Silla provides her daughter with a catechism on gender and race, struggle and social conflict: "I read someplace that this is the machine age and it's the God truth. You got to learn to run these machines to live. But some these Bajan here still don't understand that" (103). Selina, both drawn to her mother and antagonized by her, senses fundamental differences in their world views, but she acknowledges nevertheless the force of her mother's dominance in the formation of her identity.

Unlike Silla, her husband, Deighton Boyce, cannot accommodate himself to the full range of opportunities provided by his encounter with the United States. Having arrived in the United States illegally (much as Marshall's father had done following World War I), Deighton suffers from a variety of modern anomie common in the fiction depicting immigrants from colonized nations of the British Empire. The bane of Silla's existence and the focus of her hatred, he represents those exotic island pleasures—a type of Caribbean romanticism—that Silla rejects. "He's always half-studying some foolishness" (32) Silla complains to her friend Virgie Farnum, treating her "beautiful-ugly" husband, who spends most of his time in their rented brownstone in the upstairs sun room, his simulated Caribbean paradise, dreaming of projects that never come to fruition. Poor Deighton is presented ironically by Marshall as a parody of the way to wealth, a mock-Benjamin Franklin whose quest for some elusive profession that would transport him readily across cultural boundaries is frustrated by his own lack of resolve and by the inherent racism of his new and old worlds. In Bridgetown as a young man, he had encountered "white English faces" twisted with "incredulity . . . disdain . . . indignation" when he had applied for a job as a clerk. In the United States, his fleeting vision of a career as an accountant also founders on the shores of his own lack of initiative and on the bedrock of racism. As his friend Seifert Yearwood, who had come to the United States in 1920 and had lived close to the Boyces in cockroach-infested cold-water flats in South Brooklyn and who now owns a women's apparel store on Fulton Avenue counsels: "Boyce, mahn . . . you can know all accounting there is, these people still not gon have you up in their fancy office and pulling down the same money as them" (39). A charming but ultimately tragic figure in an unmanageable cultural situation, Deighton nourishes the romantic possibility of repatriation—of returning to Barbados and building his own house on two acres of land he has inherited. His dangerously attractive dream of return dooms him to conflict with Silla, gradual psychic displacement, physical and cultural loss, and eventual death.

Silla's affinity for the dynamism of America provokes a corresponding disengagement from it by Deighton, who in "The War" section, covering 1940 to 1945, progressively loses any stable sense of identity. The sequence of key episodes in Book 3 is a subtle allegory or narrative meditation on the shifting and multiform global conflicts of the war years and their corresponding refraction in urban life and also in the turbulence within the Boyce household. Holding this sequence in tension is the struggle over Deighton's land in Barbados, which Silla appropriates from him through forgery and deception, only to have him squander the money from the sale before she can invest it in property. From the time Deighton's dream of repatriation is shattered, his life begins to unravel. In the labyrinthine factory where he works with Silla, he succumbs to the lethal force of the machinery when his arm is caught and crushed in a new machine he had only half-learned how to operate. Joyce Pettis in her study *Toward Wholeness in Paule Marshall's Fiction* (1995) notes that "Silla's rapport with the machinery demonstrates her acceptance of Western values, while Deighton's mangling graphically symbolizes the spiritual injury enacted upon him and others like him" (88). His ambivalence about assimilation—he wants to succeed in America without really applying himself, and then return to Barbados to strut his success before his kinsmen, enjoying a life of leisure—violates the capitalist ethos that Silla easily embraces. Following his injury, Deighton rejects all previous career prospects for the uncertain tranquility provided by the "Father Peace" movement, Marshall's sly parody of the Father Divine phenomenon that offers a false sense of community for African Americans and African-Caribbeans disaffected by the national experience. With eyes that Marshall repeatedly describes as "glazed," "fixed," "blank," "blind," and "vacant," Deighton inhabits the world of revelation, deserting his family to work for Father Peace in a Brooklyn restaurant. His exotic encounter with a new spiritual kingdom is terminated by Silla, who turns him in to authorities because of his illegal entry into the United States. His subsequent fate is apocryphal: "On the day the war ended, a cable arrived saying that Deighton Boyce had either jumped or fallen overboard and drowned at a point within sight of the Barbados coast and that a posthumous burial service had been read at sea" (185). Deighton never situates himself authentically in America. He takes imaginary detours, and his death signifies a journey that ends appropriately between national realms.

The poignant sense of loss with which Paule Marshall invests Deighton Boyce's life in America provides the contrapuntal element in the shaping of Selina, who with her sister Ina dotes on her father while wrestling with the powerful personality of her mother. Deighton's dream of return and the construction of a house in Barbados for his "ladyfolks" clashes with Silla's more practical impulse to "buy house" in Brooklyn. Whereas certain secondary Barbadian characters (like the tenant Suggie Skeete, with her "languorous pose . . . rituals . . . and passion") complement the romantic legacies of the Caribbean that Marshall associates with Deighton, they are subordinate to the community of Bajan women who assemble in Silla's kitchen to plan their entry into American society. Marshall plots her novel so that the polarizing tendencies inherent in the conflict between Selina's parents and in the hyphenated phrase "Caribbean-American" become the terms of postcolonial dialogue that Selina, as adolescent and young adult, must balance, reconstruct, and validate before she can define herself within competing national tendencies. As Carole Boyce Davies observes, "The question of identity for Caribbean women writers involves a self-definition which takes into account both gender and heritage. In all cases it is difficult to separate heritage/identity questions from gender/identity. So for the Caribbean-American writer, cultural politics have to be worked out along with sexual politics" (60). Selina's struggle to integrate competing gender, racial, cultural, and national practices, while balancing the legacies of her father and mother, creates the oppositional narrative power of *Brown Girl, Brownstones*. More than any other character, Selina represents the task for West Indians within African-American culture to reinvent themselves by selecting discreetly from the menu of competing images presented to them by their polyglot life in the urban domains of the United States.

Selina, then, in the second decade of her life as the child of immigrant parents, must assume the task of creating a viable personal and national project for herself. She worships her father and his sun-parlor reveries, calling her mother a "Hitler" for betraying him to immigration authorities. At the same time, the battle for her soul is shaped more significantly by her mother and by Silla's female friends—the "poets in the kitchen" whom Marshall celebrates in her nonfiction and who contend with the ruptures of history and tradition. In one extended episode in the novel, this community of West Indian women assumes the stature of goddesses, talking about origins, oscillating between Old and New Worlds, declaiming on national experience for the mesmerized Selina, who observes them as they enjoy a Saturday in the kitchen. The words of these mythic figures "were living things to her. She sensed them bestriding the air and charging the room with strong odors. She wondered at the mother's strong power with words" (71). They talk about what Dorothy Hamer Denniston, reworking the double consciousness explained by W.E.B. Du Bois in *The Fiction of Paule Marshall,* terms "the *three-ness* of those who were black and Caribbean and American" (xii). Their Caribbean roots emerge from their linguistic patois and their cooking, an amalgam of Africa and the Americas: "On Saturdays the kitchen was filled with fragrances, for Silla made and sold Barbadian delicacies: black pudding, which is the intestines of the pig stuffed with grated sweet potato, beets, animal blood and spices until it is a thick sausage, then tied at the ends and boiled; also souse, which she made by pickling parts of the pig; and coconut or sweet bread, a heavy bread with coconut running in a rich vein through the center" (67). Both Ina and Selina participate in this ritual of preparation, which is also part of the ritual of self-definition. Even as Selina receives a cultural catechism through cooking, her historical and geopolitical sensibility grows intuitively from the women's conversation. For Silla, Iris Hurley, and Florrie Trotman—three oversized Barbadian Furies—talk globally about their century's discontinuities and fractures, which coalesce in wartime. They speak of Hitler and the Jews—"these white people getting on too bad," of religion and *obeah,* of patriotism and colonialism. Silla rejects any role for Barbados in the war effort, reminding her friends of the hard realities in Bimshire, with the "white people treating we like slaves still and we taking it. The rum shop and the church join together to keep we pacify and in ignorance. That's Barbados" (70). For all three, the war is an opportunity to make "big war money" and purchase property. They frame their historical condition and locate themselves in a capitalist world. For Silla and her companions the riddle of national identity can be solved by property ownership. Without rejecting Barbadian cultural experience, they embrace what Nina Baym calls the "myth of America" or "the promise offered by the idea of America" (71). They reject all legacies of domination—sexual, racial, colonial—for the pure idea or promise of material success offered ironically by their wartime world.

Caught between the romantic and carnivalesque antics of her father and her mother's fierce attempts to negotiate the African-Caribbean diaspora, Selina must construct an "American" narrative of self-identity that will enable her to integrate the hemispheres. Essentially during the second decade of her life that Marshall constructs in *Brown Girl, Brownstones*, Selina seeks a national identity in a racially heterogeneous urban world. The sharp differences between Selina and her mother, her first lover Clive, her black and white school and college girlfriends, and the closely-knit and organized Bajan community in Brooklyn suggest she is engaged in a process of cultural and national adaptation that Marshall pointedly refuses to resolve at the end of the novel. If Selina has not established a coherent framework for conceptualizing her sexual, racial, cultural and national condition, she nevertheless is self-critical as she searches for a personal platform whereby she can comprehend her transnational condition. She plans to leave Brooklyn for the "islands," not to imitate the self-destructive odyssey of enforced return that ended her father's life, but to retrace the diasporic wanderings of her mother. In one last revelatory encounter with her mother, she gently acknowledges Silla's dominance: "Everybody used to call me Deighton's Selina but they were wrong. Because you see I'm truly your child. Remember how you used to talk about how you left home and came here alone as a girl of eighteen and was your own woman? I used to love hearing that. And that's what I want. I want it!" (307). Silla, who had arrived by ship from the Caribbean to the New World "watching the city rise glittering with promise from the sea," offers her "brusque" blessing to her "soul," her daughter whose Middle Passage will take her back to her origins. Yet Selina leaves one of the two silver bangles she had always worn—her Bajan identity tag—in the rubble of a block of brownstones being demolished for urban renewal. The brownstones that now resemble the bizarre fragments of an urban world in transition from once-stable communities to the postwar phenomenon of "projects" nevertheless are part of her identity. On the voyage outward, Marshall suggests, Selina will discover the other cultural fragments required for self-definition.

The bulk of Paule Marshall's fiction constitutes a mode of cultural criticism wherein she juxtaposes multiple cultures, asking persistently what it means to be American in a postcolonial world. In an interview with Sabine Bröck, Marshall terms *Brown Girl, Brownstones* "a kind of commentary on American life" (44); and although her first novel remains her most focused critique of the immigrant experience in the United States, her subsequent fiction situates her protagonists, typically of West Indian descent, within a broader universe of cultures. Dorothy Hamer Denniston's perceptive thesis—that "the chronology of Marshall's publications suggests her intentional design to reverse the 'middle passage'; that is, she examines the experience of blacks not in transit from Africa to the New World but from the New World back toward Africa" (xii)—illuminates the diasporic consciousness that her protagonists play out against the drama of the American nation-state. The migratory panorama presented by the four novellas comprising *Soul Clap Hands and Sing* (1961), which are titled "Barbados," "Brooklyn," "British Guiana," and "Brazil," reflect the diasporic range of her fiction. Marshall implies that this diasporic diversity is not a phenomenon common only to the United States, but is rather a sign of the postcolonial network typifying modes of production in an increasingly global economy. Notably in the first story, "Barbados," a successful Bajan immigrant, Mr. Watford, separates himself from the American mainstream after fifty years of hard work to return to his homeland, reversing the Middle Passage but also setting up an involuted and ironic historical contrast. Instead of becoming reacculturated to his native land, Mr. Watford, living in his American colonial house and wearing his starched white shirts, becomes a black parody of the white Southern plantation master, advocating an Anglo-Protestant work ethic for the poor local population. Another of Marshall's protagonists, Avey Johnson, an assimilated and successful African-American woman, embarks on a reverse Middle Passage in *Praisesong for the Widow*, but unlike Mr. Watford she experiences a transcultural awakening. Rediscovering her African origins through her exposure to African-Caribbean customs, songs, dances, and religious rituals, she transforms herself into Avatara, her birthname passed down from her grandmother but Americanized for simplicity's sake. On Grenada, when questioned about her "nation," Avey can only state that she is from New York, the United States (168). But passing from Grenada

to Carriacou by boat, tossing in turbulent waters in a reinvocation of the
Middle Passage, Avey/Avatara immerses herself in older "national" cultures, her participation in African-Caribbean dances creating new affiliations and cultural loyalties. Culturally attuned to her deepest origins,
Avey plans to return to the United States with a new mission: to educate
her relatives and friends about their diasporic identities.

The creation of diasporic or transnational identity also appears as
a theme in *Daughters* (1991), where Marshall captures the constant back-
and-forth movement of West Indians that David Reimers in *Still the
Golden Door* identifies as the hallmark of Caribbean immigration patterns. A complex novel tracing the intertwined lives of several women
who form a galaxy around the figure of Primus McKenzie, the "PM" or
Prime Minister of the fictive Caribbean island of Triunion, the narrative
focuses on Ursa McKenzie, born of the PM and his African-American
wife. Because of her mother's American citizenship and her own birth
on the mainland, Ursa is not an immigrant but rather a diasporic sojourner, having grown up in Triunion before receiving her college education in the United States. Her diasporic identity thus is fluid, reacting
to the various cultural and political crosscurrents of the 1970s and 1980s
that Marshall insinuates into the novel. Ursa is at home in Triunion (whose
name captures the French, Spanish, and English colonial background of
the island) but acknowledges that her true home is polyglot New York
City. Strolling along the streets of the Upper West Side where she lives,
Ursa passes the Korean fruit stands and the "many different combinations"
of races—the faces that "flow by, black, white, Latina, Asian but mostly
white" (52). Sensing she will also be something of an exile in both nations,
she nevertheless welcomes her return to New York at the end of the novel,
following a visit to Triunion where she observes her father's defeat in an
election. Ursa "elects" the hybridized identity of the transnational wanderer. She belongs to kin and culture in the Caribbean, but she is also an
ethnic New Yorker, a part of the diasporic metropolis that, Marshall suggests, will remain the center of her shifting postcolonial world.

The West Indian Diaspora

For Paule Marshall and other novelists exploring the African-Caribbean
diaspora in the United States, the questions of identity and authority, of

First and Third World relations, of the center and the periphery are historical categories captured by the dialectics of immigration. The trajectory of Marshall's fiction, reaching back in *Brown Girl, Brownstones* to the early twentieth-century emigration of West Indians to the American metropolis and advancing through the watershed events of the 1960s, 1970s, and 1980s that serve as backdrop for the contrapuntal narrative action in *Daughters,* is anchored in the history of contemporary immigration. The turbulent dynamics of World War II precipitated in the postwar era an irreversible drive toward emigration by West Indians who suddenly were confronted by rising unemployment and economic hardship in most of the British colonies of the Caribbean. Initially, because of the restrictive immigration laws in the United States, codified in the McCarren-Walter Act of 1952, which imposed a limit of one hundred visas on each colonial dependency of Europe, thereby preventing West Indians from emigrating to North America under more liberal British quotas, migration flowed toward England. In Ransford Palmer's apt analogy, "As citizens of the United Kingdom, West Indians migrated to Britain with the same facility that Puerto Ricans migrated to the United States after the war. While population growth combined with the desperate postwar economic conditions of those colonies pushed people toward the mother country, the shortage of unskilled labor in Britain pulled them in" (10). The wry, caustic novel by Sam Selvon, *The Lovely Londoners* (1956), and Lamming's *Of Age and Innocence* (1958) capture the West Indian migrant experience in the "motherland" during this period. But with the passage by Great Britain of the Commonwealth Immigrants Act in 1962, emigration from the West Indies to England for the purpose of employment was effectively curtailed. The 1965 White Paper on Immigration, appropriately named, codified the racist logic of British policy by declaring blatantly that black people were an unwanted problem for the United Kingdom. However, the exclusionary logic of one colonial power was ameliorated both by the accelerating admission of former West Indian colonies to the Commonwealth as independent nations starting with Jamaica and Trinidad and Tobago in 1962 and by changing immigration laws and economic realities in the United States during the same period.

Even as the door closed for immigrants in England in the 1960s, it opened for them in the United States. As residents of newly formed independent nations—first Jamaica and Trinidad and Tobago in 1962, then

Barbados and Guyana in 1966, the Bahamas in 1973, Grenada in 1974, and by the 1980s an archipelago of new Caribbean states—West Indians were able to take advantage of the radically democratized policies promoted in the United States by the Immigration and Nationality Act of 1965. Prior to 1960, the door had been barely open. According to the 1970 census 10,158 West Indians had come to the United States from 1945 to 1949; and 25,737 from 1950 to 1959. By contrast, slightly more than 150,000 West Indians arrived in the decade of the 1960s, with the vast majority—112,657—arriving between 1965 and 1970. By 1990, the census totaled 682,418 West Indians in the United States—most of them residing in the metropolitan New York area. The West Indian exodus to America after 1965 confirms political scientist Aaron Segal's observation that "Caribbean peoples have become singularly adept at identifying emigration opportunities and responding to shifting policies of receiving governments" (53). The willingness of West Indians to emigrate to the United States even as their islands were liberating themselves from colonial stasis lays bare both the continuing oppressiveness of Commonwealth economic and social structures as well as the lure of life in the American metropolis.

This is not to say that contemporary West Indians, in leaving behind British imperial values, uncritically embrace the New World order. A self-critical writer like Jamaica Kincaid, for example, who was born in Antigua and whose fiction traces the legacies of domination in both the Caribbean and the United States, energetically dismantles all notions of the glory of the West. As an expatriate who enjoys Antiguan and American citizenship, Kincaid in her creative work trains an ironic and often savage eye on Western empires and on the race issues inherent in them. Investing both her fiction and nonfiction with strong autobiographical elements (as do Marshall and the Jamaican expatriate writer Michelle Cliff), Kincaid posits a continuity in the African-Caribbean-American experience of colonialism and postcolonialism, whether in the Commonwealth or in the United States. To be "colonized" or "post-colonized" is the psychic legacy that accompanies both the author and her characters as they navigate the islands and metropoles of late-twentieth-century life. In her brief but vitriolic account of Antigua in *A Small Place* (1988), Kincaid pillories with Swiftean glee imaginary tourists from the imperial centers, English and American residents whose colonial practices are steeped in racism, and indigenous black politicians whose postcolonial agendas are sad and debased simulacra of the British establishment. This sort of transnational critique of the very meaning of "nation" and national identity is at the center of Kincaid's work. With other Antiguans she insists on "knowing why they are the way they are, why they do the things they do, why they live the way they live and in the place they live, why the things that happened to them happened" (56).

Kincaid's answer to these perplexing questions specifies a need to understand the history of imperialist expansion in the Western hemisphere. Your typical Englishman, Kincaid muses sardonically, might look very sad as he contemplates "the demise of empire . . . sitting on the rubbish heap of history." She is especially incensed by North Americans who embrace England and its traditions. Kincaid by contrast imagines millions of people "made orphans: no motherland, no fatherland, no gods, no mounds of earth for holy ground . . . and worst and most painful of all, no tongue" (31). Yet she also acknowledges how thoroughly Anglicized she has become through education, religion, language, custom. Colonialism is insidious precisely because of its resurgence in the postcolonial era in various transmuted forms. In fact, the global hybridization of colonialism in the postwar era means the asymmetries of the old imperialism can reappear as easily in the new nation of Antigua as in the streets of New York.

Jamaica Kincaid's Imperial Critique

Kincaid's novels *Annie John* (1985) and *Lucy* (1990) treat the interactions of the colonizer and the colonized in the specific contexts of Antigua and the United States respectively. The protagonists of both novels, much like Kincaid, resist all attempts to impose boundaries on them or succumb to manifestations of either personal or imperial power. As a teenager in school, Annie John in the chapter titled "Columbus in Chains," commits the greatest transgression against the colonial order by penning—in old English script—a mocking caption beneath the picture of Columbus in her book, *A History of the West Indies*. Caught by her imperious history teacher Miss Edward, she subsequently is removed as prefect of her class and, as added punishment, is forced to copy Books I and II of *Paradise Lost*. As the "descendants of slaves" (76), the precocious Annie has no great admiration for Columbus, indeed sees exquisite irony in the "Great man in chains"; nor is she remorseful for her assault on the Anglicized meaning of history and Western imperialism. By the end of the novel, her secondary education finished, the seventeen-year-old Annie embarks for the imperial center—London—to study nursing, not because she loves England or desires that particular career but because she needs to reject all family and island boundaries. Traveling by boat first to Barbados and then to England, Annie John will reverse the Middle Passage, escaping one circumscribed cultural orbit for an uncertain future that nevertheless offers the possibility of self-discovery and renewal.

Whereas Annie John's voyage by boat to a European center of power suggests a necessary but transitional stage in the protagonist's confrontation with the deepest meanings of Europe's colonial empires, the arrival of Lucy by plane in the United States on a cold winter night offers a parallel but more essentially postcolonial and postmodern account of the migratory route taken by West Indians in search of a new life. Extending the themes of Kincaid's first novel, *Lucy* explores the subtle and "enlightened" forms of subjugation and servitude that West Indians encounter in the United States. Like her psychic counterpart Annie John, the teenager Lucy Josephine Potter (she is nineteen by the end of the novel), born on May 25, 1949, arrives in the United States just after Antigua had received independence from Great Britain in 1967. Whereas Annie John had embraced emigration as a possible escape from a limited world, Lucy is far more astute and attuned to the global implications of culture and society. Hired as an *au pair* by an affluent white family in New York City, Lucy defies the stereotypical contours of the African-Caribbean maid. Instead of submitting to new forms of servitude, Lucy almost immediately redefines herself as a sly and rather ascerbic ethnographer, writing in the first-person about a WASPish family whose insistent happiness and fervent liberalism mask their superficiality; their ignorance of history; their misunderstanding of class, racial, and gender divisions; and their complicity in the colonial condition.

Underscoring Lucy's role as ethnographic commentator on the colonial condition are the dichotomies that frame the novel's narrative structure. *Lucy* traces one year in the life of a young West Indian immigrant who must make sense of the contrasting ceremonies, rituals, and intertwined histories that determine relationships between men and women, black and white, colonizer and colonized. The geographical and meteorological shock of arrival in New York in the dead of winter at the outset of the novel illuminates the contrasting world views Lucy must subject to rigid critique. A native visitor rather than a native New Yorker (her employers Lewis and Mariah condescendingly call her "Poor Visitor"), Lucy realizes she is "no longer in a tropical zone" (5), that the known and familiar shores of her past are now divided irrevocably from the urban *terra incognita* that confronts her: apartment buildings instead of houses; elevators instead of stairs; cold sun instead of warm; day-old food instead of fresh; white faces instead of black. Clearly Lucy is dealing with some other place, some other human group or tribe whose appearance and behavior demand scrutiny. As an urban anthropologist of sorts, Lucy lives with these people, observes and questions them, and then, at the end of the novel, determines to write about them—and herself. A participant-observer who keeps good field notes, Lucy is writing self and writing culture. She might be a self-described "young woman from the fringes of the world" who is wrapped "in the mantle of a servant" (95), but her persistent ethnographic gaze produces an anti-colonial, anti-hegemonic reversal of fortune whereby she dissects the national traditions represented by Mariah, Lewis, and their four children (all of whose extreme whiteness and blond hair are powerful signifiers) and reconstitutes her own identity as a decolonized agent opposed to all forms of subjugating power.

As a black Antiguan and a new immigrant, Lucy can contextualize those cross-cultural forces that historically have fashioned ruling and subjugated populations. The United States from Kincaid's perspective has an imperial history and a hegemonic place in the hemisphere, and the large-scale arrival of non-Europeans in the country after World War II serves to create a postcoloniality that permits an interrogation of the Anglo-American narrative of empire. The American family Lucy serves (but also scrutinizes and subverts) is progressive and tolerant. Nevertheless, their employment of Lucy and another black maid—peoples of color—creates paradoxes and anomalies in their liberal outlook and behavior. The coolly objective Lucy perceives the cultural and racial divide separating her from her employers in the first section of the novel titled "Poor Visitor." She inhabits "a small room just off the kitchen—the maid's room" (7) that, as Kincaid describes it, is a reconfiguration of the Middle Passage. Her room is box-like—"a box in which cargo travelling a long way should be shipped. But I was not cargo." Here Lucy begins the interpretation of herself and her condition that will free her from pernicious historical circumstances whose effects linger in the postwar and postcolonial era.

As the Visitor or Other, Lucy occupies an ironic position in this generic American household (Kincaid emphasizes the point by providing no family name) that is filled with buoyant, smiling photographs of themselves: "their six yellow-haired heads of various sizes were bunched as if they were a bouquet of flowers tied together by an unseen string" (12). Lucy's persistent critique of the family—this yellow-haired tribe she lives among—and the way she stares at them with ethnographic intensity establishes the discrepant cultural and national realms they inhabit. Lewis, a lawyer, repeatedly tells Lucy a story about an uncle who preferred monkeys to humans, not realizing that the earlier generation of West Indian immigrants whom Marshall alludes to in *Brown Girl, Brownstones* were saddled with the term. Lewis's tale prompts Lucy, in an effort to bridge their two realms of experience, to share a dream she had in which Lewis chases a naked Lucy around the house until she escapes down a hole filled with snakes. Hearing the dream, Mariah and Lewis cluck, "Poor, poor Visitor . . . Dr. Freud for Visitor," ascribing a psychosexual interpretation that is beyond Lucy's province, for she has not heard of Freud. To Lucy, as Kincaid implies, the dream signifies the attempt to recapture the native, the naked savage, the monkey. Lucy's dream is not a Freudian revelation but rather a postcolonial nightmare. Kincaid's deft juxtaposition of cultural values in this dream episode epitomizes the fundamentally schismatic and unstable relationship between Lucy and her American family.

Yet Lucy must remain in close proximity to her American family because it is through them and the ethnographic activity they inspire that she can understand her relationship to American society. That Lucy perceives the American Empire as an extension of the milieu created by the British Empire in the West Indies is a conceit Kincaid probes persistently in the novel through numerous comparative motifs. Essentially Lucy puts pieces of American culture together by discovering similitudes with her Antiguan experience. The protagonist's association of the flaxen-haired family of Lewis and Mariah with flowers—specifically daffodils—is a prime example of this figurative technique. As a schoolgirl in Antigua, Lucy had rebelled (much as Annie John had) against the imposition of English cultural values. In the second section of the novel, "Mariah," she recounts the time when she was ten years old and a student at Queen

Victoria's School when she had to memorize a poem about daffodils (by Wordsworth) and recite it to the appreciation of an auditorium filled with pupils and parents. She expresses her residual anger to Mariah, who comments blithely on Lucy's strange "history." In the spring, Mariah takes Lucy to her favorite "garden," which is clearly Central Park, to show her numerous yellow flowers along the paths beneath the trees. "I did not know what these flowers were," admits Lucy, "and so it was a mystery to me why I wanted to kill them" (29). Mariah, transported by the beauty of the daffodils, which she identifies for Lucy, is confused when her *au pair* refuses a sisterly embrace. For Lucy, the daffodils are not beautiful but "wretched." They are reminders of her colonial condition, "a scene of conquered and conquests; a scene of brutes masquerading as angels and angels portrayed as brutes" (31). Lucy considers Mariah's cultural fetishization of daffodils bizarre but very much in keeping with the tendencies of the West to turn everything upside down.

From the urban garden of Central Park, Lucy next moves to the shores of Lake Michigan and Mariah's summer home, handed down to her by her parents. This movement from city to country permits Lucy to examine the artifacts of American national culture from yet another perspective. Her journey to the Middle West, the American heartland, is a trip back in time and space not just to rural national origins but also, given the garden imagery, to a mythic Eden. As a type of anticolonial field worker, in the anthropological sense, whose very name (her mother tells her that she was named after Satan himself, or Lucifer) suggests the earlier trope of "angels portrayed as brutes," Lucy is the demonic force whose mission is to demolish this Edenic myth. Aboard the train, itself a mildly anachronistic symbol of an earlier era and of that era's hardened ethnic relationships, Lucy once again must confront imperial history. In the dining car, Lucy is struck, as Mariah is not, by the strict nomenclature of race: "The other people sitting down to eat dinner all looked like Mariah's relatives; the people waiting on them all looked like mine" (32). However, the resemblance of the older, dignified black waiters to Antiguans is somewhat inaccurate, for Lucy's relatives "always gave backchat." Nevertheless, as the "native" reversing the ethnographic tables and now examining the metropolitans, Lucy/Lucifer acknowledges what she has "in common with the waiters," confirming her collective identity. Lucy's nightmares that night aboard the train, with "thousands of people on horseback . . . following me, chasing me, each of them carrying a cutlass to cut me up into small pieces"—is a proto-historical conflation of an earlier century's system of slavery. And when in the morning Mariah awakens her so that she can see "the freshly plowed fields she loved so much" (33), Lucy replies angrily is that she is glad she didn't have to work them.

Lucy's interlude at Lake Michigan spans the "Mariah" and "The Tongue" sections of the novel, evoking for the protagonist memories of people and events in Antigua that interweave with the scenes from her new locale. Always the empiricist, the ethnographic field worker who wants first-hand experience of the metropolitans enjoying their rural Eden, Lucy observes the landscape; the flora and fauna; the irreconcilable lives and loves of Mariah, Lewis and Mariah's best friend Dinah, with whom Lewis is having an affair. Mariah is oblivious to the seeds of evil and dissolution embedded in her imaginary Eden, but Lucy, capable of comparative cultural anthropology, is alert to them. For Lucy, Lake Michigan is not a pristine body of water, but mildly pestilential, not at all like Antiguan waters. Similarly, the aggressive heat, while welcomed after her first immersion in a New York winter, is unlike the soothing heat of the Caribbean. The miles and miles of countryside are "miles and miles of nothing" (34), the days are gloomy, the woods filled with biting insects. Whereas Mariah can lament the encroachment of developers into her "vanishing idyll" (72), Lucy is aware of the broader personal and national transgressions that negate any promise of paradise. Lucy challenges the myths, conventions, and power relationships of the West. She might parody the Edenic myth, as when she lies naked with her lover Hugh, the brother of Dinah, in a field perfumed with flowers, but playing Eve is not essential to her self-representation. As the constitutive "I" within this mock-Paradise, Lucy stays emotionally and analytically on the margins of this world, as much the detached observer as participant, slowly constructing out of memory and experience a selfhood adequate for the new nation she inhabits.

The last two sections of the novel, "Cold Heart" and "Lucy," reveal the protagonist resisting all forms of domination or the "master business" (143). As Moira Ferguson notes in *Jamaica Kincaid: Where the Land Meets the Body* (1994), "Lucy takes charge of her environment, right down to her sexual encounters. She fractures any attachment between sexuality and the damaging force of empire" (127). Experimenting with her sexuality by entering New York City's counterculture in the 1960s, Lucy probes power relations, continuing to assess the profound ways in which her previous life in Antigua impinges on her existence in the United States. In ways large and small, Lucy pushes past conventional boundaries of behavior; her alternative lifestyle, including her departure from Mariah's fractured household, is her way of decolonizing her identity and escaping age-old colonial practices. The very chaos and countercultural exuberance of New York City in the 1960s is a truly postcolonial experience for Lucy as she connects with her new metropolis from a minimalist perspective. Training first a camera's eye (she takes photographs and goes to work for a photographer) and finally an authorial eye on her ethnographic landscape, Lucy annexes solitude as her idea of paradise. "I understood that I was inventing myself" (134) she asserts, and that self-fashioning requires the abandonment of an "ancestral past" rooted in the "foul deed" of slavery as well as a rejection of the life she had been leading as an *au pair*. She feels "like Lucifer, doomed to build wrong upon wrong" (139), but she gives her "devil-like" or "fallen" identity a "strong embrace" (153). To be a devil is to rebel against one's subaltern condition, thereby rejecting any colonized status for a more contestatory consciousness.

Lucy also rejects any notion of the United States as an imagined community consisting of individuals with shared values and beliefs. For one year, she has observed the "ideal" American family close up, and has seen it deteriorate. Instead, she embraces—tearfully but hopefully at the end of the novel—what Gayatri C. Spivak calls strategic essentialism, a form of identity politics based on the recognition that selfhood in the postcolonial era must be contingent and negotiated. Lucy's new springtime in America finds her in oppositional terrain. Five hundred years after Columbus's landing in America—an event that she ponders as did the protagonist in *Annie John*—she prepares to explore her new metropolitan realm and her emerging self. She will become—like Kincaid herself—a metropolitan writer, operating at a key urban center of the postwar era's dominant world power. With her ethnographer's eye and new vocation as a writer, she is now prepared to interrogate the structure of her new nation and to resist the prevailing order of things. The page she begins to write in a diary (produced in the West, in Italy, a nation reminding her of former imperial supremacy) given to her by Mariah might blur with her tears. But the decision to write symbolizes Lucy's capacity to understand her newfound world by way of text. Her description of one year in her new land mimics the textual exercises by which the British Empire amplified, codified, and preserved the narratives of its conquests. Through writing and textual production, Lucy takes possession of and exercises power over her metropolitan world.

Michelle Cliff and the Postcolonial Wilderness

Just as Kincaid in *Lucy* dismantles the glories of the British empire while concurrently dissecting the wonders of the United States through the eyes of a skeptical young immigrant, Michelle Cliff in *No Telephone to Heaven* also finds in the metaphor of migration a conceptual framework whereby the postwar Anglo-American imperial mission can be evaluated. Kincaid's first-person narrative is plotted from familiar structural perspectives. By contrast, Cliff's novel is decidedly postmodern in its conjuring of anomalous and incongruous materials—the artifacts of both literary and colonialist culture—to capture the landscape of immigration and its relation to the global movement of peoples, commodities, and ideas in contemporary times. Cliff, who grew up in Jamaica and the United States and was educated in New York and London, applies her transnational experience in *No Telephone to Heaven* to survey postcolonial diasporas in a variety of settings. Cliff's insinuation of disparate materials into her shifting narrative—poetry and patois, myth and metaphor, history and naturalistic description, dream sequences and lexical definitions—is an effort to render textually the fragmented experience of her protagonist, Clare Savage, a light-skinned Jamaican-American whose diasporic wanderings serve as a symbol of the immigrant soul in search of wholeness in turbulent times. Through this strategy of textual dismantling or deconstruction, Cliff creates an experimental narrative design that advances one of her main ideological goals: the need to demythologize both the imperial mission of the West and the immigrant ethos underpinning notions of the American and British nations.

In *No Telephone to Heaven*, Cliff explores the intertwined issues of colonialism, immigration, gender and heritage from a perspective that is even more extreme than the admittedly radical visions of Marshall and Kincaid. With the novel framed at beginning and end by two poems by Derek Walcott—"Laventille" and "Jean Rhys"—that invoke the Middle Passage and the history of Caribbean slavery, Cliff constructs an anti-hegemonic critique of colonialism and postcolonialism that indicts the United States, Great Britain, and the newly created sovereign nation of Jamaica under Michael Manley. The first two chapters of the novel evoke a Jamaican landscape of wildness and almost primordial savagery as the protagonist, Clare Savage, ascends into Cockpit Country to reclaim ancestral lands and lead a motley band of revolutionaries intent on making history. Cliff describes her central character as a "light-skinned woman, daughter of landowners, native-born, slaves, émigrés, Carib, Ashanti, English" (5). In short, Clare is (like Cliff herself, who also creates Clare as an alter ego in an earlier novel about Caribbean identity, *Abeng*) the essence of hybrid Caribbean identity. Carol Boyce Davies, speaking of Cliff's autobiographical *Claiming an Identity They Taught Me to Despise* (1980), highlights this "multifaceted composition" of Caribbean personality. "The hybrid Creoleness that is essentially the Caribbean, the necessity of accepting all facets of experience, history and personhood in the definition of a self become integrated in her consciousness of her identity" (64). Moreover, her experience as an immigrant and her education in both the United States and Great Britain provide Clare with a global understanding of the conflicts inherent in the clash between Western civilization and African-Caribbean civilization. Through the migratory pattern of her life, Clare probes the liminal spaces within and between nations in order to reconstitute her own history and ultimately the history of the island where she was born.

The United States, which her family immigrates to in 1960 in order to start "a new life" (53), is Clare's "way-station" (109) in the construction of her identity. The older, at fourteen, of Boy and Kitty Savage's two daughters, Clare as a teenager spends the 1960s—a formative period in the civil rights movement that Cliff often interjects into the narrative as historical backdrop—as a witness to the politics of race in the United States. The family flies from Montego Bay to Miami, buys a used Plymouth, and embarks on a journey northward that exposes the Savages to the legacy of the South's peculiar institution. "No Statue of Liberty for them" (55), writes Cliff, but rather headlines announcing lynchings and racist motel clerks who force light-skinned Boy Savage to invoke his best English mannerisms and pass as a white sugar plantation owner in order to obtain accommodations. Boy believes fervently in the opportunity provided by the United States to metamorphose identity, whereas Kitty is far more skeptical of the promise of their new world and more readily shocked by the racial hatred in the American grain. Nevertheless, Kitty and Boy Savage are "shipmates, as surely as the slaves who crossed the Middle Passage together" (60). Together they journey to Washington, D.C., then on to the "burning excess of the refineries" (60) along the New Jersey Turnpike, until they reach their destination, New York City, and ultimately, after assistance from relatives in Queens, life in a small apartment in Brooklyn.

Although Clare's experience as an immigrant child in the United States is the focus of only two chapters in *No Telephone to Heaven,* an American presence mantels the entire novel from the start of the narrative as the small band of revolutionaries dressed in G.I. camouflage jackets trade ganja for U.S. guns and ammunition to the conclusion in which they are betrayed in their efforts to attack an Anglo-American film crew and exterminated by counterrevolutionary forces. Cliff in her essay "If I Could Write This in Fire, I Would Write This in Fire" (1988) addresses the pervasive impact of the United States on Jamaican cultural identity: "While the primary colonial identification for Jamaicans was English, American colonialism was a strong force in my childhood—and of course continues today. We were sent American movies and American music. American aluminum companies had already discovered bauxite on the island and were shipping the ore to their mainland. United Fruit bought our bananas. White Americans came to Montego Bay, Ocho Rios, and Kingston for their vacations and their cruise ships docked in Port Antonio and other places. In some ways America was seen as a better place than England by many Jamaicans" (65). Cliff structures her novel recursively so that Clare's ideological consciousness is fashioned by the constant juxtaposition of her American experience upon the many national and cultural contexts that form the brief and ultimately tragic thirty-six-year-old collage of her life. Clare's Middle Passage in the United States, where she is "[a]djusted to America after a fashion" (99), exposes her to virulent manifestations of race and class. She witnesses her mother, disillusioned by America's racism, return to Jamaica with her younger sister Jennie. Her father, adept at the "uses of camouflage" (100), blends into the American nation by passing as a white man and, after Kitty's death, marrying an Italian-American woman. Clare's own education in Brooklyn's public school system exposes her to varieties of institutionalized racism. Despite her rigorous English-style education in Jamaica, she is held back a grade by the principal, Mrs. Taylor, who believes religiously that "children from underdeveloped countries develop at a different rate than American children" (98). Mrs. Taylor repeats her physician husband's pseudo-scientific racist classification of Boy as "white chocolate," indicating there is no place for hybridized souls in the American system.

Clare, like her father, exists in the interstices of race, but ultimately identifies with the four black children killed in the Birmingham church bombing of September 16, 1963. The formation of her political identity derives from her incremental apprehension of race as the common denominator in all forms of imperialism. Her education in the United States and England is an extended journey through the metropoles of race and racism. This indoctrination into the nature of the Western world prepares her for her return to Jamaica and her effort to synthesize the "bits and pieces" or "fragments" of her existence (87) by retreating to and recovering her ancestors' plantation, signifying the "beauty, the wildness of this New World—her point of origin" (133) and the setting wherein she reconstitutes her hybrid identity as a revolutionary. She recreates an Edenic world and takes possession of it in an effort to cleanse what Georges Gusdorf calls the intellectual colonizing that has been the legacy of her life on three continents. She moves back into Jamaican history with her revolutionaries, transported into high back-country in the dilapidated truck that bears on its side the sign "No Telephone to Heaven," in order to transform Clare's abandoned matrilineal inheritance into their own makeshift paradise: "The grandmother was long since dead, and the farm had been left by the family to the forest. To *ruination*, the grandmother would have said. The family but one, were scattered through America and England and had begun new lives" (8). Cliff, who titles her first chapter "Ruinate," provides a stipulative definition of the word, drawn from Floyd's *Jamaica: An Island Microcosm* and signifying "lands which were once cleared for agricultural purposes and have now lapsed into ... 'bush.'" This wild paradise they reclaim, with its native flora and fauna, is the antidote to Anglocentric versions of Eden. The "one" who has returned to claim her inheritance and to share it with her polyglot but united group of revolutionaries, who otherwise would have been separated from each other by the contours of color and caste in Kingston and by the random and spiraling violence spawned by the Manley regime—"come Armageddon to Babylon" (20)—is Clare. Having returned from the colonial diaspora, she finds in the hybridity of her new community of revolutionaries and the lush diversity of the landscape the contours of her true past.

The paradox that Cliff creates at the conclusion of *No Telephone to Heaven* suggests, however, that reclaiming an Edenic past is ultimately futile, for the Anglo-American intrusion into the Jamaican wilderness, signified by the international film crew intent on exploiting stereotypical notions of the primitive Jamaican, results in the extermination of Clare's tiny revolutionary band. Clare remains mired in the crisis of colonialism, and her global wanderings suggest the crisis is worldwide. Michelle Cliff illustrates the civic transformations required to create a new world but grimly infers that the postcolonial context has not yet discovered the paradigm that might permit revolutionary efforts to dislodge both American and British hegemony over native cultures.

Myths of the Nation

The lens through which Marshall, Kincaid, and Cliff view contemporary American immigration reveals old forms of domination persisting in new metropolitan contexts. At the same time, instead of submitting to these neocolonial modes of domination, their characters attempt to create personal and cultural identities that shake loose from the old categories of race, gender, and national domination. By seeking ways to resist the weight of Western history, they open up space for themselves, insisting that their "otherness"—typically as female immigrants and children of immigrants of color—be accepted in the evolving civic culture of the United States. Their histories—as in *Brown Girl, Brownstones, Lucy,* and *No Telephone to Heaven*—are framed by the British colonialism they leave and the perverse forms of discrimination they encounter in their new urban environment in the United States. Paradoxically, however, the long arc of contemporary immigration to New York City traced by Marshall, Kincaid, and Cliff is epochal for their protagonists, who discover in urban life sufficient space for self-discovery, resistance, and renewal. Even as Selina and Lucy shatter the myths of the American nation by unmasking the inequalities spawned by racial difference, they inhabit an urban universe in the process of changing from a modern metropolis composed largely of white inhabitants to a postmodern one where African-Americans, West Indian and African immigrants, Latinos, and Asians create liminal spaces, hybrid notions of "nation" and new local and global affiliations. As a newly emergent group notably in the immigrant history of New York City, West Indians in fiction negotiate uneven metropolitan terrain, coping both with dominant white culture and an older native-born African-American community—as Marshall describes the situation in *Brown Girl, Brownstones*—that views them with suspicion. Their experience of the African-Caribbean diaspora, their experience of journeying to new shores, is often an unfinished project. The conclusions of *Brown Girl, Brownstones, Lucy,* and Marshall's *Daughters,* for example, suggest no closure to diasporic wandering but rather a continuous search for home and homeland.

America's "grand narrative," to once again invoke Lyotard's phrase, only partially conditions the characters in the fiction of Marshall, Kincaid, and Cliff to their own identities as they search for a spiritual and cultural home. In the case of Selina in *Brown Girl, Brownstones* and Clare in *No Telephone to Heaven* the departure from America, the return to the Caribbean, is as important as the arrival in the construction of identity. The United States is very much a part of their psychic and cultural condition, but their evolving consciousness also embraces cultural practices that carry them back to the West Indies, and through the mythic Middle Passage to Africa. As immigrants whose stories are fluid and whose lives seem caught in a continuation of events (the notable exception being, of course, the terminal condition of Clare Savage), they seem emancipated from all fixed systems of national belief, from any single ethos of the nation-state. Selena and Lucy liberate themselves from master narratives, asserting a positive liberty and individualism very much in the American grain but paradoxically interrogating the myth of American power. Even Clare before her betrayal and death escapes what Cliff in *The Land of Look Behind* (1985) calls the "hegemony of the past" (16) by reclaiming her hybrid identity and embracing revolutionary action. In the maelstrom of their diasporic lives, their Middle Passages, the West Indian characters of Marshall, Kincaid, and Cliff seek a range of experience beyond any single national boundary. Through the motif and metaphor of immigration and return, of perpetual motion across postcolonial national terrains, they seek alternative versions and visions of history.

As Elleke Boehmer suggests in *Colonial and Postcolonial Literature* (1995), contemporary narrative "has the capacity to establish new metaphors of nationhood: not only to rewrite history, but to create and frame defining symbols for the purposes of imagining the nation" (198). We have witnessed the reworking of national myths and symbols in much of the fiction treated in this study; Marshall, Kincaid, and Cliff share in this penchant for interrogating the foundational myths of the American republic, reworking ancestral histories from the uniquely gendered perspectives of women writers born of West Indian parents. The autobiographical impulse is evident in the fiction of all three writers, for they imagine their own national status—and those of their characters— through highly personalized memories transmuted into art. Thus *Lucy*, continuing the semiautobiographical foundations of *Annie John*, elevates a self-representational heroine to the status of a new and insolent Eve in the American garden, a sort of pirate queen sailing (or flying) into the United States to provide a West Indian woman's version of mythic and historical truth to the nation. Similarly, the war that is so deeply embedded in the narrative structure of *Brown Girl, Brownstones* is transformed from a masculine pursuit into a new fable in which Silla and Selina engage in a sustained battle over competing visions of the American nation. And Cliff, who constantly provides touchstones to contemporary American history in *No Telephone to Heaven*, transposes her motif of "ruinate," which is indigenous to Jamaica's colonial history, onto the American stage in such a way as to imply that the historical practice of slavery is not dead but offers instead postcolonial fables of cultural behavior and political action on a global scale.

As women of color, Marshall, Kincaid, and Cliff give meaning to West Indian immigration through narratives that focus on the formation of racial and global conditions. Their characters simultaneously demystify the immigration ethos and reclaim their mixed racial and cultural heritage. Like the creolized speech that their characters often employ, they place immigration within mixed cultural universes, creating bicultural images of existence that typify the contemporary condition. Narratives of West Indian immigration *are* representations of a hybrid and polyglot world—reflections both of the history of the Caribbean and the new, syncretic history of the American republic.

6

Gold Mountains:
The Asian-American Odyssey

He had plans. America, the big gold mountain, was where he
wanted to settle. They came to San Francisco together but
things didn't work out as fast as he wanted.
—Fae Myenne Ng, *Bone*

Contributing to the syncretic, hybrid birth of a new American nation
have been those postwar immigrants and sojourners from the Pacific
Rim and a Greater Asia, stretching across China to the Indian subcontinent and beyond to the Middle East. These strangers from distant shores,
to borrow a fine phrase coined by the Filipino writer Carlos Bulosan in
his autobiographical *America Is in the Heart,* are part of a long and varied chain in the history of American immigration. From the intrepid
Chinese miners who ventured to California in the 1850s—*gam saan haak*
or "travelers to the Gold Mountain"—to the Indian immigrants remaking the face of New York City in the 1990s, these wanderers seek a new
Promised Land. Although they emigrate from distinct cultural settings,
their common quest for the Gold Mountain—a variation on the more
familiar metaphors of the Golden Land and the Golden West—tests the
limits of American democracy while suggesting new relations among
historical agents inhabiting an evolving and rapidly changing nation. In
the fiction of Amy Tan, Bharati Mukherjee, Cynthia Kadohata, and other
contemporary writers, the internal logic and distressing contradictions
of American democracy reveal that these Asian voyagers and their off-

spring encounter in the United States unique strengths, but also profound fissures in the myth of national origins.

Bharati Mukherjee, who was born in Calcutta and first came to the United States to study at the University of Iowa in 1961, stresses the mythic notion of the American nation in her essay "American Dreamer" (1997). For Mukherjee, whose novel *Jasmine* (1989) is a cornerstone in the canon of contemporary fiction of Asian immigration to the United States, the idea of America remains a vital mythology, even in a postmodern era where all national metanarratives have been called into question, because it is still "the stage for the drama of self-transformation" (32). For an immigrant to "desire America," especially if, like Mukherjee, she comes from a homogenous and traditional society governed by lines of class and caste, customary concepts of fixed identity must be abandoned. In the "hierarchical, classification-obsessed society" of Calcutta, one's "identity was fixed, derived from religion, caste, patrimony, and mother tongue" (32). By contrast, in the United States the relation of the individual to a rapidly changing and variegated New World involves "a life of scary improvisations and heady explorations" (34). In much fiction of contemporary immigration, as we have seen, the need to adjust the language, manners, and rituals of traditional culture to the rampant pace and frenetic mood of the postwar era requires a repertoire of styles and personal choices that transcend conventional notions of who might be at the "center" of our cultural landscape and who at the "margin." Mukherjee gives central importance to the symbiotic process whereby today's immigrants are changed by the mythology of America but, in turn, alter an American paradigm once influenced largely by the dominant tradition of Eurocentric thought and public life. Today's immigrants, the products of an age of diasporas, are "minute-by-minute transforming America. The transformation is a two-way process. It affects both the individual and the national cultural identity" (35).

Asian Americans are unusually prominent in the process of immigrant dual transformation to which Mukherjee alludes. By the end of World War II, Asian American communities seemed to be at the farthest margins of national life. The Chinese community was decimated, its aging bachelor society, as Louis Chu in his seriocomic novel *Eat a Bowl of Tea* (1961) portrays it, desperately awaiting an infusion of new immigrants and a reconstitution of family life. Similarly, Japanese America, once an insular but dynamic presence, especially in the California landscape of the 1930s, lay in ruins, the result of forced internment. Korean America, as presented by Kim Ronyoung in her panoramic novel of that community from the 1920s to the 1940s, *Clay Walls*, was a numerically insignificant constituency, diasporic in mentality, its immigrants frustrated in their desire to return to their native land because of the brutal occupation of Korea by Japan. Finally, the legacy of the Philippine-American War of 1898–1902, combined with restrictive quotas that as late as 1935 limited immigrants from Philippine Commonwealth to 50 persons annually, kept these mainland "economic refugees," as E. San Juan Jr. terms them (4), at a low population level of less than 100,000 in the United States. Moreover, the Naturalization Law of 1790, which would not be repealed until 1952, had reserved citizenship for whites, and a host of other restrictive and racist state and Federal laws had forced all Asian-American cultures into the far contact zones of the nation, where power negotiations were asymmetrical and structurally unequal. Thus, as late as 1960, according to U.S. census data, there were only 877,934 people of Asian descent in the United States, less than one-half of one percent of the total national population. Yet by 1990, benefiting from the 1965 immigration law that eliminated national origins quotas, Asian America had exploded to more that 7,000,000 individuals: 1,645,000 Chinese, 1,400,000 Filipinos, 845,000 Japanese, 815,000 Asian Indians, 800,000 Koreans, 614,000 Vietnamese, 150,000 Laotians, 147,000 Cambodians, and 90,000 Hmong. Statistically the fastest growing racial group in the United States, Asian Americans will compose more than four percent of the national population by the start of the twenty-first century. Regardless of cultural attachments or the unique conditions of their arrival, Asian Americans today are dispersed across the national landscape, crossing its fault lines, and negotiating multiple contact zones that make their own cultures and hegemonic national culture susceptible to mutual influence.

Ethnic Options

In confronting the contact zones of their new nation, each Asian immigrant culture reveals different degrees of historical permeability to American influence. As a case in point, the destiny of the peoples of the Philippines resembles most closely those patterns of neocolonial influ-

ence seen in the history of Mexican and Caribbean immigration. Given
its colonial legacy, it is not surprising that major Filipino fiction would
place protagonists within a matrix of forces driving people toward various forms of independence—personal, political, social, and cultural. In
particular, the novels of Linda Ty-Casper, notably *The Three-Cornered
Sun* (1979), *Awaiting Trespass: A Passion* (1985), and *Ten Thousand Seeds*
(1987), provide readers with a panorama of resistance to colonialism
from the 1896 rebellion against Spain to the turmoil of the Marcos era.
At the same time, as Stanley Karnow and others have observed, the transition to nationhood for Filipinos resulted in a condition of "dependent
independence" (322–55). The situation in the Philippines following independence on July 4, 1946, remained neocolonial, filled with those
anomalies typical of the *pax Americana* that prevailed after the U.S. intrusion into the Caribbean. With the peso tied to the dollar, the economy
dominated by American corporations, the nation "defended" by the huge
installations at Subic Bay and Clark Air Base, and their political system
compromised, especially during the Marcos years, Filipinos remained
colonized subjects, susceptible to the forces of American hegemony.

Filipino identity both in the nation and on the American mainland
reflects a simultaneous fascination with and hostility toward American
mores. Shaped by Spanish language, culture, and religion from the six-
teenth century onward, and the inheritors as well of the English language and twentieth-century American popular culture, Filipinos are
more "Western" in their orientation than other Asian immigrant groups.
Contributing to their ambivalence as colonized subjects is their heterogeneous racial heritage. For example, the immigrant protagonist in
Bienvenido Santos's novel, *what the hell for you left your heart in san
francisco* (1987), a title whose linguistic play suggests mixed transnational
influences, reflects this composite identity: "My name is David Dante
Tolosa, a Filipino, born on February 4, 1938, on the outskirts of the
American naval base near Subic Bay in the Philippines. An oriental with
broad hints of Malay-Indonesian, perhaps Chinese, strain, a kind of racial chopsuey, that's me. Better yet, for historical and ethnic accuracy, an
oriental omelette flavored with Spanish wine" (1). Santos's novel is set in
1975, three years after martial law was declared by President Marcos. Its
immigrant narrator begins his American odyssey somewhat like the Pinoy
old-timers "aimlessly wandering the United States" (88). Like many of
the Pinoy generation, he settles in San Francisco, the archetypal city for

Asian immigrants, but he is separated from this older generation by age, class, and education. The Pinoy old-timers that Santos alludes to and sketches in several secondary characters in the novel remind readers of the restrictive immigration policies of the American nation prior to 1945. The 1934 Tydings-McDuffie Act that had granted Commonwealth status to the Philippines was designed to restrict what had been free immigration from a United States territory to the mainland. Under the new law, Filipino immigration was limited to fifty persons a year. More could enter Hawaii as labor conditions required, but Filipinos couldn't move to the mainland. They were classified as "aliens" rather than "nationals." Moreover, the 45,000 Filipino-Americans who resided in the United States in the 1930s were encouraged to return to the Philippines under the 1935 Repatriation Act.

The Filipino immigrants in Santos's novel, and also in Jessica Hagedorn's *Dogeaters* (1990) and *The Gangster of Love* (1996), are historical subjects framed by the changes in immigration policy wrought by the 1965 Act. According to Ronald Takaki (1995), "between 1965 and 1984, 665,000 Filipinos entered the United States" (111). Santos creates in David Tolosa a figure from this period of massive influx whose genealogical links with the Philippines are tested by his immersion in various levels of Filipino-American culture from immigrant affluence to abject poverty. Tolosa, the aspiring editor of a planned magazine for Filipino Americans that will be subsidized by wealthy Filipino professionals, seeks ways to remind his compatriots in the United States of their common cultural affinities despite the political divisiveness of the Marcos era. Failing in his attempt to launch the magazine, Tolosa achieves some success by teaching Filipino history and culture to second-generation Filipino-American college students. Alienated from all aspects of Filipino culture as well as from their parents, these students gradually accept Tolosa's vision of a binary relationship between the zones of their two nations. Tolosa, like his students, represents an unfinished immigrant generation. As he declares at the end of the novel, "We have left native land but our hearts are still there, not here . . . not in this golden city by the bay" (191).

The longing of Santos's protagonist for the Philippines and for an American social identity that remains true to Filipino mores is a motif that has counterparts in other zones of Asian-American fiction. At the same time, typical Filipino cultural performance, the very fabric of everyday life in the Philippines, is suffused with powerful manifestations of American popular culture. In Hagedorn's *Dogeaters*, the world of the Philippines during the Marcos era seems like a series of Hollywood scripts—some romantic, some comic, some pornographic, some nightmarish. From Hagedorn's radical perspective, American popular culture has penetrated traditional Filipino culture so thoroughly that everyone is marked by the power of the United States. Told retrospectively by Rio Gonzaga, a young woman who as a teenager immigrates with her mother to America, *Dogeaters* (a pejorative term for Filipinos) offers a serio-comic narrative of nostalgia for a former life that the more mature narrator understands had already become by 1953 a grotesque Hollywood production. For Hagedorn, Filipinos carry dual identities, but in their encounter with the two nations, the power of American culture seems dangerously definitive.

In Hagedorn's *The Gangster of Love*, the female protagonist, Rocky Rivera, is an American cultural performer, a member of a struggling rock band that travels the nation. Rocky's odyssey, starting in San Francisco, moving to New York, and retracing itself westward to Los Angeles, is an extended metaphor for the frantic and disappointing mappings of the American Dream. Just as her first sighting of the Golden Gate Bridge when she arrives by ship in America is disappointing, for the structure is shrouded in fog and not really made of gold, Rocky's American life is an imitation of artistic freedom or wild performativity that seems subversive of national norms because it is so resolutely countercultural in its artistic and sexual practices. As a countercultural "gangster," always moving "cross-country," Rocky simulates wild liberation in this postmodern novel composed of disjointed narrative, dramatic skits, jokes, poetry, and other mixed forms. However, she admits she is trapped in her "media-saturated, wayward American skin" (202). Ultimately the same questions she had tormented her psychotic brother with—What's Filipino? What's authentic? What's in the blood?—afflict her with nostalgia. Using her father's impending death as a pretext, the superficially Americanized but scarcely assimilated Rocky returns to the Philippines at the end of the novel in order to retrieve older forms of cultural performance and identity. Rocky's peripatetic departures and arrivals, along with the narrative disjunctions and multivocal musings that characterize Hagedorn's fiction, represent the reality of the Filipino diasporic condition in contemporary times. Indeed both Rio and Rocky, Hagedorn's psychic and alliterative twins, continually negotiate the borders of national experience.

Asian-American Doubleness

Despite differences in customs, languages, religions and the degree of American cultural penetration, postwar Asian-American immigrants as a collective "hyphenated" entity have had an especially graphic impact on the transformation of national identity even as they have subjected their traditional identities to intense scrutiny. American writers of Asian descent possess that acute awareness of difference that Lyotard observes is an attribute of the postmodern condition. As Amy Ling suggests, "Because they have grown up as a racial minority, imbibing the customs of two cultures, their centers are not stable and single. Their consciousness, as W.E.B. Du Bois pointed out for African Americans, is double; their vision bifocal and fluctuating" (220). The doubleness with which Asian-American novelists imbue their characters—whether of Filipino, Chinese, Japanese, Korean, Vietnamese, or Asian Indian descent—creates a familiar yet distinct dissidence in their fiction.

The theme of double, multiple, and shifting identities also reflects the tendency of Asian-American fiction to interrogate the nation in such a way that the center expands fluidly in order to accommodate a heterogeneity and plurality of peoples and voices. When, for example, Ben Loy, the comically impotent and cuckolded hero of Chu's *Eat a Bowl of Tea* (1961), leaves New York's Chinatown for San Francisco with his wife, he reaffirms both the Chinese sojourner's original quest for the Gold Mountain and the decidedly American impulse to start a new life by engaging in westward movement: "The mere thought of going away with Mei Oi had given him new hope. He saw on the horizon a chance of a new beginning" (240). With his sexual powers restored in San Francisco's Chinatown and a baby born, Ben Loy is like an original prospector from the Golden Mountain who has struck it rich in America. All scandal behind him, he is a remade American: "New frontiers, new people, new times, new ideas unfolded. He had come to a new golden mountain" (246). At the same time, Ben Loy's reverse passage from New York to San Francisco reestablishes the covenant that his ancestors had made with their new nation in the middle of the nineteenth century. Representative of a highly mobile postwar type, he moves across a spectrum of multiple histories, serving as a touchstone for the historical past and present in the evolution of the nation. His duality does not prevent him from becoming an autonomous subject. Ben Loy restores his potency through Chinese herbal cures, and also finds a place in the nation through mobility—an old-fashioned American attribute. His happy fate is a celebration of a new heterogeneous master narrative, a resolution of the challenge of doubleness that is a major motif in Asian American fiction.

Whereas the immigrant path Chu traces in *Eat a Bowl of Tea* is essentially comic and ironic, permitting converging rather than colliding cultural and national histories, there are also tragic consequences to the Asian immigrant's encounter with America. For example, a poignant presentation of immigrant origins and the crisis of doubleness unfolds in Fae Myenne Ng's *Bone* (1993), a novel that winds back through the shards and skeletons of history to uncover family and national origins. Recounted by Leila Leong, the oldest of three second-generation sisters, the family's history, which is communal and transnational in scope, converges in the inexplicable suicide of the middle sister, Ona, in San Francisco's Chinatown. Ona's suicide fragments the family even as it forces each member to reconstruct through memory those real and imagined original sins they committed that might have contributed to Ona's death. For Mah, the mother, the sin was an affair with the boss of her factory; for Leila's stepfather, Leon, the sin was his failure to return his deceased father's bones to China; for the youngest daughter, Nina, the sin was her decision to flee Chinatown for life in New York and postmodern mobility as a flight attendant. And for Leila, who has remained in Chinatown, working as a public school counselor, the sin was her failure to detect suicidal tendencies in her sister.

As a community relations specialist in her school, Leila serves as a bridge to American institutions for Chinatown's residents, visiting them in their homes. "Most of my students are recent immigrants. Both parents work. Swing shift. Graveyard. Seamstress. Dishwasher. Janitor. Waiter. One job bleeds into another" (16). Leila is a new American, comfortable in her ability to mediate between two cultural worlds. However, the immigrants with whom she deals do not want to hear about the protocols of American education, especially about parental participation in school affairs. In China, the immigrants assert, the school teacher was master. Leila uses numerous fruitless arguments to enlist these immigrants in the American educational conversation, but her "China-firsters" prefer to remain on the periphery of national life. Leila's parents are equally resistant to her professional scrutiny. They force her to piece together family memories, figuratively reassembling the "bones" of her ancestors so that she can apprehend a pattern to her family's arrival and place in American history. She learns about her actual father, Lyman Fu, who had abandoned the family after he failed to discover America's Gold Mountain: "He had plans: America, the big gold mountain, was where he wanted to settle. They came to San Francisco together but things didn't work out as fast as he wanted. Then he heard that Australia was the new gold mountain, every coolie's dream" (187). Similar secrets, buried skeletal remains, are unearthed by the narrator as she discovers and reconstructs family and immigrant history. She is a local ethnographer and recorder, wise in the ways of Western social science, scrutinizing her people but still bewildered by the mystery at the heart of Ona's suicide.

The narrator never solves the mystery of Ona's suicide, but as Ona's death hovers over this retrospective narrative, readers can infer that Ona had failed to bridge the world of Chinatown and the national landscape beyond. Ona's suicide has roots in family conflicts and evasions, including her parents' rejection of her lover, a young man who is the son of an unscrupulous business associate who brings Leon and Mah to financial ruination. Ona never solves the riddle of double consciousness. Ensnared by the conflict between traditional and contemporary mores, this lover of life, who wants to be a "smart old goddess" and sail the world like Leon, a merchant shipman, elects instead a plunge from the thirteenth floor of a Chinatown housing project. For Ona, Chinatown is not a refuge, nor is the outside world. Family bones and the harsh realities of contemporary love shape her tragic destiny.

As she seeks answers to family mysteries, Leila's act of remembrance becomes a narrative voice trying to find adequate language to express not only the doubleness of immigrant life but also the doubleness of America. One beautiful Chinese New Year's afternoon, Leila's husband, Mason, takes the family for a ride: "He drove over the Golden Gate Bridge because he knew Mah loved how the light bounced off the cables, copper into San Francisco, how when his ship passed under the Golden Gate, the light disappeared for a long minute" (109). Here Ng invokes the extraordinary symbolic power of the Golden Gate Bridge to celebrate the promise of America. As a spectacular cultural monument or icon, it rivals the Statue of Liberty, especially for immigrants from the Pacific Rim. At the same time, the image of the fragile fading light mutes this iconic scene. Moreover, the family's New Year's drive occurs against the backdrop of Ona's recent death and burial. The narrator's meditation on Ona's suicide and her reaffirmation of cultural ties, juxtaposed against her decision to leave the familiar terrain of Chinatown with Mason at the end of the novel, captures both the bond she senses with her Chinese "bones" and her willingness to test the open national road that awaits her. She embraces this dialectical doubleness as an organic part of her life.

Perhaps the epitome of the dialectics of doubleness is Wittman Ah Sing, the countercultural antihero of Maxine Hong Kingston's novel, *Tripmaster Monkey: His Fake Book* (1989). Wittman is a protean figure who resolves his problems by gradually embracing his immigrant past while singing the song of the open American road. Possessing a bifocal name, Wittman in his comically rebellious antics as a Berkeley graduate in the 1960s embodies at the outset of the novel the crisis of doubleness to which Ling alludes. He ridicules the Chinese immigrants—FOB's or Fresh Off the Boats—in San Francisco's Chinatown: "What had he to do with foreigners? With F.O.B. emigres? Fifth generation native Californian that he was. Great Great-Grandfather came on the *Nootica*, as ancestral as the *Mayflower*. . . . His province is America. America his province" (41). Wittman only thinks that he is removed from his immigrant origins. An aspiring playwright and free spirit in the tradition of his ancestors and also of Walt Whitman, the protagonist Wittman "sings" the American myth—but only by learning to blend it with Chinese culture and mythology. The play he launches improbably at a Benevolent Association house in San Francisco's Chinatown is an amalgam of Eastern and Western myths. A "master of change" (306) as the avatar of both Whitman and the Tripmaster Monkey of Chinese legend, Ah Sing is Kingston's fantastic and surreal embodiment of the state of the nation in the 1960s. He declares he is "the present-day U.S.A. incarnation of the King of the Monkeys" (33). Patricia Lin observes: "In the Chinese classic, Monkey springs *sui generis* from a stone egg. On a dare from the other monkeys in the forest he penetrates a waterfall and discovers an edenic world. For his bravado he is made king of the monkeys and leads the simians into the new kingdom" (Lim and Ling 338). By fusing Monkey and Walt Whitman, the protagonist reclaims his heritage as a "China Man" and an American man, his barbaric yawp stretching across the Pacific Rim in order to unify two myths of national origins.

In one of the skits comprising Wittman's three-day theatrical extravaganza, Kingston playfully investigates the doubleness at the core of American national identity by presenting the Siamese twins Chang and Eng, "the Double Boys, pattering away in Carolina-Siamese. Chinkus and Pinkus" (290). Imitations of the nineteenth-century Siamese twins who rose to fame and fortune with P.T. Barnum, Chang (Chinese) and Eng (English) are burlesque figures who nevertheless reveal parodically the complexities of American identity. Against the backdrop of the Civil War (while paying kaleidoscopic homage as well to Bunker Hill, Tonto and the Lone Ranger, and Confucius), the twins "make a more perfect union" (92) in their conjoined existence. As such, they are "uncommon and rare," the focus of considerable prurient fascination, for they call into question the significance, even the need for the "hyphen" in American life.

Wittman Ah Sing's staging of the "War of the Three Kingdoms," based loosely on the *Shui Hu Chuaan* or *The Wake Verge*, is an attempt to replace the hyphenization of American life and identity with a more delicate amalgamation. Just as "Englishmen and Frenchmen and Dutchmen" (326) ultimately became Americans, he yearns for a similar metamorphosis but realizes that without a "born-and-belong-in-the-U.S.A. name" (327) this change is difficult. At one point he ponders, "is there a Chinese word for Chinese American? They say 'jook tsing.' They say 'ho chi qwai.' Like 'mestizo.' Like 'pachuco'" (255). The task of transforming identity is perplexing for Wittman, who like his namesake wants to embrace all of America, without any hyphenization. A descendant of the Native Sons and Daughters of the Golden State, of the original Chinese sojourners and immigrants, Wittman wants to make "the entire U.S.A." (327) a part of his being. As Tripmaster Monkey, Wittman learns to alter identities, play at multiple roles, pick and choose from a potpourri of cultural possibilities. Like a transcendental Walt Whitman, he becomes what he wills, as if this is the apotheosis of American identity, and in the end he makes up his mind not to go to the Vietnam War, which would be tantamount to a betrayal of the Asian site of his double identity.

Wittman Ah Sing, tall and lanky like Abraham Lincoln, his long hair and general demeanor in the tradition of artistic American iconoclasts from Walt Whitman to the Beats, his finely chiseled Asian features suggesting a composite of Chinese and Japanese genealogy (he delights in passing as Japanese), is Maxine Hong Kingston's vision of the future complexion of American society. He is the incarnation of Walt Whitman's "teeming Nation of nations" extolled in the poem "By Blue Ontario's Shore" in *Leaves of Grass*; his soul, as Whitman writes in "Passage to India," "Tying the Eastern and Western sea/The road between Europe and Asia." The epic play he produces, steeped in American and Asian wars, similarly depicts the battle to achieve a multiethnic American nation. As the multiethnic cast in Wittman Ah Sing's play makes its transcontinental and trans-Pacific odyssey across time and space, Kingston posits a new national dynamic in which American history becomes a composite of disparate and often clashing cultures and traditions. Asians who, as Kingston asserts in *Tripmaster Monkey* were here before Columbus, have always been a part of this volatile national mix, although it was only in the events of World War II and the postwar changes in immigration policy that they were able to claim a significant place in the American landscape.

In both its large and small historical allusions and motifs, the prototypical Asian-American novel presents the immigrant encounter as the core of experience for the original voyagers to the New World and their descendants. Kingston's postmodern time traveler, Wittman, constantly conflates and superimposes various immigrant encounters as when, recounting one of his numerous Chinese tales, he tells the story of the invention of the ritual of friendship: "That friendship ritual was one thousand six hundred and twenty nine years old when the forty-niners, our great-great grandfathers, brought it to the Gold Rush. Every matinee or evening for a hundred years, somewhere in America, some acting company was performing *The Oath in the Peach Orchard*. . . . then it disappeared, I don't know why, the words of that oath used to be printed in programs, and it was inscribed on walls for the World War II audience" (141). Here, in a passage typical of her stylistic dexterity in *Tripmaster Monkey*, Kingston holds thousands of years of cultural and national history in delicate suspension, not attempting to simplify this history but rather to suggest that Chinese immigrants and their descendants have been involved in a continuous process of preserving their culture *and* negotiating their passage through American society. Similarly when, in the Chang and Eng skit, she raises the issue of miscegenation against the backdrop of the Civil War, Kingston tests readers' own knowledge of the history of America's anti-miscegenation laws, which persisted in the United States well beyond World War II. In fact, they were not repealed in California until 1948 (Melendy 52–53), almost one hundred years after the first Chinese miners entered California in 1849 in search of the Gold Mountain. (Kingston devotes eight pages of *China Men* to a catalogue of all exclusionary laws against Chinese Americans in the nation's history.) Seen from the perspective of the immigrant encounter, Asian-American fiction makes problematic, in modes we have already seen but also in discretely different forms, the unequal power relationship in United States history between peoples of the East and those of the West.

East and West

Kingston's persistent allusions to the Chinese forty-niners who helped open the rivers and mountains of northern California to the Gold Rush conflates notions of East and West while inscribing parallel histories of white and Asian communities as the western United States developed. In the wake of the Mexican War, the now American West opened rapidly in the 1850s to both white immigrants, pushing swiftly to the Pacific shore, propelled by its Manifest Destiny or "divine command" to create, as Senator Thomas Hart Benton of Missouri declared, an "American road to India," and to free Chinese immigrants to California who were among the original forty-niners seeking their fortune on the Gold Mountain. For these Chinese immigrants, as Ronald Takaki writes in *A Different Mirror: A History of Multicultural America* (1993), "America possessed an alluring boundlessness, promising not only gold but opportunities for employment." According to Takaki, there were 325 Chinese migrants, mostly men, among the original forty-niners. Another 450 came in 1850, 2,716 in 1851, 20,026 in 1852, until by 1870 there were 63,000 Chinese in United States, with 77 percent of them in California (192–194). By 1930, approximately 400,000 Chinese had crossed the Pacific to America, and more than half had stayed, mining the gold, building the first transcontinental railroad, opening businesses from San Francisco to New York, and cultivating agricultural lands from California to Idaho. The legend of the Gold Mountain that had first captured the imaginations of the original Chinese forty-niners would remain a seductive myth, a fiction luring subsequent waves of Asian immigrants to American shores in the aftermath of World War II, and compelling writers like Maxine Hong Kingston to interrogate, as she does in *The Woman Warrior*, *China Men*, and *Tripmaster Monkey*, the sinister allure of this shimmering archetype.

Kingston's contemporary, Shawn Hsu Wong, also wrestles with the ambiguous resonance of the Gold Mountain myth for generations of

Chinese Americans. In his short fable, "Each Year Grain," published in the first major Asian-American literary anthology, *Aiiieeeee* (1983), Wong implicitly invokes the myth of the Gold Mountain while creating an Odyssian figure out of the narrator's great-grandfather: "Your great-grandfather's country was a rich land, the river's sand had gold dust in it. The water was fresh and clear, the sand sparkling beneath the surface of the water like the shiny skin of the trout that swam in the deep pools. This was California's gold country in 1850s and your great-grandfather was there to reap the riches that California offered and to return home a rich man to live in comfort with his family" (171). In the expanding dream-vision experienced by the narrator as a child, the great-grandfather becomes the apotheosis of all early Chinese immigrants seeking the Golden Land but who were ultimately "rejected" by their adoptive nation as the gold ran out and the railroad was finished. "They were allowed to live but not marry. The law was designed so that the Chinese would gradually die out, leaving no sons or daughters" (175).

Wong submits actual and archetypal history to a more extended scrutiny in his first novel, *Homebase* (1979), in which the protagonist, Rainford Chan, fourth generation on his father's side and second on his mother's, travels psychically through time and physically across the continent, seeking a central point of cultural origin. As in "Each Year Grain," Wong's character in *Homebase* faces a world in which past and present converge at the Gold Mountain. A traveler in America from the time that he was four years old and his parents drove from Berkeley to New York and back, Rainford is the sum of his family's history. His great-grandfather "built the railroad through the Sierra Nevada in difficult seasons" (11); his grandfather was a Chinese *vaquero* in California; his father was an engineer on the mainland and in Guam. An orphan in America by the age of fifteen, he intends to create "the whole vision of my life in America, of our lives in America" (57) by reconstructing the journeys of his ancestors. He finds on Angel Island, where Chinese immigrants were detained, "a haunted house" (103); and on Guam, where a crashed World War II fighter plane is lodged in the back yard, memories of this turbulent period. He concludes that Chinese Americans "are on the run through America" (76) and that the antidote is a "homebase," a stable sense of identity and rootedness in a shifting world: "And today, after 125 years of life here, I do not want just a home that time allowed to have. America must give me legends with spirit. I take myths to name this country's canyons, dry riverbeds, mountains, after my father, grandfather, great-grandfather. We are old enough to haunt this land" (111). By "haunting" America, Wong suggests Americans of Chinese descent can merge with Anglocentric national myths. Rainford, the child of an immigrant mother and a descendant of the original sojourners, inherits and extends this integrated history. A contemporary American, he pieces the fragments of family and national history into a coherent whole, one that embraces heritage, myth, and the often opposing demands of the majority culture. He becomes part of a national foundation narrative.

Wong's allusion in "Each Year Grain" to the series of nineteenth- and twentieth-century exclusion laws that effectively barred Chinese wives from joining their husbands in the United States raises the issue of institutionalized discrimination against Asians that permeates the history of American immigration. The Page Law, passed by Congress in 1875 ostensibly to prevent the entry of Chinese prostitutes, was implemented so vigorously that it effectively cut off the bare trickle of immigrant women from China that already by the 1870s had created the "bachelor societies" of the nation's Chinatowns. Moreover, the Chinese Exclusion Act of 1882 codified the principle of excluding immigrants based on nationality. It also denied the promise of naturalization, stating that "hereafter no state court of the United States may admit Chinese to citizenship." Passed during a period of rabid nativism and anti-Chinese xenophobia, at a time when hundreds of thousands of European immigrants were arriving in the United States annually, the Exclusion Act was renewed in 1892 and then indefinitely in 1902. The Immigration Act of 1924, which barred the entry of "aliens ineligible for citizenship" and set up quotas based on two percent of foreign-born individuals of each nationality residing in the United States in 1890, virtually ended Chinese immigration as well as immigration from Japan, India, Korea, and other Asian nations. Thus Shawn Hsu Wong's vision of a nation intent on making its fragile Chinese immigrant population "disappear" just as completely as the great-grandfather's bones decomposed in northern California soil, never to be returned for burial in China, is the fictive rendition of a trend in immigration policy that prevailed up to the bombing of Pearl Harbor by Japan in 1941 and the subsequent repeal of the exclusion laws in 1943 when China became an ally of the United States.

The myth of America as a Golden Land for Asian Americans changed with the disruptions and displacements of World War II. Out of the Holocaust of World War II emerge transnational survivors who, scarred by scarcely speakable horrors, imagine America as a continuation of their nightmares. In Nora Okja Keller's *Comfort Woman* (1997), narrated from the dual perspectives of a mother and daughter, the quest for wholeness is framed by the mother's secret past as a teenage Korean prostitute in Japanese "recreation camps." Slowly, the daughter, Beccah, pieces together the trauma of her mother Akiko's life, including her rescue by a depraved American missionary and her unhappy marriage to him. After the war, Akiko and her husband are spiritually adrift in America. "For years, we traveled from the east coast to the west coast, from north to south, to every state in the Union" (107). Often mistaken for "a poor little orphan Jap" but shielded from the more virulent forms of anti-Japanese sentiment by her tortured and mildly psychotic husband, Akiko is not mesmerized by this "country of excess and extravaganza" (108). Debased by Japanese troops, shuttled around the United States in endless circles by a husband without a permanent religious mission, Akiko experiences dislocation rather than wholeness in America: "When you see it for the first time, it glitters, beautiful, like a dream, but then, the longer you walk through it, the more you realize that the dream is empty, false, sterile. You realize that you have no face and no place in this country" (110). In Hawaii, their final destination, it is Beccah's task to "claw" through memory and story to understand the "atrocities" afflicted on her mother (196). Beccah is nearly thirty when her mother dies; their relationship has survived numerous "death thoughts," as her mother characterizes the world spawned by World War II. Spreading her mother's ashes in the stream behind their house in Honolulu, Beccah accepts the myths and mysteries of Akiko's tormented life, acknowledges the love that sustained their relationship, and accepts her own identity born of the diasporic forces of twentieth-century life.

World War II also constitutes a watershed for the immigrant generation in Amy Tan's fiction, but from a more promising perspective than the one posited by Keller. When, for example, the second-generation daughter, Jing-mei "June" Woo recalls the flight of her mother out of war-torn China in Tan's *The Joy Luck Club* (1989), the trope of the Promised Land suggests a new horizon for peoples dispossessed by contemporary history: "My mother believed you could be anything you wanted to be in America. You could open a restaurant. You could work for the government and get good retirement. You could buy a home with almost no

money down. You could become rich. You could become instantly famous" (132). Suyuan Woo's unambiguous faith in the United States, which
is shared by her three female immigrant companions and their husbands
who comprise the Joy Luck Club and who meet regularly to play mahjong,
eat and converse, and decide on investment opportunities, is counterpoised against the traumas inherent in the global situation that unfolded
in the 1930s and 1940s. Having lost her first husband, her parents, and
her home following the Japanese invasion of China in 1937, and having
abandoned her twin baby daughters in a frantic effort to escape, Suyuan
Woo reconstructs a life and a society in San Francisco's Chinatown.
Whereas certain writers, most typically Frank Chin in his short story
collection *The Chinaman Pacific & Frisco R.R. Co.* (1988) and his novel
Donald Duk (1991), view the Chinatowns of America as oppressive internal colonies or as sites of grotesque cultural behavior, Tan situates the
Woos and the other three families—the Hsus, Jongs, and St. Clairs—in a
postwar urban enclave that is as sustaining for them as was the Brooklyn
depicted by Paule Marshall in *Brown Girl, Brownstones.* Although Suyuan
Woo is recently deceased at the beginning of Tan's novel, her spirit nevertheless speaks most emphatically for the Joy Luck Club's desire to preserve traditions while preparing their children for life in a new nation. In
death, she exerts an especially powerful influence on her daughter, who
must learn to balance her Americanized identity as June against the
competing claims of her mother and the force of tradition her mother
represents.

The generational contestations that form the core of *The Joy Luck
Club* are once again forged on the borderlines of the contemporary immigrant experience, with the daughters of dominant and domineering
mothers who demand filial devotion moving from the Chinatown of
their youth to the interstices of urban America and outward to engagement as college students and professionals in the collective experiences
of the nation. What Sau-ling Cynthia Wong terms the conflicts of
"ethnicized gender" signals their push-and-pull sense of identity and affiliation with the nation. "Gender roles, invested with strong emotions
concerning what is 'naturally fitting,' become as convenient a locus for
testing out and codifying cultural meaning. Thus characters' actions,
depicted along a spectrum of gender appropriateness, are assigned varying shades of 'Chineseness' or 'Americanness' to indicate their at-homeness
in the adopted land" (14). Jing-Mei and the other daughters in Tan's novel

engage in various degrees of intergenerational conflict, tumbling persistently as children and adults into the abyss of disrespect as they become more and more Americanized. As Jing-Mei declares rebelliously in refusing to practice the piano at her mother's command, "I didn't have to do what my mother said anymore. I wasn't her slave. This wasn't China" (141). In this episode from the frequently anthologized chapter "Two Kinds," Jing-Mei's apostasy is matched by her mother's demand for respect: "Only two kinds of daughters,' she shouted in Chinese. 'Those who are obedient and those who follow their own mind" (142). As women in their thirties who have confronted American culture with varying degrees of professional and personal success and disappointment, the daughters' lives are sparked constantly by their shared family histories and the struggle to reconcile obedience and independence.

The daughters of immigrant parents in *The Joy Luck Club* are condemned to lives and identities typified by cultural fluidity, a constant push-and-pull movement away from family origins and back to them. When, for example, Lena St. Clair (who is part Chinese and part American of English-Irish descent and who, unlike her other family friends, grew up in Oakland and San Francisco's North Beach rather than Chinatown) examines a photograph of her mother, she equates the "scared" look of her interracial appearance with that of her mother in the picture: "I have a photo of my mother with this same scared look. My father said the picture was taken when Ma was first released from Angel Island Immigration Station. She stayed there for three weeks, until they could process her papers and determine whether she was a War Bride, a Displaced Person, a Student, or the wife of a Chinese-American citizen. My father said they didn't have rules for dealing with the Chinese wife of a Caucasian citizen. Somehow, in the end, they declared her a Displaced Person, lost in a sea of immigration categories" (104). Lena, who is married to an American architect named Harold and is largely responsible for his success although he deprecates her contribution by measuring out their married lives in separate expense statements, sees in the photograph of her mother a capsulated history of the immigrant experience and the "displacements" visited on Ying-Ying St. Clair. Lena's mother was once part of a wealthy family in China, but through an unfortunate first marriage and the outbreak of war, her life had become permeable. Her daughter now enjoys affluence on a four-acre estate in Woodside, but Ying-Ying senses, along with her daughter, a similar displacement inherent in a house that to the mother seems unbalanced, not right, falling apart. Ying-Ying's daughter knows that "everything she's said is true" (151), and that their mutual fear is rooted in their perception of a world—and in Lena's case a marriage—whose essential condition or architecture is disruptive, dissonant, and insubstantial.

In order to manage the diasporic dilemmas of their New World, the immigrant mothers in *The Joy Luck Club* implore their daughters to meditate on myths of cultural and national origin, the narratives of immigration, the grim but sustaining histories of families. These filial injunctions to remember their origins create the intertextual unity for the alternating stories of the four families Tan weaves into her novel. The Woo, Hsu, Jong, and St. Clair daughters are exposed to two cultures and are bivocal in their experience of the world. However, only Jing-Mei, or June May, whose stories open and close *The Joy Luck Club*, literally encounters the East by traveling to China and meeting the twin daughters of her mother's first marriage who had miraculously survived the vicissitudes of the wartime years and the Maoist ascendancy. As her mother had predicted, Jing-Mei becomes Chinese, for it is in her blood, and when the three daughters embrace, they see in the Polaroid snapshot that Jing-Mei's father, Canning Woo, takes of them the undeniable image of their mother. By retrieving the history of her mother, the daughter unites the dichotomized identities of Jing-Mei and June May, recreating an identity by creatively juxtaposing and integrating experience from both sides of her diasporic world.

Suyuan Woo had conceived her first Joy Luck Club in China in the late 1930s as a refuge from the onslaught of Japan's invading army, and the conflict between these two nations (which is a strong element in Tan's second novel, *The Kitchen God's Wife*, 1991) underscores their intertwined destinies. In the American context, the passage of Chinese and Japanese immigrants to the United States also is reflected in these nations' interconnected histories. Even as the Western powers were expanding their imperial hold over China in the nineteenth century, Japan, following Commodore Matthew Perry's forcible entry into Tokyo Bay in 1853, had to deal with the economic and political realities forced on it by the West. With the restoration of the Meiji emperor in 1868 and the creation of a strong centralized government intent on rapid militarization and industrialization, Japan soon became a power that the West—especially the United States—had to contend with. At the same time, Japan's rapid development created severe economic dislocations for its agricultural class as thousands of farmers, unable to pay their taxes, lost their holdings. As Page Smith writes, "By 1890 the pressures of population in Japan led that country, inherently hostile to foreigners, to permit emigration. . . . A trickle at first, by 1900 there were over 24,000 Japanese in a California population of 1,485,053. Ten years later the number in the United States had swelled to 72,157, of whom 41,356 were in California" (48). The same stories of the Gold Mountain that had lured Chinese newcomers to California in the middle decades of the nineteenth century now created in the 1890s a similar *netsu* or fever as Takaki describes it in *A Different Mirror* among Japanese laborers. By 1924, 200,000 Japanese had left for Hawaii and 180,00 for the United States mainland. These voyagers had "huge dreams of fortune" as one haiku of the period indicates. The imagined nation for both Japanese and Chinese immigrants was one of fabulous wealth, but the American community they encountered would confound and often suppress their dreams of departure and arrival.

Both the Issei, or first-generation Japanese, and the second-generation Nisei experienced the same racial discrimination encountered by the Chinese, which had been codified in the Chinese Exclusion Act of 1882. The early inscription of Chinese and Japanese newcomers as "Chinks" and "Japs" by white America reflects a pervasive racism in the nation as it confronted cohorts of immigrants from different shores. More often than not, white America attempted to extend anti-Chinese agitation and legislation to the Japanese immigrants, as when workers, led by the American Federation of Labor under Samuel Gompers, advocated the renewal of the Chinese Exclusion Act in 1902 and its expansion to ban all Japanese. Similarly, the 1906 decision of the San Francisco Board of Education to send all Chinese, Japanese, and Korean children to Oriental School precipitated an international crisis for the Roosevelt administration: Japan, a rising power, protested this attempt to segregate Japanese schoolchildren. While Roosevelt clearly advocated the civilizing mission of white America throughout the world, and was especially critical of the influx of Japanese into Hawaii, he worked assiduously to defuse the San Francisco School Board crisis. Ultimately, the School Board rescinded the segregation order for Japanese Americans, but Roosevelt in turn extracted from Japan the 1908 Gentlemen's Agreement under which Japan would no longer permit the emigration of laborers to the United States. That only a handful of Japanese schoolchildren had been involved in the original San Francisco School Board's initiative is strongly representative of the fear and antipathy felt by white Americans over imaginary Asiatic hordes. Yet these racist fantasies had desired effects, forcing the Issei away from mainstream metropolitan society into the Little Tokyos of Los Angeles, San Francisco, and Seattle and increasingly into the agricultural regions of the western states. Anti-Japanese sentiment also added to the catalog of restrictive immigration laws, including a series of alien land provisions which under California law and the statutes of twelve other western states made it increasingly difficult for Japanese to own property. Moreover, the 1921 Ladies' Agreement under which Japan barred "picture brides" from emigrating to the United States effectively ended Japanese arrivals even before the exclusionary 1924 Immigration Act went into effect. To preserve the myth of white national culture, the United States had effectively marginalized the Japanese long before the events of World War II.

Enemy Aliens

The internment of Japanese Americans during World War II haunts the nation's history, disturbing its normative myths and signifying yet another atavistic juncture in the nation's definition of itself. The forced internment years of 1942 to 1944 disrupted the lives of 120,000 Japanese Americans—some 50,000 Issei and 70,000 Nisei—who were evacuated from the West Coast and detained in ten relocation centers inland. The writer and theologian Daisuke Kitagawa is one of numerous commentators who assert that the state-organized oppression of Japanese Americans during World War II was the nation's final enunciation of an immigration policy that condemned them to be aliens: "The Japanese community came to be an insulated cultural island in American society, not by choice but as a result of rejection and social ostracism by American society" (11). Thus Executive Order 9066, signed by President Franklin D. Roosevelt on February 19, 1942, was in one sense the culmination of national policy that had effectively created racial ghettoes and the condition of apartheid for Japanese Americans long before they were interned. Yet at the historical moment precipitated by Pearl Harbor, this condition of apartheid was profoundly altered. Suddenly the immigrants of the Issei generation were labeled "enemy aliens," their assets frozen; while their Nisei children, who had been envisioned as a bridge to the national experience, were caught in the most extreme form of doubleness: American citizens by birth but potential enemies because of their parents' origins.

The attack on Pearl Harbor on December 7, 1941, which sank or damaged nineteen ships of the United States Navy and killed 2,300 Americans, created a national hysteria against Japanese Americans and the imagined danger they posed to the security of the West Coast. This hysteria was fueled by the press, notably the Los Angeles *Times*, which warned that California was a zone of danger, and by influential syndicated columnists including Westbrook Pegler and Walter Lippman. Moreover, West Coast military authorities, California politicians such as Attorney General Earl Warren, patriotic organizations, and powerful figures in Washington, D.C., contributed to the panic. Roger Daniels, a foremost historian of the internment, assesses this historic watershed: "The reasons for the establishment of these concentration camps is clear. A deteriorating military situation created the opportunity for American racists to get their views accepted by the national leadership. The Constitution was treated as a scrap of paper not only by . . . Roosevelt but also by the entire Congress, which approved and implemented everything done to Japanese Americans, and by the Supreme Court, which in December 1944, nearly three years after the fact, in effect sanctioned the incarceration of the Japanese Americans" (1993: 47). History harbors ambiguities, but the logic of wartime incarceration of mainland Japanese Americans unravels when their fate is measured against the more benign treatment of their counterparts in Hawaii, where 150,000 Japanese Americans never were sent to internment camps, despite the fact that the islands were in the Pacific theater of wartime operations.

The removal of all persons of Japanese ancestry from the western halves of California, Oregon, and Washington and their relocation and internment in desolate interior defense zones was a transformational moment for the Issei and Nisei. This radical displacement of humanity also became a dominant trope for Japanese American writers, as powerful for them as the motif of the Middle Passage for African-American artists. In autobiography, fiction, poetry, and drama, the evacuation, relocation, and incarceration experience is the cathartic moment situating two generations of Japanese Americans in the field of American history. Prior to Pearl Harbor and the internment, Japanese Americans, while facing discrimination and disenfranchisement, nevertheless had been able "to build orderly and meaningful lives," relying on "the support of ... a cohesive ethnic community for meeting both material and emotional psychological needs" (O'Brien and Fugita 27). Unlike the disproportionately male bachelor societies typifying early Chinese immigration patterns, which persisted into the 1950s and are configured comically in Louis Chu's *Eat a Bowl of Tea*, the substantial immigration of women and picture brides to the United States provided strong Japanese-American family networks while their heavy engagement in agriculture and rural lifestyles created an insularity that strengthened the ethnic community. In the short fiction of Toshio Mori, written in the 1930s and 1940s and collected in *Yokohama, California* (1949), the strong collective identity of Japanese Americans during the decade of the Great Depression contrasts with stories set in the disruptive realm of World War II and the internment camps. At the same time, Mori's best short fiction invokes the rapidity of change in twentieth-century America and the dilemma for ethnic groups that rely on a "homebase" even as a mobile nation impinges on the ethnic community. Mori's "The Woman Who Makes Swell Doughnuts" captures this dynamic as the center and the margins collide:

> Sometimes I sit and gaze out the window and watch the Southern Pacific trains rumble by and the vehicles whiz with speed. And sometimes she catches me doing this and she nods her head and I know she understands that the silence in the room is great, and also the rain and the dust of the outside is great, and when she is nodding I understand that she is saying that this, her little room, her little circle, is a depot, a pause, for the weary traveler, but outside, outside of her little world there is dissonance, hugeness of another kind, and the travel to do. (24–25)

Mori's narrator embraces all of America, both the static and stable pleasures of the ethnic community and the "dissonance" of the nation rushing by the window. Specific immigrant histories might be discrepant, but they also merge with powerful national histories. Several of Mori's short story titles—"The All-American Girl," "Notes on America," "Slant-Eyed Americans"—suggest these diasporic tensions and intersections. Other stories like "The Finance Over at Doi's" reveal the Japanese immigrant's obsession with American institutions—in this case a shoe repairman's neglect of his business as he invests imaginary money in the stock market. Mori's authorial inclination to mediate between these worlds is filled with ironic tenderness, yet when the Japanese-American universe explodes after Pearl Harbor, an event alluded to in "Slant-Eyed Americans," where a Nisei son visits home one last time before going to war, the tone is more funereal than buoyant, suggestive of a community constricted by national and global politics. Mori's stories, as Sau-ling Cynthia Wong observes, "provide snapshots of a way of life before internment capable of serving as a touchstone of at-homeness in America" (75), a paradise lost because of the traumas of the Second World War.

We see the traumas of the war and the profoundly disruptive consequences of internment in John Okada's *No-No Boy* (1976), a novel interrogating the contradictions of a democratic nation. The "no-no boy" of Okada's raw, disquieting novel is a twenty-five-year-old Japanese American, Ichiro Yamada, who has just returned to Seattle following two years in an internment camp and two years in a federal penitentiary for having refused to serve in the military. As the double negative of the novel's title implies, Ichiro has been twice incarcerated: first for being of Japanese ancestry and second for protesting the denial of his citizenship and rejecting the opportunity to demonstrate his loyalty to the United States by defending his country. That Okada, who served in the U.S. military during the Second World War along with 33,000 other Japanese Americans, should focus on a no-no boy in his only novel underscores the theme of resistance. (Okada died of a heart attack at the age of 47; the manuscript of a second novel dealing with the Issei generation was burned by his wife.) In point of fact, there was resistance to the mass internment: legal challenges by Japanese-American dissidents, four of which reached the Supreme Court and were rejected; riots at the camps in Manzanar and Tule Lake in California and Topaz in Utah; demands for repatriation to Japan; and opposition to loyalty oaths and the military draft which was offered to all Japanese-American citizens in January 1944. Resistance to the draft was not significant in terms of numbers except at Heart Mountain, Wyoming, but within the context of an entire community singled out for internment, such resistance is a striking indication of the willingness of individuals to say "no" to the lie at the heart of the incarceration, for detainment, finally acknowledged in 1981 by the Presidential Commission on the Wartime Relocation and Internment of Civilians, was grotesque and unnecessary. Okada's protagonist stands for the 291 Nisei who were tried for draft resistance and the 263 who were convicted and sent to federal penitentiaries (Daniels 1993: 64). However, Okada presents him not as a hero but rather as a disillusioned soul seeking a refuge in postwar America.

The figure who emerges in *No-No Boy*, having transgressed national boundaries and cultural expectations, is the emblem of the severe postwar fissures afflicting Japanese Americans. He is, as Fanon puts it nicely, "a stranger to his environment . . . an alien in his own country" (63). Returning to a city that strikes him as gray, grimy, and palpably claustrophobic, Ichiro re-enters the Japanese section of Seattle and his parents' grocery store in a state of ambivalence and lethargy. He is doubly marginalized and doubly conflicted because he rejects both his Japanese and his American identities. As noted by Jeffrey Chan and the other authors of "An Introduction to Chinese-American and Japanese-American Authors," "Okada's hero, embodying his vision of the Japanese-American, cannot be defined by the concept of the dual personality that would make a whole from two incompatible parts. This hero of the double and hyphenated 'No' is both a restatement of and a rejection of the term 'Japanese-American'—'No' to Japanese and 'No' to American" (215). Unable to reconcile or integrate his divided selves, Ichiro exists in a condition of *hopelessness*, a word Okada underscores throughout the novel. His challenge is to emerge from this estranged condition and the dialectic of doubleness that destabilizes his life. He feels "like an intruder in a world to which he had no claim" (1), a subject without any social destiny. Surrounded by people in various stages of metropolitan delirium, he senses that not only his doubleness but his otherness might be an inescapable fate.

Ichiro's predicament reveals the perilous situation of the children of immigrants who doubly negate their identities, rejecting ancestry as well as nation as marks of identification. Although once loyal to his parents, aging Issei who had ventured to America as sojourners seeking riches and planning to return to Japan, he is now estranged from them. At the basic level of communication, there is a binary conflict, for his parents "spoke virtually no English. On the other hand, the children, like Ichiro, spoke almost no Japanese" (7). Nevertheless, Ichiro had submitted to his mother's total rejection of American national identity by refusing to sign the loyalty oath or submit to military service. His mother, clearly deracinated by the war and the internment, believes Japan was victorious and that ships will be sent to take them home. His father, portrayed by Okada as pliant and feminine in a symbolic reversal of Japanese patriarchal patterns, seeks solace in alcohol. By explicitly renouncing his mother's pro-Japanese sympathies, the protagonist removes himself as a dutiful son from the refuge of the family. To construct a new identity, Ichiro thinks he must reject or lose family history, but the conflicts he encounters within the Japanese-American community and the continuing forms of racism existing in the larger society make his options and his future tenuous. Casting himself from the family, he enters an even more hostile realm. Moreover, given his sense of hopelessness and exhaustion, he seems—in a trope Okada weaves into the narrative—to be moving or driving without a map.

There was a time in childhood when Ichiro's map of cultural understanding was almost exclusively Japanese, fueled by his mother's mythic "stories about gallant and fierce warriors who protected their lords with blades of shining steel and about the old woman who found a peach in the stream and took it home, and, when her husband split it in half, a husky little boy tumbled out to fill their hearts with boundless joy" (15). Okada's allusion to the tale of Momotaro, familiar to generations of Japanese schoolchildren, is a narrative of nation that extols family, culture, and country. As Gayle K. Fujita Sato argues, the story of Momotaro invokes one form or myth of national loyalty that is the counterpart to the loyalty oath forced on Ichiro as a young man during the internment (239–58). Thus Ichiro confronts two national myths, neither of which he can embrace, which is the cause of his aimless wandering and anomie. From existing wholly as Japanese during childhood, he becomes only half Japanese and half American. "But it is not enough . . . to be only half an American and know that it is an empty half. . . . I am not Japanese and I am not American" (16). Lacking loyalty to either frame of culture, indeed disloyal to them, Ichiro, the child of immigrants, is a striking emblem of the deeply disassociated self seeking a viable myth of the nation.

Searching for an authentic national identity, Ichiro embarks on a postwar errand into the wilderness, "plunging down" Jackson Street, roaming the inner city, traveling by bus to the University of Washington, where he had once been an engineering major, visiting the country with his friend Kenji, and accompanying Kenji, a wounded veteran with a gangrenous leg stump that is slowly killing him, to a hospital in Portland.

His frantic wandering, suggestive of his psychic condition, is a parody of the myth of American mobility and the promise that individuals can reinvent themselves if given sufficient territory. Even some of the Issei generation, "living in America and being denied a place as citizens, nevertheless had become inextricably a part of the country which by its vastness and goodness and fairness and plenitude drew them into its fold...." (52). Yet Ichiro's effort to imagine a paradisical nation where, in keeping with the Turner thesis, immigrants in the "crucible of the frontier" are Americanized and create a "mixed race," clashes with the sobering realities of his condition—reviled and ostracized by any members of his immediate community and caught in the cauldron of continuing racial conflict emblematic of postwar society. His abiding "tolerance for the Negroes and the Jews and the Mexicans and the Chinese" (5–6) is an implicit recognition that Turner's mixed-race vision of the prototypical American is unrealized. Nevertheless, the power of this myth—the same motivating force that brought his parents to America—propels Ichiro across the postwar urban and rural landscapes of Washington and Oregon, turning him into a grim picaresque wanderer in search of any small personal and national promise of deliverance.

Even as *No-No Boy* is a parody of the myth of American mobility (Ichiro tellingly begins and ends his odyssey on the streets of Seattle), the author offers a more serious discourse on American identity. Okada's penchant for editorializing evokes the extremes of the Nisei state of mind in the aftermath of the Second World War's disruptions. In this connection, Ichiro's relationship with his friend Kenji, who is both his opposite and his desired double, frames the dilemma confronting the children of immigrant parents: "They were two extremes, the Japanese who was more American than most Americans because he had crept to the brink of death for America, and the other who was neither Japanese nor American because he had failed to recognize the gift of his birthright when recognition meant everything" (73). Okada's configuration of Ichiro and Kenji as interconnected halves or polarities in the puzzle of American immigrant identity offers in their close friendship a possible solution to the doubleness the protagonist experiences. Ichiro wants to believe in "the great compassionate stream of life that is America" (153). But first he must empathize with the suffering of his dying friend and the grief and stoicism of Kenji's highly Americanized and assimilated father; and then with the love freely offered by a woman, Emi, to whom Kenji introduces Ichiro. Emi, whose father was repatriated to Japan and whose husband, a Japanese-American soldier who had signed up for a second tour of duty and will never return to her, is both compassionate and loving. Refusing to accept Ichiro's sense of hopelessness, she reminds Ichiro that "this is a country with a big heart" (95). Both Kenji and Emi are integral to Ichiro's "quest for completeness" (134). At the end of the novel, as Ichiro extends his own compassion to a former adversary injured in a barroom brawl that is fatal to yet another "no-no boy," Okada offers a carefully nuanced note of hope: "He walked along, thinking, searching, thinking and probing, and, in the darkness of the alley of the community that was a tiny bit of America, he chased that faint and elusive promise as it continued to take shape in mind and in heart" (251). Ichiro's excursion into the heart of America comes full circle: no longer immobile physically, emotionally, or intellectually, in constant motion after years of internment and incarceration, he is now prepared to begin a journey that is not parodic but instead a heroic venture toward reconciliation and reintegration into the postwar geography of the nation. As Lawson Fusao Inada observes, Ichiro, the no-no boy, "is an underground figure, the conscience of Japanese America. And he is what the novel is all about. The quest by Japanese America to be whole again" (263).

The Quest for Wholeness

This quest to be whole is a dominant theme in Asian-American fiction, linking the motif of journey with the paradox of duality as immigrants and American-born children of immigrant parents and grandparents attempt to locate themselves in national culture. Sau-Ling Cynthia Wong in her highly original study *Reading Asian American Literature* (1993) emphasizes in successive chapters the ways in which "encounters with the racial shadow" often play themselves out against the "politics of mobility." As this study suggests, immigration in itself triggers the myth of mobility, bringing "outsiders" or "others" to the United States but also locating them typically in the rural margins or inner city landscapes of the nation, forcing upon these new strangers in paradise an acute sense of duality or what Maxine Hong Kingston in *The Woman Warrior* describes trenchantly as seeing double. The very landscape of America, filled with uncertainties, illusions, and contradictory promises, fuels this double consciousness. Asian immigrants come to America but then are confined on Angel Island or interned in a camp. The city welcomes sojourners, but then traps them in the Chinatowns, Little Tokyos, Little Manilas, Little Saigons, and other metropolitan ghettoes of the nation. The Gold Mountain beckons but withholds its riches. The nation becomes, as Cynthia Kadohata describes it, a "floating world" of elusive promises for immigrants participating in the American saga.

Kadohata's *The Floating World* (1989), a novel embracing three generations of Japanese Americans—Issei, Nisei, and Sansei—chronicles the distinctive experiences of one family as its members search for America in the 1950s. Told from the perspective of Olivia, or Livvie, who is twelve when the peripatetic events begin and twenty-one when they end, the novel captures the cultural adaptations and unique generational responses of the Usaka family as it discovers America. The sociologist Darrel Montero states that "the Japanese are the only ethnic group to emphasize generational distinctions by a separate nomenclature and a belief in the unique character structure of each generational group" (O'Brien and Fugita 15). In *The Floating World*, Livvie's grandmother, Hisae Fujitano or Obaṣan, who has had three husbands and several lovers, is the iconoclastic force molding the family's American odyssey: "My grandmother liked to tell us about herself during evenings while we all sat talking in front of the motels and houses we stayed at. We were travelling then in what she called Ukiyo, the floating world. The floating world was the gas station attendants, restaurants, and jobs we depended on, the motel towns floating in the middle of fields and mountains. In old Japan, ukiyo meant the districts full of brothels, teahouses, and public baths, but it also referred to change and the pleasures and loneliness change brings" (3). Obasan, who is Livvie's "tormentor" in life and death, is the family's immigrant touchstone: hardened by her passage from Japan to Hawaii and then to the mainland, rebellious in her lifestyle, tyrannical in her hold over her daughter and her daughter's four children. Obasan breaks boundaries by inculcating in her family the myth of the floating world, of movement from place to place. Always in transit, Obasan creates for her family a parable of the immigrant experience. The Osakas are restless and rootless wanderers drifting across a continent which, at midcentury, was not especially hospitable to Japanese Americans or other groups excluded from the American mainstream.

The highways of America beckon the Osakas: on the road, their numerous problems, many of them the outcome of the troubled relationship between Livvie's parents, tend to defuse, while new horizons offer promise and opportunity. Motels, boarding houses, camps, the interiors of cars circumscribe their existence. They "traveled a lot" (1) declares the narrator at the outset of the novel, moving up and down the western states; scattering occasionally as when Livvie and her brothers Walker and Ben are sent to a foster home in Nebraska; and finally in a nicely conceived reversal of the myth of westward expansion, turning back through the Southwest to rural Arkansas where they join the small community of Japanese Americans employed by the state's chicken hatcheries. Livvie, who represents the most recent generation, carries with her the luggage of mixed origins (her "dad," Charlie-O, is actually her stepfather), the lifestyle of the migrant, the psychology of the perpetual wanderer who values freedom more than anything else. Indeed, Livvie identifies with immigrant and migrant rootlessness, which she equates with the essence of the American landscape and the American experience: "I read once that there were three main rivers in the country, one on the West Coast, one on the East, and one in the Midwest. The rivers, made up of migrant farmworkers, traveled down the country every year during the growing season" (177). Livvie's life—and that of her family—resembles points on the map of America. (They constantly read and reread maps while on the road.) The narrator charts her life in America by points on this map, preserving certain family connections but also gradually severing many of them. She watches Obasan die on the bathroom floor of a motel in Fresno without calling for help, thereby assuring through guilt that her grandmother's ghost will haunt her forever. She settles in Arkansas during her early teenage years but wants "badly to leave" (133). Following high school graduation, she postpones college and takes a bus to Los Angeles, where she leads a "disorderly life" (153) in an apartment close to the freeway, taking up with a Chinese American named Andy Chan in what amounts to yet another rupture of intergenerational tradition.

Livvie Osaka remains faithful to the floating world of her immigrant forebears even as her parents settle into relatively comfortable—easily "assimilated"—lives in Arkansas. When her birth-father Jack dies in Barstow, California, she takes over his vending machine service route, wandering California, Arizona, and Nevada. Her stepfather Charlie-O accompanies her part of the way but then returns to what is now the

other world of settled existence. Kadohata allegorizes her narrator as a
protean figure who willingly embraces the American epic of mobility.
Communing with the ghost of her father at the very end of the novel, she
pays homage to the spirits of her immigrant past but also knows it is
time to leave. She alone in the novel remains a picaresque national heroine, buoyant upon the floating world that characterizes America and the
American character at mid-century.

Travel—whether it is urban wandering or transcontinental quest—
is the norm in Asian-American fiction, as protagonists cross cultures and
generations in their search for new homelands and identities commen-
surate with the frontiers they explore. The nation, the floating world,
forces a fluidity of identity, an ability or willingness to remake one's life
upon individuals who do not acculturate in any traditional sense but
must weave in and out of the hybrid cultures that increasingly signify the
postmodern nation-state. They become cultural performers—like
Wittman Ah Sing in *Tripmaster Monkey* or Raymond Ding in Shawn
Wong's second novel *American Knees* (1995)—in the contact zones of
the nation, subverting absolutist notions of what it means to be American. In Wong's comic critique of ethnic and national identity, Raymond
Ding, in the throes of a messy divorce, is told by his attorney that he
"won't even be Chinese" (11) when his estranged wife's lawyer gets
through with him. Third-generation on his father's side and second-generation on his mother's, Ding inherits the twists and turns of immigration history. His father Woodrow (named after President Wilson) was a
"rarity—born in the late twenties in New York's Chinatown, a Chinatown
that was still reeling from the effects of immigration laws, a Chinatown
of aging bachelors" (24). His mother arrived in America after the U.S.
government had repealed the Chinese Exclusion Act. With a father born
on American shores and a mother born in China, Ding is a cultural and
national hybrid—pulled by a traditional sense of what it means to be
Chinese and a more poignant sense that he is a "lapsed Chinese." Living
in the San Francisco Bay area, Ding contends with a "version of American history" stretching from memories of "the transcontinental railroad
built by Chinese workers" (23), to "a dozen different exclusionary immigration laws" (24), to the postwar era in which the Chinese, once reviled,
are now "loyal Americans." The task for Raymond Ding, at the age of 37,
is to find an inhabitable social and cultural field that might help him
resolve his fragile sense of self.

In *American Knees*, Shawn Wong plays with the notion of ethnic, racial, and national identity. In contemporary America, the sense of self is not fixed but rather involves a series of choices and "options," one of which for the protagonist is the option of not being Chinese: "Certainly it was easy enough to change your mind and decide to be some other Asian ethnicity, such as Japanese, Korean, Vietnamese, Thai, Cambodian, Malaysian, or even a different kind of Chinese, such as Taiwanese. What non-Asian would know?" (12). From the perspective of white America, all Asians look alike, and indeed the title of Wong's novel is a play on the refrain that students used to taunt the protagonist with during his childhood: "What are you—Chinese, Japanese, or American Knees?" (12). Raymond didn't like any of these options as a child, and as an adult his continuing dilemma is to create a self that is psychically and culturally whole.

By divorcing his Chinese wife, who "gets custody" of his ethnicity, and moving from Los Angeles to San Francisco, Raymond situates himself as a nomad who is in physical and psychic transit, lighting out for new territory like a contemporary Huck Finn. For Ding, the Bay Area is "the promised land for those confused about their identity" (54). Ding locates himself in a landscape that celebrates the complexities of diversity. He enters into a relationship with Aurora Crane, who is half Japanese and half Irish. As an assistant director of affirmative action at a college in Oakland, he confronts the ethnic and racial carnival that surrounds him and that Wong treats parodically. The cross-cultural characters moving in and out of Ding's life are, to differing degrees, representative parts of the new American mosaic. They collide, converse, and frequently copulate in a ritual of interaction. Wong subjects their various traditions and histories to satiric assessment, typically probing the realm of interracial sexuality and romance for fresh revelations about the character of the contemporary nation. Ethnic and racial identity, often complicated by gendered difference, both unites and separates these individuals, who travel into unexplored territory with each new interracial relationship.

The broad humor Wong applies to these shifting alignments, this mixing of national types, reads like a parodic gloss on Edward Said's *Orientalism*, a canonical text alluded to in *American Knees*. Everyone in the novel seems preoccupied with the exotic psychosexual contours of race and ethnicity. Aurora's friend, Brenda Nishitani, is a Sansei who grew up in the suburbs and has trouble with all varieties of Asian men. Brenda's aunt, who had been interned at Minidoka Relocation Center during World War II, believes in "marrying out" so that when the next roundup comes, the Japanese can pass as Hispanics or Jews. A white activist, "fresh out of Stanford with an Asian Studies degree" (94), babbles about Asian culture with his "Oriental" friends. Raymond, separating from Aurora, takes up with Betty Nguyen, a Vietnamese refugee with hidden scars from the war that fascinate him but that she wants to forget. Raymond's father plans to return to China to interview for a second wife. Wong presents a panorama of "mutual stereotypes," posing an ironic critique of the polarities within Asian and American culture: "Japanese practiced gaman and euryo, meaning no one took the last piece of chicken no matter what. . . . Fight over the bill until you tear it in half. . . . Chinese scrimped on things at home, clipped coupons at home, never bought retail . . . but they too, would fight to the death over the bill" (90–91). Such passages offering comic presentations of customs and rituals capture the unique attributes of various groups and also the intertwined roots of their behavior and their lives in America.

Raymond Ding, a traveler in the world of love, is also a voyager whose wanderlust is sated only at the end of the novel, when he settles into lyrical and relatively permanent domestic bliss with Aurora, to whom he returns. He also reunites with his father, who is recovering from an aneurysm and has given up any ideas of his own voyage to the "East." All are situated together in the "West," but Woodrow "transplants a forty-year-old *bonsai* pine from his house to theirs" (239). Here is the "equilibrium" and "tensile strength"—terms reflecting Wood's career as an engineer—undergirding the structure of this New World family. Raymond still needs a "map" to situate his life and his many loves, and to "discover a sense of place, reach home" (240). One reaches home, Wong suggests, by mixing "tradition, custom, history, superstition" (192) with the culture of the nation. One then becomes "Americanese," an almost paradisical possibility: at the end of the novel Ding and Aurora become, as the garden imagery implies, the new Adam and Eve in a multicultural American Eden.

The search for wholeness, for a coherent and authentic identity, cuts across all fictions of Asian America. In Chang-Rae Lee's *Native Speaker* (1995), for example, the Korean-American protagonist's quest for identity, family, and community involves a process of shedding multiple roles before arriving at a viable sense of self and a place in contemporary America. Lee, who was born in Seoul, South Korea, and educated at Yale University, signals at the start of the novel that his main character, Henry Park, possesses an "alien" identity: "The day my wife left, she gave me a list of who I was" (1). The list, composed by Lelia, his American wife, in free verse, is an indictment of his behavior: "illegal alien, emotional alien . . . poppa's boy . . . stranger . . . traitor, spy." Park is a "false speaker of language" (5) in his hidden and inauthentic existence, for among other things he is an industrial and corporate spy, adept at assembling, hiding, and shifting identities. Park travels the nation with false identity papers, insinuating himself into the confidence of others, uncovering mysteries, reporting revelations to his boss. He is, in keeping with the subtly ambiguous and ironic title devised by Lee, a "native speaker" of myriad talents, but confused about his own true identity or "ontological bearing" (20).

As the well-educated child of hardworking immigrant parents, Park must mediate between two cultures: one traditional, stressing such virtues as honor, love, and loyalty, and the other, late-twentieth-century American society, embracing various myths of fluidity, reinvention, and mobility. The trajectory of Park's life is fueled by these binary opposites. Park's father, who had crossed to the New World with practically nothing and who had spent a quarter of a century building up his greengrocer business, is a modern-day Gold Mountain sojourner possessing faith in the American immigrant saga: "For him, the world—and by that I must mean this very land, his chosen nation—operated on a determined set of procedures, certain rules of engagement. These were the inalienable rights of the immigrant" (42). With the early death of his mother, Henry is raised by this coarse immigrant father, who brings a Korean maid to assist him in household duties and, gradually, comfort him in his middle years. Park's father "was the kind of man who subscribed to that old-fashioned idea of nation as personal test—and, by extension, a test of family—and not only because he was an immigrant" (126). The narrator sympathizes with his father's immigrant passage into middle class America, but Henry disobeys and dishonors him in the son's failure to sustain family life or select a vocation that might reaffirm the national myth. Park is the true alien, the emotional Other, keeping to the margins of human commitments, even after his young son dies in an unfortunate accident and Lelia requires more attention that he can provide.

Park's vocation uproots and displaces him from loyalty to family and community. He willfully dislocates himself from traditional values and from home and homeland, haunting instead the netherworld of global intrigue, of false and shifting identities, of languages spoken falsely. As a displaced person, Park cannot embrace the sustaining values of either the East or the West, preferring instead to exploit his knowledge of both worlds and to refine his talent for disguised identities in order to complete his assignments. Amiable and charming, Park is "hardly seen" (16), adept at exploiting the identities of others and exposing them for profit. Only when he is given the "simple" assignment of reporting on a Korean-American politician named John Kwang, a New York City councilman, does Park discover that those "rules of engagement" that had guided his father's life cannot be persistently breached without risk, terrifying loss, and personal tragedy.

Councilman Kwang serves as the narrator's father-figure and his psychological double. Born in South Korea, Kwang has become fluent in the ways of his new nation—as much a "native speaker" as Henry Park. Like the protagonist, he is also affable and charming, charismatic, adept at becoming whatever his admirers—his transnational community in Queens—expect of him. At the same time, the narrator sees in the politician, this Korean-American luminary who moves close to the core of political power in New York City by contesting for the mayoralty, the powerful forces of loyalty and tradition that governed his deceased father's life and that link Kwang to his constituency in Flushing. The newcomers in Flushing who constitute Kwang's power base are a reflection of the changing demography of American cities in the late twentieth century. Main Street, Flushing, is the polyglot heart of the new American metropolis: "They were all kinds, these streaming and working and dealing, these various platoons of Koreans, Indians, Vietnamese, Haitians, Colombians, Nigerians, these brown and yellow whatever, whoever, countless unheard nobodies, each offering to the marketplace their gross of kimchee, lichee, plantain, black bean, soy milk, coconut milk, ginger, grouper, ahi, yellow curry, cuchifrito, jalapeno . . ." (77). These are Councilman Kwang's "people," the newer immigrants who, especially in the era after 1965, have transformed America's cities—no more so than New York. Chang-Rae Lee in *Native Speaker* skillfully traces the metamorphosis of the very idea of America as the United States absorbs transnational immigrant populations in such laboratories of the new nation as northern Queens. Some 800,000 immigrants settled in New York in the 1970s; nearly a million in the 1980s; and, following another liberalization of the immigration law in 1990, some 100,000 newcomers annually in the last decade of the twentieth century (Binder and Reimers 225–26). The 1990 census lists 512,000 Asians in New York City, an influx that has transformed Flushing from its white ethnic moorings to a polyglot community of exploding populations from south and east Asia, the Middle East, the Caribbean, and Central America. Councilman Kwang plays to this new immigrant population. He brings Park into his inner circle, his multiethnic political family. And when Park betrays him by uncovering computerized files of Kwang's contributors, precipitating the wholesale deportation of undocumented aliens, the protagonist discovers belatedly the tragic results of his betrayal of both a surrogate father and his own immigrant roots.

Kwang, his political career ruined, returns to South Korea, to a distant realm Henry Park can scarcely imagine. Park, even as he has stripped away the masks of others, experiences a metamorphosis. This transformation develops gradually, spurred by the dark tragedy framing his time in Flushing. Quitting his job and reuniting with Lelia toward the end of the novel, this solitary pilgrim learns to speak the communal language of the heart. He assists Lelia in teaching English to immigrant children. His final disguise is that of the "Speech Monster," but he takes off his mask at the end of each lesson to embrace and kiss these young immigrant children, helping them to become good citizens. No longer a lonely exile in a strange land, he can now embark on a New World journey that promises regeneration.

Jasmine's New World Metamorphosis

The promise of regeneration, of constant metamorphosis, is intrinsic to the myth of contemporary American immigration. Immigrants and the descendants of immigrants do not arrive on the North American continent as newly-minted citizens but rather as voyagers seeking remade selves and viable paths into the heartland. Often, as we have seen, these transformations and routes carry contemporary immigrant voyagers into bizarre realms. For example, in Bharati Mukherjee's *Jasmine* (1989), a novel whose global vision embraces a transnational terrain stretching from India to California, the heroine experiences multiple departures and arrivals and transformations of character and destiny. Jasmine, raised in rural Hasnapur and named Jyoti (or Light), renamed variously in America as Jasmine, Jane, or Jase, is presented by Mukherjee as the epitome of diasporic humanity. She is the late-twentieth-century goddess of "adventure, risk, transformation: the frontier" (240). A self-defined "sage" of the Punjab, set in global motion by cataclysmic events that test and deepen her understanding of those fates that are "so intertwined in the modern world" (15), Jasmine travels through a violent and grotesque universe, an exile or refugee who, on account of gender, nationality, religion, and social and economic origins, seems destined to be in constant, haphazard motion. The epigraph for Mukherjee's novel, taken from James Gleick's *Chaos*, sets the tone for Jasmine's bizarre odyssey: "The new geometry mirrors a universe that is rough, not rounded, scabrous, not smooth. It is a geometry of the pitted, pocked, and broken up, the twisted, tangled, and intertwined." In *Jasmine*, the geometry of Asian immigration, the passage from East to West, along with the parallel trope of American migration from East to West, is not a straight line but rather a maze of lines, perplexing routes, unknown destinations. For the heroine, "the promise of America" (24) is this shifting national map, a powerful topography that rewards immigrant voyagers if only they have the fortitude to navigate its twisted and scabrous routes.

Jasmine's history, cutting across cultures, nations, and continents, presents a version of the myth of mobility that is among the most complex and grotesque in the fiction of contemporary immigration. Mukherjee in the novel investigates those powerful global forces, at root economic and political, that have resulted in an unprecedented movement of peoples across national frontiers in the late twentieth century. To trace a map of the heroine's wanderings is to be reminded of the extreme forms of identity and survival that displaced persons must assume to navigate routes through contemporary global chaos. Jasmine's family, uprooted from its ancestral home in Lahore by the Partition Riots, never adjusts fully to life in the rural Punjab. At the age of fourteen, Jasmine marries an educated and enlightened man who dreams of moving to America but who is blown up by a Sikh extremist, the victim of "vengeful, catastrophic politics" (63). With forged travel documents, the heroine then enters the netherworld of "international vagabondage," moving not with any linear certainty across the Middle East, Africa, Europe, until finally she embarks on a steamer for the New World. She envisions herself as part of a vast sea of unknown and undocumented immigrants, slipping across borders, testing contact zones, searching not so much for a final destination as for the opportunity to continue their movement across frontiers: "We are the outcasts and deportees, strange pilgrims visiting outlandish shrines, landing at the end of tarmacs, ferried in old army trucks where we are roughly handled.... We ask only one thing: to be allowed to land; to pass through; to continue. ... We must sneak in, land by night in little-used strips" (101). Thus positioned, Jyoti/Jasmine imagines she is a "phantom" in time and space, a fluid traveler who, because of the clash of cultures and civilizations, must be in perpetual transit.

Jasmine's strange and circuitous voyage has the United States as its final destination, but on arrival her imagined nation turns out to be an extension of the harrowing global domain she has experienced. Prior to her arrival, Jasmine had possessed a vague sense of America: "I didn't know what to think of America. I'd read only *Shane* and seen only one movie" (81). Her limited exposure to American popular culture—one Western novel and a film, *Seven Brides for Seven Brothers*—scarcely prepares Jasmine for the raw encounter with a Promised Land as an undocumented immigrant. Landing on the Florida coast aboard a freighter captained by a monstrous figure named Half-Face, a disfigured Vietnam War veteran, Jasmine immediately perceives the praxis of dream and reality that will govern her American life. "The first thing I saw were the two cones of a nuclear plant, and smoke spreading from them in complicated but seemingly purposeful patterns, edges lit by the rising sun, like a gray, intricate map of an unexplored island continent, against the pale unscratched blue of the sky. I waded through Eden's waste: plastic bottles, floating oranges, boards, sodden boxes, white and green plastic sacks tied shut but picked open by birds and pulled apart by crabs" (107). The dream of America as Eden that fuels the immigrant quest has been transformed at the end of the nuclear century into a nautical and terrestrial garbage dump. Instead of a pastoral Paradise, this tainted or fallen world spews forth images of a satanic realm. Hurled upon this continent like so much flotsam and jetsam, confined and raped by Half-Face, himself a corollary of the disfigured landscape and perverted national myth, Jasmine immediately enters an "underworld of evil" (116). Yet the protagonist refuses to be immobilized by this initial encounter with the violent underside of the national experience. Slicing her tongue and dripping blood from her mouth like the avenging goddess Kali, she slits Half-Face's throat and sets out on her American odyssey "with the first streaks of dawn, my first full American day . . . traveling light" (121).

Jasmine's encounter with the New World and her peregrinations across the continent constitute an exemplary instance in contemporary American fiction of the myth of national mobility. Her national wandering is an ambiguous attempt to escape boundaries and constraints, yet ironically through movement to embrace "the promise of America" (240). Her odyssey is haphazard, random, filled with bizarre, inexplicable turns. Recounting her tangled travels from the deceptively stable homebase of Baden, Iowa—the American heartland writ large—the twenty-four-year-old protagonist conceives of her new nation as a continent constantly dispersing and reconstituting itself. As an undocumented immigrant who has traversed continents and who almost miraculously has become the pregnant common-law wife of a Midwestern banker, Jasmine embraces "the speed of transformation, the fluidity of American character and American landscape" (140). Her immigrant style thus is compatible with an emerging style of national culture in which leaving home is as important as finding a home in America. For Jasmine, "home" is a decidedly provisional concept: whether in Florida, New York, or Iowa, she seems to be just passing through, inventing herself as she goes, translating cultural practices from her "alien" perspective. Each of her geographic domains conveys its own truths about a nation still fashioning itself. Her backwater hideout for undocumented aliens in Florida, for example, ultimately will become Paradise Bay, "a sanctuary turned into a hotel; hell turned into paradise—to me this seems very American" (138). New York, "an archipelago of ghettoes seething with aliens" (140), her second destination, is another landscape to pass through as she invents and reinvents herself. And Iowa, her third national site, rooted in traditional values but overrun by Aryan militias, anti-tax and anti-bank apostles, and deranged farmers on the fringes of bankruptcy also fails to offer final refuge.

In each national site, with each new set of relationships, Jasmine develops fresh tactics and practices, redefining herself as a national and global citizen. White Americans see her as different, part of the "teeming millions with wide hips breeding like roaches on wide-hipped continents" (33). During her three years in Iowa, in a heavily German community, she also is perceived as "inscrutable," a term applied with shifting degrees of emphasis and meaning to Americans of Danish, Swedish, Dutch, and other un-German ethnic backgrounds. Her consort Bud Ripplemeyer courts Jasmine because she is an exotic alien. "I am darkness, mystery, inscrutability. The East plugs me into instant vitality and wisdom" (200). From a mainstream perspective, Jasmine is the generic Other: as she acknowledges, she might be Iranian, Afghani, Greek, Caribbean. She is the alien in the midst of Middle America, but as a "fighter and adapter" (40) she is caught up in the process of personal and national redefinition.

At the core of Jasmine's sense of self in a rapidly changing nation is her kinship with other Asians who have been hurled around the globe by various geopolitical eruptions. In Baden, Iowa, there is a Vietnamese network and a Hmong community. In this context, Jasmine's decision along with Bud to adopt a fourteen-year-old Vietnamese refugee, Du Thien, reaffirms a personal "center" that is Asian, not Euro-American. The young Du, who is so fixated with hoarding and repairing gadgets that Jasmine imagines he is computer-generated, survived the horrors of the Vietnam War, the butchery of family members, and survival in a sequence of camps before reaching America. Jasmine sees him, with his loner's penchant for American technology, as "hyphenated . . . a hybrid, like the fantasy appliances he wants to build" (223). Jasmine and Du are spiritual twins who have "survived every degradation known to this century. . . . Once upon a time, like me, he was someone else. We've been many selves. We've survived hideous times. I envy Bud the straight lines and smooth planes of history" (215). Du's passage westward to join a sister in Los Angeles prefigures Jasmine's own decision to leave Bud for another man whom she had met in New York and who is on his way west to reclaim her. "New York's over," he declares. "We're heading West" (239).

In *Jasmine*, which despite its horrors and disruptions retains a spirited buoyancy, Bharati Mukherjee posits a new American type rooted in the cosmic rhythms of the Indian subcontinent and also in the rhythms of adventure and mobility so central to the mythology of the North American continent. This dual immigrant personality is not hyphenated in the conventional sense or bifurcated in the mode proposed by W.E.B. Du Bois. Instead, this new unitary personality derives strength from both mythologies, reinventing itself in order to contend with new circumstances. America today, as Jasmine understands, is a tangled and intertwined landscape. She shuttles between identities that are interconnected, treating every second and incident of her existence in her New World "as a possible assignment from God" (61). As such, she is divinely inspired, interacting wondrously with a changing society (interfacing with it as Du might say) in an odyssey that defies all constraints and boundaries.

Vietnamese Exiles

The presence of Du Thien in Mukherjee's novel, although his searing experience as a Vietnamese refugee is not fully particularized, confronts readers nevertheless with yet another global fissure and diasporic movement that typifies the contemporary geopolitical condition. When Saigon fell to North Vietnamese troops and Vietcong forces on April 30, 1975, a new mythology of departure and arrival was immediately superimposed on the American experience as hundreds of thousands of South Vietnamese (529,706 by 1987 according to *Refugee Reports*), many of them boat people, ventured through hazardous seas and perilous way stations to reach the United States. The terrors Du Thien survived during the exodus prepare him for any contingency in his new land, where he claims a new identity and struggles, as his departure for California suggests, for the sort of autonomy fostered by a mobile, rapidly transforming society. Du, the fix-it genius, is the reincarnation of Franklin and Edison, perhaps a future Bill Gates. He is undaunted by the minor problems of American life. Yet for other Vietnamese, whose exodus continues to this day, often the third or fourth largest annual total of immigrants from any country (41,752, for example, in 1995), the fresh, luminous Promised Land hides its own demons and ghosts.

The demonic world of the Vietnam War (or the American War as the Vietnamese term it) hovers over Lan Cao's *Monkey Bridge* (1997), a novel that weaves back and forth, like a narrow bridge made of bamboo and vines that serves as the novel's controlling metaphor, over the perilous landscapes of Asia and the United States. Cao, who was born in Vietnam, left the country in 1975, and is now a professor of international law at Brooklyn Law School, reconstructs through almost kinesthetic memory the landscapes of war-torn Saigon and the Mekong Delta, and the new American setting that absorbs a mother and daughter who enter the Little Saigon of Falls Church, Virginia, during the first year of the exodus. Cao pinpoints the moment of this exodus: "There was the South China Sea on April 30, 1975. There was the exodus by air, with the Seventh Fleet and the aircraft carriers *Enterprise* and *Coral Sea* providing air support and cover. The was the exodus by sea, a lurching protuberance of South Vietnamese Navy vessels, barges, tugboats, junks, sampans, fishing boats, and other makeshift vessels, all heading away from the coast of Vietnam, toward the Philippines, then, it was hoped, to Guam" (165). For the narrator, Mai Nguyen, who escapes Saigon in February of 1975 at the age of fourteen with the assistance of an American colonel who had become a friend of her family, traditional Vietnamese culture contends with her place as a rapidly assimilating young refugee in the United States. As Cao suggests in her novel's extended metaphor, Mai is on a monkey bridge that takes her across jumbled and dangerous national terrains. Her challenge is to get from one side of that bridge to the other, carrying with her a previous history while contending with the promise of her new world.

Told from the perspective of a daughter who views her mother sympathetically but with a measure of trepidation because of the family secrets Mrs. Nguyen carries with her and that are revealed in a series of diary entries Mai uncovers in the course of the novel, *Monkey Bridge* traces the nightmare of contemporary Vietnamese immigration. The imagery of blood and of "ghosts, bones, and funerals" (1) permeating the novel, combined with the motif of wounded memories and tortured dreams, conveys Mai's sense of diasporic dislocation as she deals with her mother's agitated existence in America. Whereas Mrs. Nguyen suffers from what she perceives as bad Karma, Mai rebels slowly against this sense of unalterable fate or powerlessness. Steeped in the Vietnamese immigrant community's customs and traditions, she manages during a four-year period stretching from 1975 to 1979 to remain obedient while carving out a separate American identity. Mai's mother is overwhelmed by a sense of immigrant impermanence. She declares: "They'd jump at the chance to send us all back. Nomads, that's what we've all become" (15). By contrast, with her green card, Mai tries to take comfort in her status as resident alien, her emergence as an honors student bound for Mount Holyoke College, and the protective mantel provided by Colonel MacMahon and his wife—her "umbilical cord"(99) to the American experience. Whereas her mother, despite frenetic attempts to embrace the spirit of American capitalism in Little Saigon, succumbs to the burden of her Vietnamese past and finally commits suicide, Mai learns the "new terminologies" of the United States, moving away from the refugee margins toward the national center, acknowledging that "the American Dream was exerting a sly but seductive pull" (37). Mai can imagine an American future.

Political winds blowing from ancient times to the present, embracing the French and American defeats in Indochina, have tossed the Nguyen family "here" and "there": from harsh farm life in the Mekong Delta; to strategic hamlets; to Saigon; to America and northern Virginia's Little Saigon, a "world in and of itself, a world that census takers had documented, one hundred thousand strong and growing" (203). A people not adept at "crossing boundaries" (29) must traverse international borders, pushed out of their country by wartime and postwar events. They become wandering spirits, altered by the changing course of history and disoriented by "a shifting world." Those who survive learn how to "sustain a new identity . . . relocate one's roots and bend one's body in a new direction" (39). Others, like Mai's mother, live life in reverse, becoming dependent on the adaptability of their children and the support systems provided by the Little Saigons that sustain life on the margins of their refugee nation. They try to "hang onto their Vietnam lives" like amputees still feeling their missing limbs, but they have been "exiled into a space that could not be reached" (255). The most enterprising and flexible exiles in Cao's immigrant community are those who contrive "a truly uncluttered beginning, the complete absence of identity, of history" (41) by burning identification papers, reinventing lives, changing birth dates. However, Mrs. Nguyen cannot forget the historical and political dissonance of her previous existence or her rootedness in Vietnamese traditions. She prefers Karma, with its basis in moral duty and obligations to destiny. Recovering painfully from a stroke at the beginning of *Monkey Bridge* and committing suicide at the end of the novel, Mrs. Nguyen is not seduced by the American dream. In her series of extended written remembrances to her daughter, she lays out their twisted inheritance, their historical burden, and Mai's "American future" that awaits her teenage daughter with a mother's final blessing.

Typical American

The heroines in Cao's novel and in Mukherjee's *Jasmine* accept the contradictions of contemporary American life, refashioning the myth of mobility by constantly seeking new settings and new opportunities. Such protagonists form a galaxy of immigrant types in Asian-American fiction. For example, the characters in Gish Jen's seriocomic novel *Typical American* (1991), alluded to in the opening chapter, struggle with these contradictions and are almost overwhelmed by them. Labeled "an American story" on the first page, *Typical American* commences in 1947, in the aftermath of what Jen terms the Anti-Japanese War, with a young man, Yifeng Chang, soon to be Ralph Chang, coming to America to study advanced engineering. Chang dreams of the "splendor" and "radiance" of the Golden Gate Bridge as he sails from Shanghai to San Francisco, but in a trope we have already seen in other novels, he arrives in San Francisco Bay on a day when fog covers the bridge—the first sign of the paradoxical nature of the Golden Land he will encounter. Chang then sets out across the New World for New York City: "Famous mountains lumbered by, famous rivers, plains, canyons, the whole holy American spectacle" (7), but Chang rarely gazes upon his new Promised Land. He awakens to the national pulse only in New York, which with his scientific bent he envisions as an intricate American machine, almost mythopoeic in its mechanical grandeur, the antithesis of his rural Chinese upbringing. In New York, Yifeng becomes Ralph, a name given to him by a secretary at Columbia University where he studies for his advanced degree. In the city and surrounding suburbs, Ralph enacts a quirky quest to become a typical American. His quest, to employ an extended trope introduced by Gish Jen, is a roller-coaster ride, characterized by loops, death-defying rises and falls, and potential derailments. For Gish Jen (much like Mukherjee), mobility and identity formation for the Asian-American immigrant are not linear processes but instead convoluted, haphazard, transient.

Typical American is composed in a series of seriocomic acts, divided into five parts, with each part constructed of several inherently absurdist scenes. Each part and scene has a title that establishes ironic juxtapositions within the narrative wherein Chang appears "typically" as a bewildered, gullible, frequently disoriented buffoon confronting the ambiguities of America. Often deceived by others but also self-deluded, he nevertheless manages to reunite with a sister, marry, have children, obtain his doctorate, become a professor, migrate from the city to the suburbs, move from "no status" as a refugee from the Communist takeover of China to American citizen, and dabble in unrestrained American capitalism as the owner of a fried chicken palace. This newly minted

American, a parody of the myth of immigrant success and mobility, but also a curious affirmation of the myth, accepts the powerful and unpredictable undercurrents of life in the United States. "He lay waiting to see what happened. Anything could happen, this was America. He gave himself to the country, and dreamt" (42). Mixing Chinese philosophy and folklore with the positive thinking of Norman Vincent Peale, whose wisdom he memorizes, Ralph uncritically embraces the promise of American life. Even when he is tricked and cuckolded by a demonic double, Grover Ding, ruined in his fried chicken fiasco, and in danger of losing his family to a bizarre series of catastrophes, Ralph finds ways to rebound. Fascinated by American cars and the American penchant for speed, he keeps moving. At the intersection of hope and despair, he learns that "this New World . . . this . . . continent . . . a paradise . . . the great blue American sky" (158–59) also has limits. To lose oneself in "spread-out America, this loose-knit country, where one could do as one pleased" (178), is to forget one's knowledge of good and evil. To drive with a car's convertible top down in a driving rain, as Ralph does in one scene, is to risk more than a passing cold.

Ralph Chang's hubris is to believe uncritically that his "fortune was to live in the other America, the legendary America that was every wish come true" (236). He zooms along the road of American mobility and success, scarcely aware of what Fredric Jameson terms the "embattled situation" of all Third World protagonists caught up in national allegories. Only through a series of near-disasters does Ralph near the end of the novel rediscover his cultural origins and correctly perceive the myth of the nation. He accepts his destiny (as will his children in Jen's comic sequel, *Mona in the Promised Land*, 1996), concluding, "a man was as doomed here as he was in China. *Kan bu jian. Ting bu jian.* He could not always see, could not always hear. He was not what he made up his mind to be. A man was the sum of his limits; freedom only made him see how much so. America was no America" (296). Ralph had listened to the siren sounds of America but had not heard the rhythms of its darker, potentially tragic heart. The Chinese phrases represent the "old culture talking" (4) that Ralph's mother had attempted to instill in him when he was a child. Yet this "bleak understanding" is tempered or balanced (another Chinese virtue) by the lingering national promise. Opposites begin in one another, as Ralph's father had stated long ago. By the end of the novel, in a scene redolent of suburban summer pleasures, Chang seems prepared for a synthesis of Chinese and American values, an authentic reconstruction of his national identity.

The numerous frontiers of Asian-American fiction reveal a common concern with historical and national identity framed by the boundaries of East and West. Immigrants and their descendants cope with the weeping ghosts of their past (as Maxine Hong Kingston terms it in *The Woman Warrior*) and the equally demanding demons of the New World. These competing ancestral and contemporary forces prompt protagonists to manage antipodal elements through transformative practices. Typically, like Ralph or Jasmine or Livvie, they plunge into the maelstrom of modern experience, testing the boundaries of ethnic and national culture and reinventing themselves in a world that encourages—indeed requires—the adjustment of self to a rapidly evolving, polyglot, transnational nation. Their odysseys across boundaries, often involving bizarre and grotesque action, are metaphors for this inherently dynamic contemporary condition. The Asian-American encounter with the Gold Mountain dramatizes the continuing search for America that is at the heart of the immigrant experience.

7

Searching for America

The small crowded boat plows northward through choppy,
slate-blue sea, toward America. . . .
—Russell Banks, *Continental Drift*

"This is an American story of the late twentieth century," writes Russell
Banks in the invocation to *Continental Drift*, a brilliant canonical novel
pitting migrants against immigrants within the complex, unfinished narrative of the nation. At the end of the century, as Banks and the numerous writers treated in this study assert, a new nation is being called into
existence, even as Banks would call into being the Haitian *vaudou loas* to
help him "mouth" his tale. The old Muses, Eurocentric and Homeric, are
still with us, but they can no longer capture fully this new national condition, this emerging multicultural America that is more mosaic than
melting pot. Instead, as older white ethnic Americans, once again on the
move across the national landscape, compete with newer immigrants for
enhanced cultural space, multiple myths of old and new lands must be
reconstituted in order to capture and explain global realities and a nation's
heritage as it attains a new millennium.

Animated by multiple myths spanning ages, continents, and cultures, all humankind in *Continental Drift* is in motion at the end of the
century. Within the dichotomous scheme of the novel, where chapters
elucidating the search of a white American male of French-Canadian
descent for a new life in Florida alternate with chapters tracing the tortured Middle Passage of a Haitian woman across the Caribbean to the
same Florida shores, a fierce postmodern anarchy seems unleashed around

the world. This anarchy of movement is geological in its deepest terrestrial underpinnings; political as teeming millions are displaced across nations and continents by wars, famines, and natural disasters; and ultimately epistemological as the psychic and spiritual nomads try to locate stability in an inherently unstable universe. With so much movement threatening the very foundations of the globe, the totalizing power of any myth or system of belief is suspect. Yet immigrants and their migrant counterparts embrace with irrational, almost mystical fervor the myth of a Promised Land, a new Golden Shore that awaits them if only they can keep moving toward it. The immigrant-migrant cosmology, as Banks posits in his novel, which parodies and critiques but ultimately validates numerous national myths, is sacred; and immigration itself is, to invoke one of his chapter titles, an *action de grâce*. The world's dispossessed might be "pushed" out of their familiar surroundings by countless forces but they are "pulled" toward their imagined Eden in America by faith. If, ironically, they are violated like Vanise or even killed like Bob Dubois in their quest for Paradise, their fates merely remind us that postmodern destinies are as old as ancient memory. Sex and death, prevalent in *Continental Drift*, are not new: they are the twin constituents in the myth of the Garden of Eden. Thus immigration and migration at the end of the century, framed by new routes and old myths, constitute a powerful ideology, a universal movement of peoples that mirrors the fate of nations and the collective fate of the planet.

Peoples on the Move

The ideological and geopolitical sweep of *Continental Drift* makes Banks's novel, as suggested in the introductory chapter, the paradigmatic presentation of late-twentieth-century immigration, and a text that achieves a confluence of the major themes that have guided this study. Unlike most contemporary writers who permit their narratives of immigration to reveal meanings, Banks in *Continental Drift* actually theorizes and philosophizes about the subject, offering a parodic postmodern turn on traditional modes of fiction. Exploding celebrated modernist aesthetic conventions that postulate the imitative power of narrative art, Banks resurrects the eighteenth-century omniscient narrator to editorialize and speculate about national and global manifestations of migratory movement. Yet he makes this intrusive narrative gambit, rejected by mimetic modernist aesthetics, fresh and original by invoking the *loas,* the voodoo deities, to animate and give power to his incantatory tale. To tell the complex, contradictory, intersectory, and paradoxical story of immigration in the late twentieth century requires the intercession of an author who, like his heroine Vanise Dorsinville, presents himself as a *serviteur*, the divinely inspired mouthpiece for peoples on the move. Having spent time in the mid-1960s in the backcountry of Jamaica with the Maroons, the descendants of escaped slaves who preserve the vestiges of West African culture (a motif that both Michelle Cliff in *No Telephone to Heaven* and Banks in his earlier novel *The Book of Jamaica* interrogate), Banks appropriates a "mouth-man" or type of village griot to help him with his narrative. As the author acknowledged in a 1987 interview with Trish Reeves, this attempt to explain events through a speaker drawn from West African and African-Caribbean culture is no more or less artifice than the other conventions of fiction, but an original form of "intrusive" narrative nevertheless (45–59). Throughout the novel, Banks, possessed by Legba, the *loa* who is the protector of children and guardian of the crossroads, a deity who sees backward and forward in time, intercedes to shape, guide, and illuminate action and meaning, even to comment on future events. Above all, as a writer conscious of history, Banks wants to explain to readers that they are entering a historical realm: they are encountering a form of narrative that Linda Hutcheon, alluded to earlier, defines as historiographic metafiction, a postmodern, problematizing amalgam of fiction and history that attempts to reveal the current human condition.

When Banks steps outside and above his narrative, his intent is to convey an epic historical dimension to the fictive enterprise. Alluding in his interview with Reeves to two American novelists with whom he feels kinship—E.L. Doctorow and Robert Stone—Banks celebrates the metafiction they produce: "It's fiction with a sense of history—and a willingness to fight their way through a maze of histories. . . . A vision of the history of our country is crucial to our understanding of ourselves. This kind of obligation is Homeric. That's what writers have always done: told us who we were, where we came from, where the ends of our lands were" (49). An attempt to understand history, both national and global, is the basis of the narrator's discourse to the reader in *Continental Drift*. Banks ponders catastrophe and cataclysmic change through the lens of continental upheavals. Migration, disruption, displacement, exodus: these are the mediating agents of the physical and human universe Banks creates in his global canvas. Indeed the migration of humans is as fundamental and inevitable as the movement of the earth, as Banks observes in an early chapter, "Battérie Maconnique":

> It's as if the poor forked creatures who walk, sail, and ride on donkeys and camels, in trucks, buses and trains from one spot on this earth to another were all responding to unseen, natural forces, as if it were gravity and not war, famine or flood that made them move in trickles from hillside villages to gather along the broad, muddy riverbanks lower down and wait for passage on rafts down the river to the sea and over the sea on leaky boats to where they collect in eddies, regather their lost families and few possessions, set down homes, raise children and become fruitful once again. (34)

This extraordinary extended paragraph, Faulknerian in its stylistic rhythms, presents Banks's vision of contemporary global history. The troubled, violent years of the late twentieth century are startling in themselves but primitive, primeval, almost biblical in their ageless origins, with allusions to floods and famines that reach backward in time to the oldest myths. At the same time, the "creatures" who clamor for the right to exist are a subplot in the cosmic drama of birth, death, and rebirth. Banks in the "Battérie Maconnique" chapter asks readers to come to terms with mythic, scientific, and political realities in "these years, the early 1980's," during which "most events and processes that have been occurring for millennia continue to occur, some of them silently, slowly, taking place an inch at a time miles below the surface of the earth, others noisily, with smoke and fire, revolution, war and invasion, taking place on the surface" (36). The conscious and unconscious forces of the age create a clash of global relationships embracing peoples, races, classes, ethnic groups. Somalis, Cubans, Russians, Iranians, Thais, Israelis, Grenadians, Indians, Pakistanis, Chinese, the peoples of the Caribbean whom Banks catalogs: all are caught in an unstable, eruptive drift whose geological consequences embrace continents and seas, moving inevitably and "eventually to America" (37).

Signaling to his readers that his novel will subvert the strict conventions of realistic and naturalistic fiction, Banks invites readers to become part of this universal flow of humanity toward America—a collective "us" or "we" who, as part of a volatile, constantly changing process provides "the only argument against entropy" (39). The people, families, tribes, entire nations converging on America's shores become a moral and planetary imperative: "To continue, just to go on, with entropy lurking out there, takes an old-fashioned, Biblical kind of heroism" (39). Thus Banks's migratory drama, as implacable as cosmic destiny, makes possible a provisional "Heroic Age" in which the allegory of movement, the dream of arrival in an imagined Eden or simply in a better place, is the one metanarrative that might fashion forms of resistance to the forces of decline, entropy, and extinction. "Go on through the darkness," writes Wallace Stevens in a line from "Farewell to Florida" that Banks presents as one of two epigraphs for his novel (counterpointing a second epigraph, a musical refrain from Northrup's *Twelve Years a Slave*). In movement, Banks suggests, there is the possibility of transformation, the promise of release from servitude, and the opportunity to be free.

Continental Drift unfolds as a contemporary history of migration and immigration, set specifically in a period from December of 1979 to February of 1981 when the "sad story of Robert Raymond Dubois . . . a good American man" (1) is juxtaposed against and ultimately converges with the harrowing story of Vanise Dorsinville, a Haitian boat person drifting erratically toward Florida. It is significant that Banks establishes the historicity of his novel at the precise time when Florida's shores were receiving armadas of boat people from Cuba and Haiti. The Mariel boat lift, which as we have seen serves as the historical backdrop for a significant body of Latino fiction, constitutes one half of this particular Caribbean odyssey. Banks takes up the other part in *Continental Drift*, centering half of the novel on Vanise's nightmarish 600–mile passage, along with her infant son and her nephew Claude, from an area on the northwest coast of Haiti to North Caicos Island; thence in a second harrowing segment to the Bahamas; and finally in a cataclysmic series of events to Florida as the sole survivor of a boatload of Haitians captained by "Destiny's Darling," one Bob Raymond Dubois. As a representation of contemporary historical realities, Vanise serves to remind readers of a specific moment in the saga of American immigration that for Banks assumes allegorical, mythic, and metahistorical significance. Banks finds traces of the past in the compressed contemporary period that frames his novel, locating in one boatload of Haitian refugees a complex metaphor signifying the dual epics of New World discovery and the Middle Passage. Capturing recent events, *Continental Drift* presents the influx of Haitian refugees in the 1970's and 1980's as an ideological phenomenon, one that problematizes both immigration history and notions of the American nation. The Haitian boat people who made their way to Florida during this period, many in rickety vessels that cost numerous lives, entered the American nation as pariahs, as black refugees who experienced some of the worst forms of recent discrimination by politicians, immigration officials, and society at large.

It is evident that the world of the Haitian boat people, those who managed to survive the contemporary Middle Passage, was circumscribed by patterns of official discrimination that set them apart from the Cuban refugees of the same period. In the spring of 1980, coterminous with the "fictive" events in *Continental Drift*, numerous boatloads of Cubans and Haitians were arriving in the same Florida ports. The United States, under the United Nations Protocol relating the status of refugees that had been ratified by the Senate in 1968, granted refugee status to Cubans fleeing the Castro regime but withheld it from black Haitian refugees escaping the conditions spawned by the Duvalier regime. A refugee, according to U.S. immigration policy, is any person who has fled a country "because of persecution on account of race, religion, or political opinion." Such individuals entering the country without proper immigration papers whom the INS determines are refugees normally are granted temporary asylum or legal residency. Yet Haitian boat people, who have numbered more than 200,000 souls since the first major wave traveled across the Windward Passage to the shores of south Florida in the late 1970's and spring of 1980, have been the nation's least welcomed immigrants. Some were granted amnesty under the Immigration Reform and Control Act of 1986, but many others, those who did not escape to Miami's Little Haiti or into Florida's rural enclaves, were jailed for illegal entry and deported. In a 1980 case brought by the Haitian Refugee Center against the INS, Judge James Lawrence King in his Final Order Granting Relief found a pervasive pattern of racism and discrimination in the way immigration officials and judges were denying refugee status to Haitian nationals. Noting the disparity between the treatment of Cubans, who were routinely granted asylum, and more than four thousand Haitians who were denied asylum, Judge King ascribed this discriminatory practice to the fact that the Haitians were "part of the first substantial flights of black refugees from a repressive regime to this country." Characterizing INS policy as "shocking," "brutal," and "callous," King declared: "The manner in which INS treated the more than 4,000 Haitian plaintiffs violated the Constitution, the immigration statutes, international agreements, INS regulations and INS operating procedures. It must stop" (Laquerre 176). The plight of the Haitian boat people, distilled and symbolized in the figure of Vanise and her small band of compatriots, presents certain inescapable truths about the history of the American nation and the arbitrary power of its institutions to offer or deny hope for people representing a new immigrant generation.

New World Voyagers

Banks's genius in *Continental Drift* is to situate the fictive action in a concrete historical time of migration and immigration and monumental change in the American nation. His heroine and hero engage with history although they might not apprehend their encounter in national historical terms. As exilic figures estranged from their homes and homelands respectively, Bob and Vanise must improvise their lives and seek destinations in the same wondrous and contingent ways characterizing the original voyagers to the New World Banks puts forward as part of his historiographic method. Vanise, leaving the "familiar dark green hills" of Haiti in search of America, an abstract point on her imaginary compass, thinks of a New World "rising from the sea." Her dream merges with those of the first explorers and adventurers whose own maps of the unknown world were as indistinct as hers but who were driven across oceans and seas by fantasies of a Golden Land:

> For centuries, men and women have sailed this passage north of Hispaniola waiting for the sight of one idea or another rising all aglitter with tangible substance from the turquoise sea. Columbus approaches from the east in search of Cathay, and Ponce de Leon cruises north from Puerto Rico looking for the fabled Bimini, and now comes Vanise, huddled by the low rail in the bow of a small wooden fishing boat out of Haiti, scouring the horizon for a glimpse of America. None of them is lost. All three know they'll recognize the substance of their

idea as soon as they see it, Columbus his Cathay, Ponce his
Bimini, Vanise her Florida. (107)

With subtle use of the present tense here and throughout the novel, Banks
unites Vanise, a New World woman of African descent, with the Old World
explorers whose dreams foundered on the reefs and land masses of their
imagined geography but whose visions of Paradise were never extinguished entirely. In this chapter, "À Table, Dabord, Olande, Adonai" (to
the east, to the west, in the north, in the south), Vanise enters a warp in
time and space. Her "map" of the world is "a living, coiling and uncoiling
thing" (114) adjusting constantly to the unknown and provisionally
known. At their present historical moment, Vanise discovers, as had Columbus and Ponce de Leon, that she has not yet reached her imagined
Eden, America, but has been tossed up instead on North Caicos Island, a
discontinuity in her dream she must endure for several months in de-
grading physical and sexual circumstances before escaping and embarking on the second perilous stage of her journey. Hoping to join her brother
in Miami, animated by the same winds that breathed hope into the sails
of the original New World explorers, Vanise is a contemporary emana-
tion of the project of immigration that continues to uncoil and unfold
into the American future—that "age that lies before us" as Hegel proph-
esied in *The Philosophy of History*, where "the burden of the world's history will reveal itself" (86).

Banks problematizes the world's history in Hegelian terms, with
the binary frame of *Continental Drift* suggesting a historically conditioned dialectic of oppositional forces struggling for reconciliation or
synthesis. To apply a familiar Hegelian term, Banks seeks to "mediate"
between two individuals whose identities—in terms of race, language,
gender, class, culture and more—seem to exist in utterly different realms
of experience. If we were to diagram the oppositional identities and binary worlds of Vanise Dorsinville and Bob Dubois, the resulting scheme
would reveal a radical discontinuity that ostensibly erodes all totalizing impulses. Vanise is Haitian, black, female, sexually exploited, French
Creole-speaking, poor, uneducated, illiterate, a practitioner of voodoo.
In contrast, Bob is American, white, male, sexually exploitative, English-speaking, working class, educated, literate, a lapsed Catholic. Contained within Banks's mutually exclusive dual narrative format, the sagas
of Vanise and Bob apparently do not share the same public, national,

or historical space. They possess "different" histories or narratives, one ostensibly peripheral and the other central to traditional American experience. Yet Vanise and Bob are alike in that both are on the move, immigrant and migrant, their destinies slowly converging in this era of late-twentieth-century commodity capitalism. In their own ways they are diasporic protagonists, as are all Americans and their hemispheric counterparts who experience the vagaries of exile, enslavement, displacement, emigration, and resettlement. Banks instructs readers to recognize the reciprocal and paradoxical interactions common to his two protagonists' distinct quests for America. Both are part of the same historical process. Both are subjected to various structures of domination rooted in racism, sexism, class struggle, and economic and political subjugation. Both persist in their search for the Golden Shore.

The aspirations of Bob Dubois, third-generation descendant of French-Canadian immigrants to New Hampshire's mill towns, are cast by Banks as part of a larger demographic movement of the citizens of the Northeast seeking a new life in the nation's Sun Belt. Bob's historical crisis might not seem as acute as the one embodied in Vanise, but he nevertheless is the vivid bearer of working-class angst in the era of late capitalism. His radical and violent rebellion against a dead-end existence as an oil burner repairman in Catamount, New Hampshire, one snowy evening near Christmas hurls Bob and his family into a migratory world of social, economic, and spiritual decline. Separating himself with wild abandon from the logic of his working-class life, Bob "feels he's riding a horse-drawn wagon somewhere in Siberia, as if he were being carted late at night from one prison to another." Imagining himself in a frozen Gulag of the soul, Bob merges with the millions of diasporic peoples in the twentieth century who are lost in the depths of the nation, kept "in transit from one cold, isolated place to another" (20). Rejecting the fates of his father and grandfather, "dumb Frenchmen" who had yoked themselves to mill lathes all their lives, Bob Dubois sells virtually all material possessions and leaves, as had his brother Eddie and best friend Avery Boone, for Florida. Like Vanise, he abandons the known world for a realm of uncertain promise, joining those "creatures residing on this planet" who, constantly moving, seek better conditions elsewhere. With Vanise he enters a category of humankind distinguished by its struggle to reject one moment in history—for Vanise the totalitarian realm spawned by the Duvaliers and for Bob the epochal decline of industrial New England—and invent another world, another history for himself.

With contempt for his ancestry, his origins, his place in the Republic, Bob Dubois as late twentieth-century migrant re-enacts the archetypal movement that typifies the American experience. No longer traveling west as had the earlier settlers, he moves frantically south and, as he continues to shed possessions and decline economically, away from the center and toward the margins. His migratory situation becomes a mirror image of the immigrant odyssey, for the history of American immigration, as Oscar Handlin observed in *The Uprooted*, is the history of "alienation and its consequences" (4). Banks, himself a product of a New England working-class environment, is quite adept in positioning Bob Dubois in imitative relationship to Vanise's diasporic journey. Bob both contemporarizes and parodies R.W.B. Lewis's classic American Adam, for as this common man, essentially innocent of changing national life, travels south, he leaves the white world of his wintry New England for more profoundly variegated terrain. As the contemporary avatar or allegorical representation of the old European settlement of the Americas, and through patrimony the reminder of France's expansionist reach not only into the Caribbean but also into Canada and what would become the United States, Dubois runs into a new national history as he discovers those territories to the tropical south populated increasingly by darker, hyphenated Others, new *habitants* from less-developed worlds. In the dialectic Banks establishes in *Continental Drift*, his protagonist becomes enmeshed in the immigrant revolution that is reshaping America. Progressively dispossessed, he also assumes a type of postcolonial migrant status. As an alienated migrant, Bob merges with what Fredric Jameson (1979) terms "the collective experience of marginal pockets of the social life of the world system" (40). His new frontier in Florida turns out to be the reverse of what he had imagined—a simulacrum of his brother Eddie's garish existence. Frustrated in his attempts to secure the fruits of mass culture, a discouraged consumer, Bob emerges slowly from a closed American understanding of race to a more informed perception of the nation as whole continents of memory wash over him.

Instead of discovering new frontiers of capitalism in Florida, Bob Dubois and his wife Elaine encounter new frontiers of cultural production. Bob's "road map" into the new American experience is framed by a distressing "glut of McDonalds and Burger Kings, Kentucky Fried Chickens and Pizza Huts" (53) which, along with car lots, strip malls, and trailer parks, constitute the nondescript central Florida towns they pass through and that reveal the desiccation of high-commodity culture. Scarcely cognizant of black Americans or other minority groups when he resided in New Hampshire during the first thirty years of his life, Bob discovers a world of color in Florida. In his ignorance about race, Bob provokes the same problem concerning historical knowledge that governs Doctorow's *Ragtime*, a novel that begins with the author's ironic observation that in the year 1902, "there were no Negroes. There were no immigrants" (4). Populating Bob's new American map are peoples who had been abstractions to him in Catamount but who now dominate the Florida landscape: "These black- and brown-skinned people, the American blacks in the department stores and supermarkets, the Jamaicans and Haitians in the fields, the Cubans in the filling stations—these working people, who got here first, belong here, not Bob and Elaine Dubois and their daughters Ruthie and Emma. It's Bob and his family who are the newcomers at the Florida trough, and Bob is embarrassed by his lateness" (55). Until the late 1970's, Bob had lived in a cocoon of historical amnesia. In Florida, he awakens to discover he too is different, separated impossibly from a confident American future. He misreads the map, stumbles upon new routes, and ultimately enters a sphere of existence where the burdens of gender, ethnicity, and race determine his tragic destiny.

The destiny of Bob Dubois is to drift away from white America, away from a life fueled by outlandish dreams of material success embodied in the banal figure of Bob's foul-mouthed, felonious brother, "Fast Eddie." Bob's brother, superficially successful in his all-American wheeling and dealing, is a grotesque monument to capitalism run wild. Installed by Banks as a mock petit-bourgeois crook, the stereotype of white American greed, sexism, and racism, Eddie fears the nation's new historical condition: "We got niggers with guns and razors here. . . . We got Cubans who cut your balls off, we got Haitians with their fucking voodoo sacrifices and Jamaicans with machetes as long as your fucking arm. . . . We got Colombians, for Christ's sake, with fucking *machine guns!*" (58–59). In his comic and histrionic ravings about the altered state of the nation, Eddie is a parody of white cultural supremacy, a pathetic, ultimately doomed figure trapped in a field of new historical forces that overwhelm him.

Whereas Eddie has an exaggerated fear of "dark-skinned crazies of all types" (58), Bob is drawn toward the other America whose peoples represent cultural and historical formations that are changing the nation in the last quarter of the American Century. Managing one of Eddie's liquor stores, Bob learns the "languages" of his black, Cuban, and Haitian customers. Whereas his destiny had been circumscribed by exclusively white cultural formations in Catamount, New Hampshire, he now perceives, since arriving in Florida, that he must grasp the "big system" (68) of multicultural America if he is to succeed. His destiny, although he does not apprehend it fully, merges with the black Atlantic, away from the center and toward the ethnic and racial margins. His liaison with Marguerite Dill, the daughter of the store's black janitor, carries him across the Great American Divide of race into new territory he must negotiate. For Bob, sex with Marguerite is like washing up on the tropical shores of the New World. This conceit, while undercut by inequalities in their relationship, nevertheless positions Bob Dubois as an explorer, like Columbus, on the fringes of the new American experience. His slow discoveries about basic human nature, his attempt to decipher the hieroglyphics of race, gender, and class, inscribe Bob Dubois as a paradoxical but persistent voyager in a rapidly changing civilization. As the omniscient author observes: "Men and women seek the love of the other so that the old, cracked and smoky self can be left behind, like a sloughed-off snakeskin, and a new self brought forward, clean, shining, glistening wetly with promise and talents the old self never owned" (132). That Bob fails to shed his old skin, ending his relationship with Marguerite after the birth of his son, suggests that he must travel farther south from Oleander Park, all the way to the Florida Keys, deeper into the tropics of race before meeting his American destiny.

Bob Dubois's fate and ultimate redemption are entwined with that of Vanise Dorsinville. As Bob descends toward the Keys, invited there by his childhood friend Avery Boone to buy a share in a fishing excursion boat that Ave in actuality has overleveraged to a bank, Vanise in her jarring odyssey across the Caribbean also searches for an acceptable national fiction. At each stage in her journey, there are echoes of the Middle Passage and of the history of slavery and colonialism in the Caribbean. Vanise traverses liminal spaces between Anglophonic and Francophonic islands; survives multiple instances of imprisonment, servitude, and rape; apprehends the characteristic unpredictability of her new universe. Each stage in her journey is an unresolved beginning and ending, disorienting and potentially destructive, but pointing resolutely toward her imagined Golden Shore. Moving from one island to the next, "surrounded in darkness as if buried" (178) in the hold of one ship bound for the Bahamas, Vanise in her *grand chemin* becomes the contemporary symbol of the millions of souls condemned by the history of slavery in the New World: "They had come over three hundred miles as if chained in darkness, a middle passage . . ." (188). A castaway, subjugated and violated by virtue of her race and sex, Vanise places her destiny in the hands of *les Invisibles* and *les Morts,* the potent force of *vaudou* that "connects her sad, suffering moment on earth to universal time, ties the stingy ground she stands on to the huge, fecund continent of Africa, makes an impoverished, illiterate black woman's troubles the pressing concerns of the gods" (209). The bearer of powerful transcontinental histories and unique spiritual forces, Vanise articulates a system of belief that enables her to survive the multiple horrors of her Middle Passage. As Banks acknowledges, Vanise survives because she has "a connection to the spiritual world" (Reeves 46).

Sailing north as Bob Dubois travels south, Vanise places her destiny in the hands of the voodoo gods: Agwe, Legba, Baron Cimitiere. Her embrace of voodoo links Vanise to a realm of culture and myth that is African in origin but encapsulates the imperial history of the Caribbean. According to Patrick Taylor, "A form of mythical narrative, vaudou always remained bound to the drama of colonialism and its neocolonial aftermath" (96). It is "the classic example of the mythic encoding of experience in the Caribbean" (98). Voodoo was an animating force in the overthrow of slave society in colonial Haiti and, conversely, an instrument of oppression during the Duvalier era. Viewed as a syncretic and creolized amalgam of West African religions and Catholicism, Haitian voodoo, which Banks invokes in significant sections of *Continental Drift*, each of whose chapter headings replicates *vaudou* iconography, serves to order Vanise's temporal passage from the Old World to the New. Voodoo is the spiritual stream that parallels the ocean currents linking islands and continents: "Where the stream enters the sea, the Haitians come alone and in twos and threes. . . . In the bay, a half mile away, the trawler rocks lightly in the soft lavender pre-dawn light, and beyond the hook of beach that protects the bay, open sea stretches straight to Africa, where the eastern sky is born, cream-colored near the horizon, fading to zinc sky overhead. In the west, above Florida, the sky deepens to purple, with glints of stars" (300). In this scene, Vanise boards Bob's trawler immediately after attending a voodoo ceremony deep in the Barrens of the Bahamas. Carrying with her the blessing of her mambo, or priestess, who invests her with the protective mantel of Agwe, Lord of the Sea, Vanise places her destiny in the hands of spiritual forces. Unlike Bob, who subscribes to luck and fanciful notions about the myth of American success, Vanise is nourished by a community of faith, a fundamentally religious culture that enables her to survive the multiple attempts of her new colonizers, black and white, to shackle and oppress her. Seemingly passive in her immigrant odyssey, especially when juxtaposed against Bob's increasingly frenetic behavior, Vanise retreats from consciousness of the world into the realm of voodoo mysticism. As Banks puts it, she loses her immediate "narrative history," her sense of day-to-day events, and is submerged within the deeper, more mysterious texture of mythic history. Possessed or "mounted" by voodoo gods during dances and heightened religious rituals (much as Avey Johnson, in her reverse passage to African-Caribbean roots in Marshall's *Praisesong of the Widow,* is danced into a mythic realm), she transcends oppression by becoming an almost disembodied allegorical voyager. Leaving her temporal fate in the hands of Bon Dieu and the various *loas,* Vanise enacts a ritualistic drama of arrival that interrogates the myth of the American nation and the forces that draw immigrants to it.

Vanise's ritualistic and mythic movement toward America, filled with the familiar voices of *vaudou* deities and the strange polyvocal voices of the non-French Caribbean peoples she encounters, ultimately converges with Bob's increasingly hopeless movement away from America as he sails his trawler toward the Bahamas to pick up Vanise, her infant and nephew, and a group of Haitians paying for their fateful passage to Miami. The Haitians sustain a dream of American plentitude: "Every day there were boats going across to Florida with Haitians on board, boats operated by Americans who knew how to carry you over to Miami itself, where there was a whole city of Haitians living in their own neighborhoods just like Americans, with automobiles and plenty of food to eat and nice clothes to wear" (204). Bob, on the other hand, "a stranger in a new world . . . his life a useless, valueless jumble of broken plans, frustrated ambitions, empty dreams" (283), sails out to meet the Haitians. He does not have a myth, a community, a system of belief to sustain him. Yet his fate, as he attempts to cross the transcultural divide by speaking a smattering of Quebecois to the Haitians, is inextricably joined with that of his human cargo. He stands in awe of these desperate voyagers who are prepared to throw away everything in order to get to America, and he fears for their safety. He also envies their fatalism: "The Haitians know something, about themselves, about history, about human life, that he doesn't know" (305). Attuned to the spiritual powers in the world, the Haitians move with their deities toward their destiny while Bob remains spiritually adrift.

At the crossroads of life and death, of arrivals and departures, a realm governed typically by Legba but also by Baron Samedi and the deities of the Ghede family in the *vaudou* pantheon who determine who will live, die, or be reborn, Bob, Vanise, and the other Haitians enact a poignant, tragic ceremony. Nearing the United States mainland, Bob searches for the Gulf Stream, "the green river that flows from Mexico to Newfoundland and east to Europe with the force and clarity of a great river draining half a continent." Bob's project, like that of his father before him and the Haitians aboard his boat, involves an archetypal "searching for America." The "rich green streak on the horizon" (311), so reminiscent of Fitzgerald's metaphor for the American Eden at the end of *The Great Gatsby*, offers a mirror up to the nation that historically has transfixed all voyagers. Yet the Edenic history of the nation is interrupted by fierce swells, a pursuing Coast Guard cutter, and the dispatch of Bob's human cargo into the ocean, where all except Vanise drown, to be washed up on the Florida sands south of Bal Harbour in subsequent days like a bloated, mutilated record of the failed American Dream. Vanise avoids the terrible fate of the other Haitians. Taken by a Haitian who finds her wandering aimlessly along the side of a highway to her brother in Little Haiti, she slowly reenters the human community, taking up a new American life not authorized by immigration policy but another variation of the experience of voyagers to the New World who risk everything for the mere fact of arrival.

As for Bob, who escapes the debacle even as his criminal associates wind up jailed or deported, the jarring impact of the cataclysm and the self-recognition that he has become a "monster" sends him into the Haitian community in Miami in search of absolution. Little Haiti is a realm that forces Bob to re-envision his own life and the life of the nation. It is "a forty-block section of the city squeezed on the west of Liberty City, where impoverished blacks boil in rage, and on the other three sides by neat neighborhoods of bungalows, where middle-class Cubans and whites deliver themselves and their children anxiously over to the ongoing history of the New World" (332). This New World is polyglot, filled with anxiety and apocalyptic undercurrents at the end of the century, yet an unfinished narrative with redemptive promise. Bob wants to return the money he has taken from the Haitians in exchange for another chance in this New World—a humble reverse passage to New Hampshire. His hope is for redemption, but his rejection by Vanise and murder by a group of young Haitians ends his dark, labyrinthine quest.

Reconstructing the Nation

By constructing the slowly converging narratives of a contemporary American migrant and a Haitian immigrant, Russell Banks in *Continental Drift* retells and reinvents the nation's story. By merging interacting cultures, with their colliding myths and histories, he draws attention to the ways in which a hybrid nation is reassembling itself, even as continents are in a continual process of assemblage, at the end of the century. The mingled voices speaking to the reader throughout the novel—English, French, Creole in several Anglophone and Francophone variants, and Banks's own incantatory voice—inscribe a new nation that is no more fixed in its linguistic practices than it is in its racial and ethnic composition. Diverse cultures and the personal histories originating in them will remake the American future, and Banks would hope that fiction itself might contribute to the subversion of those historical, political, and economic abuses that force people like Bob Dubois and Vanise Dorsinville to embark on "heroic" journeys or quests for salvation. Rather than despairing of their fates, Banks would have us celebrate their lives: Bob accepts his fate and in death finds absolution while Vanise, having survived the Middle Passage, has arrived in America, the survivor and embodiment of all immigrants who, "drowned, brutalized, cheated and exploited" (365), continue to search for America's shores.

If, as Banks suggests in *Continental Drift*, the Statue of Liberty competes at the end of the century with shady real estate developers who would sell this national icon and any other tract of land to unsuspecting newcomers, this anomaly highlights the fact that reconstructing the nation through the absorption of new immigrant groups is a complex process filled with ironic twists and ambiguous outcomes. The imaginative landscape of contemporary immigrant fiction challenges historical assertions about the univocal American nation but also in surprising ways celebrates the life of a new nation grappling with issues of class, race, ethnicity, gender, and nationality. What we see in postwar fiction is an emerging immigrant narrative of a hybrid United States in which diverse groups call into question and force a revision of the national project. The most distinctive feature of these new immigrant fictions is the degree to which their protagonists bring Asian, African, Caribbean, Mexican, and South American civilizations to bear on the course of contemporary American history. Works like *Continental Drift*, Kingston's *Tripmaster Monkey*, Singer's *Enemies, A Love Story*, and García's *Dreaming in Cuban* link contemporary history to the global immigrant enterprise of the postwar years and also to the concrete demographic trends that are reconstituting the nation. These new immigrant stories are not mere codicils to American history or exotic cultural accretions sticking to the margins of the literary canon like superficial formations. Rather, the new immigrant fiction signifies what Cornel West perceives as a cultural crisis but what can also be viewed as a cultural challenge. Speaking of the decolonization of the Third World, West in his essay "Canon Formation" points to "a world-historical process that has fundamentally changed not only our conceptions of ourselves and those constituted as 'Others' . . . but, more important, our understanding of how we have constructed and do construct conceptions of ourselves and others as selves, subjects and peoples" (35). West speaks of the eclipse, dwarfing, and demystifying of European cultural hegemony and its hold on American consciousness. This study attempts to demonstrate that with the ascendancy of the United States after World War II and its emergence as the sole superpower, the peoples of the entire planet now gravitate to the American national project as they search for a map into an uncertain future. The vagaries of this new immigrant experience are frequently harrowing, fantastical, or extreme—departures from the American commonplace—but as the narrator of Wong's *Homebase* observes, "all points along a journey should be named" (71). By naming the journeys of these new strangers as they search for America, we define a transformative national condition.

This new national condition, influenced by discrete but interacting patterns of immigration, reveals a transnational American landscape whose permeable borders provide entry for immigrants, exiles, expatriates, guest workers, temporary migrants, diasporic wanderers—all participating in the evolution of a pluralistic nation-state. Their arrival from virtually every point on the global compass, all striving toward a safe "homebase," forces a reconceptualization, as suggested in the opening chapter, of the postmodern condition. Despite their differences, most well-known proponents of postmodern polemics assert that the essence of postmodernism is the decline of grand narratives. As Lyotard states in *The Postmodern Condition,* "Most people have lost the nostalgia for the lost narrative" (41). Lyotard's self-proclaimed "war on totality" derives from his fear that universalizing forces tend to submerge difference and diversity. Yet as we have seen, the immigrants depicted in contemporary American fiction espouse unique mythologies of the self and of their community that enrich and expand the social order. Such immigrants project a new grand narrative, a historical actuality that Trinh T. Minh-Ha terms the "heterogeneous reality we all live today, in postmodern times—a reality, therefore, that is not a mere crossing from one border-line to the other or that is not merely double, but a reality that involves the crossing of an indeterminate number of borderlines, one that remains multiple in its hyphenization" (1991: 107). In such a hyphenated world, fresh myths can compete for a place in the national mythology. When the Punjabi heroine in Mukherjee's *Jasmine* arrives in the New World, she embodies mythologies of creation and destruction that are older than any Edenic trope. Her temporary union with a disabled American banker suggests allegorically the erosion of an exclusively Eurocentric base for the national epic, while her adoption of the Vietnamese boy Du installs a new level of transnational history into the memory of the nation. Is this not an even grander narrative than the narratives of the past? Do we not read "America" in *Jasmine* and so many other contemporary immigrant allegories as a national project from a broadly inclusive but manifestly totalizing perspective?

Like Jasmine, who for a time dwells in a bizarre Florida realm that is eerily reminiscent of Banks's vision of the state as a chaotic and anarchic parody of El Dorado, the characters in immigrant fiction engage in national reconstruction. Some live in perpetual exile. Others, afflicted with diasporic nostalgia, as are certain characters in *Brown Girl, Brownstones, The Joy Luck Club,* and *Dreaming in Cuban,* return provisionally to sites of origin. Reverse immigration, of course, is not a new characteristic of the American immigrant experience, but today the peoples and the sites of return are different. In Nahid Rachlin's *Foreigner* (1978), for example, an Iranian-born scientist leaves her job and her husband in the "green backyard" of her alienated life in America for what turns out to be a permanent return to the deepest sources of her native culture. More typically, however, immigrants bring their discrepant origins with them and remain in their new nation. Outsiders now on the inside of the nation, searching for a place in America, they roam the cities and the continent, plunging into a maelstrom of uncertainty and promise, reworking the national mythology. Like the immigrants in Mukherjee's *Jasmine* and her two major collections of short fiction about immigrants, *Darkness* (1985) and *The Middleman and Other Stories* (1988), they arrive from everywhere: India, Vietnam, the Philippines, the Caribbean, Italy, Afghanistan. These new immigrants disperse into the vast American landscape, no longer situated exclusively in the inner cities, scarcely poor, huddled masses of an earlier era, animated instead by the drama and exuberance of their traditional cultures contending with the seductive postmodern lure of the nation. Scarcely marginalized, notably the women, they move through the seams of the nation and stream toward its center, transforming both themselves, as Mukherjee observes, and the national culture.

As archetypal narratives signifying the end of one phase of the national epoch and the beginning of another, that radical break described whimsically by Jameson as "the end of this or that" and signifying a new era characterized by chaos and heterogeneity (53), postwar fictions of immigration anatomize the creation of a revolutionary American society. This transformation or mutation in the sphere of culture, as Jameson phrases it, gives voice to constituencies formerly absent from or historically silenced by the Eurocentric narrative of the nation. In fact, it is the task of white America to acknowledge and align its destiny (as does Bob Dubois) with this turbulent historical period in which new immigrant groups are struggling for a place in the national community. As once-privileged origins erode, as white society no longer dominates contemporary life or the national world view, a revised and more inclusive vision of the nation emerges with different parts creating a new whole. As the embodiment of white ethnic America, Bob Dubois (whose last name when pronounced in Anglicized fashion signifies his stature as one of America's prototypical "boys"), is "heroic" to the extent that his perspective alters from that of a person who is blind to the changing national landscape to one who apprehends difference and heterogeneity. Throughout most of the novel, Bob's appreciation of difference is limited by his persistent failure of imagination and his slavish pursuit of the bourgeois and commodified American Dream. Nevertheless, the last brief stage of this migrant's quest—the heroic part—reveals Bob Dubois as a supplicant seeking salvation—some sort of absolution that might mitigate the seemingly irreconcilable differences of race, gender, and nationality that have come to determine his end. In the end, he finds salvation in the diasporic realm of the nation. His death therefore should not be viewed, suggests Banks, as a tragedy, but rather as a sign of the unavoidable conflicts inherent in the unfinished national project, which continues to unfold as transfiguring waves of immigrants from around the globe arrive at America's shores.

As the literal and allegorical agents of national metamorphosis, the immigrant characters in contemporary fiction alter the horizons of the American experience. Linda Hutcheon acknowledges that the United States is "a land of immigration," but more perceptively than most critics she asserts that today's land of immigration has been transformed. In Hutcheon's words, "The 'ex-centric'—as both off-center and de-centered—gets attention. That which is 'different' is valorized in opposition both to elitist, alienated 'otherness' and also to the uniforming impulse of mass culture" (1988: 130). Hutcheon's intertextual play on the words "center" and "eccentric" derives from a similar trope established by Maxine Hong Kingston in *The Woman Warrior*, wherein the narrator, recalling her childhood in her parents' laundry, ponders the place of the Chinese in American society. The galaxy of immigrant women and men who populate today's fiction signify the "ex-centricity" of the nation—the radical turn in what formerly was a linear story of American civilization deriving from relatively homogenous and Eurocentric sources. Vanise, Dottie, Jasmine, Silla and Selina, the García girls, the mothers and daughters in Tan's fiction: all bring discrete cultural memories and myths to the project of the nation, expanding its foundations. By conflating issues of race, class, and gender, they and their male counterparts interrogate the old totalizing narrative of the nation and postulate a new nation emerging from global catastrophe, disaporic wandering, racial and ethnic resurgence, and vast cultural change.

With an array of late-twentieth-century immigrant histories contending for a place in the American nation, it is not surprising that the country's newcomers retain multiple identities and cultural loyalties. Experiencing plural, contrapuntal lives in what James Clifford aptly terms "the current transnational moment," they search for America in selective ways that often enable them to retain communal languages and customs while negotiating the degree of assimilation they desire. Alluding to *Brown Girl, Brownstones* in a provocative essay titled "Diasporas" (1997), Clifford writes of the tendencies of the Bajan women depicted by Marshall who are "caught between patriarchies, ambiguous pasts, and futures," to engage with America in provisional ways. As diasporic agents, they "connect and disconnect, forget and remember, in complex, strategic ways" (257). Similarly the Chicana writer Gloria Anzaldúa, speaking of borderlands culture, equates the complex search for Mexican-American identity with the search for America: "Chicano, indio, American Indian, mojado, mexicano, immigrant Latino, Anglo in power, working class Anglo, Black, Asian—our psyches resemble the border towns and are populated by the same people" (87). Within the polyglot culture of everyday immigrant life, not even "double consciousness" captures fully the fluidity of identity required to shape a new life in the nation. Suffice it to say that immigrants and the children of immigrants, facing the turbulent historical currents of the late twentieth century—what Salman Rushdie, himself no stranger to the transnational immigrant project, terms "the increasing storm"—require supple, highly pluralized conceptions of the self as they manage shifting power relations and attempt to control their destinies within the multiple public and private spheres of the American nation.

By creating the possibility of a new nation and a new national identity based on intersecting global histories, the fiction of contemporary American immigration captures and codifies the anarchy of arrival and dispersal, the unending search for a place in the nation. Today in the United States, where according to the Census Bureau almost one out of every ten people is foreign-born, with 27 percent from Mexico, another 27 percent from Asia, and 12 percent from Central or South America, it is clear that the "West" has met the "Rest." These new immigrants are in constant physical, psychic, and spiritual motion. They are transnational travelers, a new species of immigrant who, in Edward Said's assessment (1994), "crosses over, traverses territory, and abandons fixed positions, all the time" (17). As such the new immigrant tests the national terrain, shakes the North American continent's tectonic plates, as Russell Banks avers.

As the continent shifts imperceptibly even as the metabolic rate of history accelerates, this fourth wave of immigrants, some 8.5 million in the last decade of the American Century, cross and recross boundaries in search of their places in the nation. Blood ties, religious practices and creeds, family values, and their own diasporic spaces sustain them. At the same time, they interact with society and the nation's myths, rituals, and ideologies. They embrace democratic vistas and transcendent national meanings: opportunity, social mobility, self-reliance, the dreams inherent in their new Promised Land. In this paradoxical postwar Eden, the harbinger of polyglot global democracy, the immigrant men and women passing to and fro are voyagers from every nation on the planet. Like continents drifting, they contribute in their search for America to the slow but inevitable reshaping of the nation's complex fate.

Bibliography

Acosta-Belén, Edna. "Beyond Island Boundaries: Ethnicity, Gender, and Cultural Revitalization in Nuyorican Literature." *Callaloo* 15.4 (1992): 979–98.

Acuña, Rodolfo F. *Occupied America: The Chicano's Struggle Toward Liberation.* 1972. New York: Harper, 1988.

Ahmad, Aijaz. *In Theory: Classes, Nations, Literatures.* London: Verso, 1994.

Alvarez, Julia. *How the García Girls Lost Their Accents.* Chapel Hill: Algonquin Books, 1991.

———. *Yo.* New York: Algonquin, 1997.

Anaya, Rudolfo A. *Alburquerque.* Albuquerque: U of New Mexico P, 1992.

———. *Bless Me, Ultima.* Berkeley: Quinto Sol, 1972.

Anaya, Rudolfo, and Francisco Lomelí. *Aztlán: Essays on the Chicano Homeland.* Albuquerque: U of New Mexico P, 1989.

Anderson, Benedict. *Imagined Communities: Reflections on the Origin and Spread of Nationalism.* London: Verso, 1983.

Antin, Mary. *The Promised Land.* 1912. Boston: Houghton, 1969.

Anzaldúa, Gloria. *Borderlands/La Frontera: The New Mestiza.* San Francisco: Aunt Lute, 1987.

Appelfeld, Aharon. *Beyond Despair.* Trans. Jeffrey Green. New York: Fromer, 1994.

Arenas, Reinaldo. *The Doorman.* New York: Grove Weidenfeld, 1991.

Arias, Ron. *The Road to Tamazunchale.* 1975. Reno: West Coast Poetry Review, 1987.

Ashcroft, Bill, Gareth Griffiths, and Helen Tiffin. *The Empire Writes Back: Theory and Practice in Post-colonial Literatures.* London: Routledge, 1989.

Baker, Beth. "Stirring the Melting Pot." *AARP Bulletin,* 34 (Dec. 1993): 16.

Baker, Houston A. Jr., ed. *Three American Literatures.* New York: MLA, 1987.

Bakhtin, Mikhail. *The Dialogic Imagination.* Trans. Michael Holquist and Caryl Emerson. Austin: U of Texas P, 1981.

———. *Rabelais and His World.* Trans. Helene Iswolsky. Cambridge: MIT P, 1968.

Banks, Russell. *Continental Drift.* New York: Harper, 1985.

Barkin, Elliot Robert. *Asian and Pacific Islander Migration to the United States: A Model of New Global Patterns.* Westport: Greenwood, 1992.

Barrera, Mario. *Race and Class in the Southwest: A Theory of Racial Inequality.* Notre Dame: U of Notre Dame P, 1979.

Barrio, Raymond. *The Plum Plum Pickers.* 1969. Tempe: Bilingual, 1984.

Barry, Tom. *The Other Side of Paradise: Foreign Control in the Caribbean.* New York: Grove, 1984.

Barthold, Bonnie J. *Black Time: Fiction of Africa, the Caribbean, and the United States.* New Haven: Yale UP, 1981.

Baumgarten, Murray, and Barbara Gottfried. *Understanding Philip Roth.* Columbia: U of South Carolina P, 1990.

Baym, Nina. "Melodramas of Beset Manhood: How Theories of American Fiction Exclude Women Authors." *The New Feminist Criticism.* Ed. Elaine Showalter. 63–80.

Bell, Christine. *The Pérez Family.* New York: Norton, 1990.

Bellah, Robert, et al. *Habits of the Heart: Individualism and Commitment in American Life.* Berkeley: U of California P, 1985.

Bellow, Saul. *Mr. Sammler's Planet.* New York: Viking, 1970.

———. "Some Notes on Recent American Fiction." *The American Novel Since World War II.* Ed. Marcus Klein. Westport: Fawcett, 1964.

Benitez-Rojo, Antonio. *The Repeating Island: The Caribbean and the Postmodern Perspective.* Durham: Duke UP, 1992.

Benston, Kimberly. "Architectural Imagery in Paule Marshall's *Brown Girl, Brownstones.*" *Negro American Literature Forum* 9 (Fall 1975): 67–76.

Berger, Alan L. *Crisis and Covenant: The Holocaust in American Jewish Fiction.* Albany: State U of New York P, 1985.

Bhaba, Homi K. *The Location of Culture.* London: Routledge, 1994.

———. *Nation and Narration.* New York: Routledge, 1990.

Bilik, Dorothy. *Immigrant Survivors: Post-Holocaust Consciousness in Recent Jewish American Fiction.* Middletown: Wesleyan UP, 1981.

Binder, Frederick M., and David M. Reimers. *All the Nations Under Heaven: An Ethnic and Racial History of New York City.* New York: Columbia UP, 1995.

Blauner, Robert. *Racial Oppression in America.* New York: Harper, 1972.

Bodnar, John. *The Transplanted: A History of Immigrants in Urban America.* Bloomington: Indiana UP, 1985.

Boehmer, Elleke. *Colonial and Postcolonial Literature: Migrant Metaphors.* New York: Oxford UP, 1995.

Boelhower, William. *Through a Glass Darkly: Ethnic Semiosis in American Literature.* New York: Oxford UP, 1987.

Bouscaren, Anthony T. *International Migrations Since 1945.* New York: Praeger, 1963.

Bowen, Elizabeth. *Immigration in New York.* New York: Praeger, 1987.

Briggs, Vernon M., and Stephen Moore. *Still an Open Door? U.S. Immigration Policy and the American Economy.* Washington: American UP, 1994.

Bröck, Sabine. "Talk as a Form of Action." (Interview with Paule Marshall.) *History and Tradition in Afro-American Literature.* Ed. Günter Lenz. 196–202.

Bruce-Novoa, Juan. *Chicano Authors: Inquiry by Interview.* Austin: U of Texas P, 1980.

Bulosan, Carlos. *America Is in the Heart.* 1943. Seattle: U of Washington P, 1973.

Butler, Robert Olen. *A Good Scent from a Strange Mountain.* New York: Holt, 1992.

Calavita, Kitty. *Inside the State: The Bracero Program, Immigration, and the I.N.S.* New York: Routledge, 1992.

Calderon, Héctor, and José David Saldívar, eds. *Criticism in the Borderlands: Studies in Chicano Literature, Culture, and Ideology.* Durham: Duke UP, 1991.

Camarillo, Albert. *Chicanos in California: A History of Mexican Americans in California.* San Francisco: Boyd and Fraser, 1984.

Cao, Lan. *Monkey Bridge.* New York: Viking, 1997.

Carr, Raymond. *Puerto Rico: A Colonial Experiment.* New York: New York UP, 1984.

Carroll, Raymond. *The Caribbean: Issues in U.S. Relations.* New York: Franklin Watts, 1984.

Chambers, Iain, and Lidia Curti, eds. *The Post-Colonial Question: Common Skies, Divided Horizons.* London: Routledge, 1996.

Chan, Jeffrey Paul, et al. "An Introduction to Chinese-American and Japanese-American Literatures." *Three American Literatures.* Ed. Houston A. Baker, Jr. New York: MLA, 1987.

Chan, Sucheng. *Asian Americans: An Interpretative History.* Boston: Twayne, 1991.

Chang, Gordon H. "Asian Americans and the Writing of Their History." *Radical History Review* 53 (1992): 105–14.

Chatterjee, Partha. *The Nation and Its Fragments: Colonial and Postcolonial Societies.* Princeton: Princeton UP, 1993.

Chin, Frank. *The Chinaman Pacific & Frisco R.R. Co.* Minneapolis: Coffee House, 1988.

———. *Donald Duk.* St. Paul: Coffee House, 1991.

Chin, Frank, et al. *Aiiieeeee!: An Anthology of Asian-American Writers.* Washington: Howard UP, 1983.

———. "Come All Ye Asian American Writers of the Real and the Fake." *The Big Aiiieeeee! An Anthology of Chinese American and Japanese American Literature.* New York: Penguin, 1991.

Christian, Barbara. *Black Women Novelists: The Development of a Tradition, 1892–1976.* Westport: Greenwood P, 1980.

Christian, Karen. *Show and Tell: Identity as Performance in U.S. Latina/Latino Fiction.* Albuquerque: U of New Mexico P, 1997.

Chu, Louis. *Eat a Bowl of Tea*. 1961, 1979. New York: Carol, 1995.

Cisneros, Sandra. *The House on Mango Street*. Houston: Arte Público P, 1983.

Cliff, Michelle. *Abeng*. Trumansburg: Crossing, 1984.

———. "If I Could Write This in Fire, I Would Write This in Fire." *The Graywolf Annual Five: Multicultural Literacy*. Ed. Rick Simonson and Scott Walker. St. Paul: Graywolf, 1988. 63–81.

———. *The Land of Look Behind*. Ithaca: Firebrand, 1985.

———. *No Telephone to Heaven*. New York: Vintage, 1989.

Clifford, James. *The Predicament of Culture: Twentieth-Century Ethnography, Literature, and Art*. Cambridge: Harvard UP, 1988.

———. *Routes: Travel and Translation in the Late Twentieth Century*. Cambridge: Harvard UP, 1997.

Clifford, James, and George E. Marcus, eds. *Writing Culture: The Poetics and Politics of Ethnography*. Berkeley: U of California P, 1986.

Cockcroft, James D. *Latinos in the Making of the United States*. New York: Franklin Watts, 1995.

———. *Outlaws in the Promised Land: Mexican Immigrant Workers and America's Future*. New York: Grove, 1986.

Cofer, Judith Ortiz. *An Island Like You*. New York: Orchard, 1995.

———. *The Line of the Sun*. Athens: U of Georgia P, 1989.

Cook, William W. "Writing in the Spaces Left." *CCC* 44.1 (Feb. 1993): 9–12.

Cose, Ellis. *A Nation of Strangers: Prejudice, Politics, and the Populating of America*. New York: Morrow, 1992.

Coser, Stelamaris. *Bridging the Americas: The Literature of Paule Marshall, Toni Morrison, and Gayl Jones*. Philadelphia: Temple UP, 1995.

Cudjoe, Selwyn R. "Jamaica Kincaid and the Modernist Project: An Interview." *Callaloo* 12 (Spring 1989): 396–411.

Daniels, Roger. *Asian America: Chinese and Japanese in the United States since 1850*. Seattle: U of Washington P, 1988.

———. *Coming to America: A History of Immigration and Ethnicity in American Life*. New York: HarperCollins, 1990.

———. *Prisoners without Trial: Japanese Americans in World War II*. New York: Hill and Wang, 1993.

Daniels, Stephen. *Fields of Vision: Landscape Imagery and National Identity in England and the United States*. Princeton: Princeton UP, 1993.

Davies, Carole Boyce, and Elaine Savorn Fido, eds. *Out of the Kumbla: Caribbean Women and Literature*. Trenton: Africa World, 1990.

Denniston, Dorothy Hamer. *The Fiction of Paule Marshall: Reconstructions of History, Culture, and Gender*. Knoxville: U of Tennessee P, 1995.

Des Pres, Terrence. "Holocaust Laughter?" *Writing and the Holocaust*. Ed. Berel Lang. 216–33.

Dinnerstein, Leonard. *America and the Survivors of the Holocaust*. New York: Columbia UP, 1982.

———. *Antisemitism in America*. New York: Oxford UP, 1994.

Dinnerstein, Leonard, and David M. Reimers. *Ethnic Americans: A History of Immigration and Assimilation*. New York: Harper, 1982.

Dirks, Nicholas B., ed. *Colonialism and Culture*. Ann Arbor: U of Michigan P, 1992.

Diza-Briquets, Sergio, and Sidney Weintraub, eds. *Determinants of Emigration from Mexico, Central America, and the Caribbean*. Boulder: Westview, 1991.

Doctorow, E.L. *Ragtime*. New York: Random, 1975.

Dominquez, V.R. *From Neighbor to Stranger: The Dilemma of Caribbean Peoples in the United States*. New Haven: Antilles Research Program, 1975.

Downing, Christine. *Women's Mysteries. Toward a Poetics of Gender*. New York: Crossroad, 1992.

Ezrahi, Sidra DeVoen. *By Words Alone: The Holocaust in Literature*. Chicago: U of Chicago P, 1980.

Fanon, Franz. *Toward the African Revolution*. Harmondsworth: Pelican, 1967.

———. *The Wretched of the Earth*. 1961. Trans. Constance Farrington. New York: Grove, 1968.

Ferguson, Moira. *Jamaica Kincaid: Where the Land Meets the Body*. Charlottesville: U of Virginia P, 1994.

Fernández, Roberto. *Raining Backwards*. Houston: Arte Público, 1988.

Fernandez, Ronald. *The Disenchanted Island: Puerto Rico and the United States in the Twentieth Century*. New York: Praeger, 1992.

Ferraro, Thomas J. *Ethnic Passages: Literary Immigrants in Twentieth-century America*. Chicago: U of Chicago P, 1993.

Fine, David M. *The City, the Immigrant and American Fiction, 1880–1920*. Metuchen, NJ: Scarecrow, 1977.

Finnegan, William. "The New Americans." *New Yorker* 25 March 1996: 53–62.

Firmat, Gustavo Pérez. *Life on the Hyphen: The Cuban-American Way*. Austin: U of Texas P, 1994.

Firmat, Gustavo Pérez, ed. *Do the Americas Have a Common Literature?* Durham: Duke UP, 1990.

Fitzpatrick, Joseph P. *Puerto Rican Americans: The Meaning of Migration*. Englewood Cliffs: Prentice-Hall, 1987.

Fix, Michael, et al. *Immigration and Immigrants: Setting the Record Straight*. Washington: Urban Institute, 1994.

Fix, Michael, and Jeffrey S. Passel. *The Door Remains Open: Recent Immigration to the United States and a Preliminary Analysis of the Immigration Act of 1990*. Washington: Urban Institute, 1991.

Foner, Nancy. *New Immigrants in New York*. New York: Columbia UP, 1987.

Fox, Geoffrey. *Hispanic Nation: Culture, Politics and the Construction of Identity*. Secaucus, NJ: Birch Lane, 1996.

Friedländer, Saul. "Historical Writing and the Memory of the Holocaust." *Writing and the Holocaust*. Ed. Berel Lang. 66–78.

————. *Nazi Germany and the Jews.* New York: HarperCollins, 1997.

Fuentes, Carlos. *A New Time for Mexico.* Trans. Marina Gutman Castaneda. New York: Farrar, Straus, Giroux, 1996.

Fusco, Coco. *English Is Broken Here: Notes on Cultural Fusion in the Americas.* New York: New P, 1995.

Galarza, Ernesto. *Barrio Boy.* Notre Dame: U of Notre Dame P, 1971.

————. *Merchants of Labor: The Mexican Bracero Program.* Charlotte, Santa Barbara: McNally & Loftin, 1964.

Gann, L.H., and Peter Duignan. *The Hispanics of the United States: A History.* Boulder: Westview, 1986.

García, Christina. *Dreaming in Cuban.* New York: Knopf, 1992.

García, Juan Ramon. *Operation Wetback: The Mass Deportation of Mexican Undocumented Workers in 1954.* Westport: Greenwood, 1980.

García, Mario. "La Frontera: The Border as Symbol and Reality in Mexican American Thought." *Mexican Studies/Estudios Mexicanos* 1 (Summer 1985): 196–205.

Garver, Susan. *Coming to North America: from Mexico, Cuba, and Puerto Rico.* New York: Delacorte, 1981.

Garza, Hedda. *Latinas: Hispanic Women in the United States.* New York: Franklin Watts, 1994.

Gates, Henry Louis, Jr. *Figures in Black: Words, Signs, and the "Racial" Self.* New York: Oxford UP, 1987.

————. *Race, Writing, and Difference.* Chicago: U of Chicago P, 1986.

Geertz, Clifford. *The Interpretation of Cultures.* New York: Basic, 1973.

————. *Works and Lives: The Anthropologist as Author.* Stanford: Stanford UP, 1988.

Giddens, Anthony. *The Consequences of Modernity.* Stanford: Stanford UP, 1990.

Gikandi, Simon. *Writing in Limbo: Modernism and Caribbean Literature.* Ithaca: Cornell UP, 1992.

Gilroy, Paul. *The Black Atlantic: Modernity and Double Consciousness.* Cambridge: Harvard UP, 1993.

Glazer, Nathan, and Daniel P. Moynihan, eds. *Ethnicity: Theory and Experience.* Cambridge: Harvard UP, 1975.

Gordon, Milton M. *Assimilation in American Life: The Role of Race, Religion, and National Origin.* New York: Oxford UP, 1964.

Grasmuck, Sherri and Patricia Pessan. *Between Two Islands: Dominican International Migration.* Berkeley: U of California P, 1991.

Grebler, Leo, and Joan W. Moore. *The Mexican-American People: The Nation's Second Largest Minority.* New York: Free, 1970.

Grenier, Guillermo, and Alex Stepick, eds. *Miami Now! Immigration, Ethnicity and Social Change.* Miami: UP of Florida, 1992.

Griffiths, Gareth. *A Double Exile: African and West Indian Writing between Two Cultures.* London: Marion Boyars, 1978.

Griswold del Castillo, Richard, and Arnoldo De León. *North to Aztlán: A History of Mexican Americans in the United States*. New York: Twayne, 1996.

Guha, Ramajiti and Grayatri Spivak, eds. *Selected Subaltern Studies*. New York: Oxford UP, 1988.

Gusdorf, Georges. *Speaking*. Trans. Paul T. Brockelman. Evanston: Northwestern UP, 1965.

Gutiérrez, David G. *Walls and Mirrors: Mexican Americans, Mexican Immigrants and the Politics of Ethnicity*. Berkeley: U of California P, 1995.

Gutiérrez, Ramón, and Genaro Padilla, eds. *Recovering the U. S. Hispanic Literary Heritage*. Houston: Arte Público, 1993.

Habermas, Jurgen. "Modernity versus Postmodernity." *New German Critique* 22 (1981): 3–14.

———. *The New Conservatism: Cultural Criticism and the Historians' Debate*. Cambridge: Harvard UP, 1989.

Hagedorn, Jessica. *Dogeaters*. New York: Pantheon, 1990.

———. *The Gangster of Love*. Boston: Houghton, 1996.

Hall, Stuart. "Cultural Identity and Diaspora." *Identity: Community, Culture, Difference*. Ed. Jonathan Rutherford. London: Lawrence & Wishart, 1990: 222–37.

Hamm, Mark S. *The Abandoned Ones: The Imprisonment and Uprising of the Mariel Boat People*. Boston: Northeastern UP, 1995.

Handlin, Oscar. *The Uprooted: The Epic Story of the Great Migrations that Made the American People*. 1951. 2nd ed. enlarged. Boston: Little, Brown, 1973.

Hartman, Geoffrey, ed. *Holocaust Remembrance: The Shapes of Memory*. Cambridge: Blackwell, 1993.

Hassan, Ihab. *The Dismemberment of Orpheus: Toward a Postmodern Literature*. 2nd ed. Madison: U of Wisconsin P, 1982.

Hegel, Georg Wilhelm Friedrich. *The Philosophy of History*. Trans. J. Sibree. New York: Dover, 1956.

Henry, William A., III. "Beyond the Melting Pot." *Time* 9 April 90: 28–35.

Hernandez, Irene Beltran. *Across the Great River*. Houston: Arte Público, 1989.

Hernández-Gutiérrez, Manuel de Jesús. *El colonialismo interno en la narrativa: chicana: el barrio, el anti-barrio y el exterior*. Tempe: Bilingual, 1994.

Higham, John. *Send These to Me: Immigrants in Urban America*. Baltimore: Johns Hopkins UP, 1989.

———. *Strangers in the Land: Patterns of American Nativism 1860–1925*. New York: Atheneum, 1963.

Hijuelos, Oscar. *The Fourteen Sisters of Emilio Montez O'Brien*. New York: Farrar, Straus, Giroux, 1993.

———. *The Mambo Kings Play Songs of Love*. New York: Farrar, Straus, Giroux, 1989.

———. *Our House in the Last World*. New York: Persea, 1984.

Hinojosa, Rolando. *Dear Rafe*. Houston: Arte Público, 1985.

———. *Klail City*. Houston: Arte Público, 1985.

Hobsbawn, E.J. *Primitive Rebels: Studies in Archaic Forms of Social Movement in the 19th and 20th Centuries*. New York: Norton, 1959.

Hollinger, David A. *Postethnic America*. New York: Basic, 1995.

hooks, bell. *Black Looks: Race and Representation*. Boston: South End, 1992.

———. *Yearning: Race, Gender, and Cultural Politics*. Boston: South End, 1990.

Horno-Delgado, Asunción, Eliana Ortega, Nina M. Scott, and Nancy Saporta Sternback, eds. *Breaking Boundaries: Latina Writings and Critical Readings*. Amherst: U of Massachusetts P, 1989.

Horowitz, Michael M., ed. *People and Cultures of the Caribbean*. Garden City: Natural History, 1971.

Hutcheon, Linda. *Narcissistic Narrative: The Metafictional Paradox*. New York: Methuen, 1984.

———. *A Poetics of Postmodernism: History, Theory, Fiction*. New York: Routledge, 1988.

Inada, Lawson Fusao. "Of Place and Displacement: The Range of Japanese American Literature." *Three American Literatures*. Ed. Houston Baker, Jr. 254–65.

Islas, Arturo. *Migrant Souls*. New York: Morrow, 1990.

———. *The Rain God: A Desert Tale*. Stanford: Alexandrian, 1985.

Jameson, Fredric. "Postmodernism, or, the Cultural Logic of Late Capitalism." *New Left Review* 146 (1984): 53–93.

———. *Postmodernism, or, The Cultural Logic of Late Capitalism*. Durham: Duke UP, 1991.

———. "Reification and Utopia in Mass Culture." *Social Text* 1 (Winter 1979): 130–48.

———. "Third World Literature in the Era of Multinational Capital." *Social Text* 15 (Fall 1986): 65–88.

Jasso, Guillermina, and Mark P. Rozenzweig. *New Chosen People: Immigrants in the United States*. New York: Russell Sage, 1990.

Jen, Gish. *Mona in the Promised Land*. New York: Knopf, 1996.

———. *Typical American*. Boston: Houghton, 1991.

Jiménez, Francisco, ed. *The Identification and Analysis of Chicano Literature*. New York: Bilingual, 1979.

Johnson, Charles. *Middle Passage*. New York: Atheneum, 1990.

Jones, Maldwyn Allen. *American Immigration*. Chicago: U of Chicago P, 1992.

Jussawalla, Feroza, and Reed Way Dasenbrock. *Interviews with Writers of the Post-Colonial World*. Jackson: UP of Mississippi, 1992.

Kadohata, Cynthia. *The Floating World*. New York: Viking, 1989.

Karnow, Stanley. *In Our Image: America's Empire in the Philippines*. New York: 1989.

Kasinitz, Philip. *Caribbean New York: Black Immigrants and the Politics of Race.* Ithaca: Cornell UP, 1992.

Keefe, Susan E., and Amado Padilla. *Chicano Ethnicity.* Albuquerque: U of New Mexico P, 1987.

Keller, Nora Okja. *Comfort Woman.* New York: Viking, 1997.

Kellner, David. *Postmodern Theory: Critical Interrogations.* New York: Guilford, 1991.

Kim, Elaine H. *Asian American Literature: An Introduction to the Writings and Their Social Context.* Philadelphia: Temple UP, 1982.

Kim, Illsoo. *New Urban Immigrants: The Korean Community in New York City.* Princeton: Princeton UP, 1981.

Kim, Ronyoung. *Clay Walls.* New York: Permanent, 1986.

Kincaid, Jamaica. *Annie John.* New York: Farrar, Straus, Giroux, 1985.

———. *Lucy.* New York: HarperCollins, 1990.

———. *A Small Place.* New York: New American Library, 1988.

Kingston, Maxine Hong. *China Men.* New York: Ballantine, 1981.

———. *Tripmaster Monkey: His Fake Book.* New York: Knopf, 1989.

———. *The Woman Warrior: Memoirs of a Girlhood among Ghosts.* New York: Vintage, 1977.

Kitagawa, Daisuke. *Issei and Nisei: The Internment Years.* New York: Seabury, 1967.

Kitano, Harry H.L. *Japanese Americans: The Evolution of a Subculture.* 1969. Englewood Cliffs: Prentice-Hall, 1976.

LaCapra, Dominick. *History and Politics.* Ithaca: Cornell UP, 1987.

Lamming, George. *The Emigrants.* London: Michael Joseph, 1954.

———. *In the Castle of My Skin.* London: Longman, 1970.

———. *Of Age and Innocence.* London: Allison and Busby, 1958.

———. *The Pleasures of Exile.* 1960. Ann Arbor: U of Michigan P, 1992.

———. "The West Indian People." *Caribbean Essays* Ed. Andrew Salkey. London: Evans, 1973.

Lang, Berel, ed. *Writing and the Holocaust.* London/New York: Holmes & Meier, 1988.

Langer, Lawrence L. *Admitting the Holocaust: Collected Essays.* New York: Oxford UP, 1995.

———. *The Holocaust and the Literary Imagination.* New Haven: Yale UP, 1975.

———. *Holocaust Testimonies: The Ruins of Memory.* New Haven: Yale UP, 1991.

———. "Interpreting Survivor Testimony." *Writing and the Holocaust.* Ed. Berel Lang. 26–40.

———. *Versions of Survival: The Holocaust and the Human Spirit.* SUNY P, 1982.

Langley, Lester D. *The United States and the Caribbean in the Twentieth Century.* Athens: U of Georgia P, 1982.

Laquerre, Michel S. *American Odyssey: Haitians in New York City.* Ithaca: Cornell UP, 1984.

Lauter, Paul. *Canons and Contexts.* New York: Oxford UP, 1991.

Lee, Chang-Rae. *Native Speaker.* New York: Riverhead, 1995.

Lee, Gus. *China Boy.* New York: Dutton, 1991.

Lenz, Günter H., ed. *History and Tradition in Afro-American Culture.* Frankfort: Campus-Verlag, 1984.

Levine, Barry, ed. *The Caribbean Exodus.* New York: Praeger, 1987.

Levine, Lawrence. *The Opening of the American Mind.* Boston: Beacon P, 1996.

Lewis, Gordon K. *The Growth of the Modern West Indies.* New York: Monthly Review, 1968.

———. *Main Currents in Caribbean Thought.* Baltimore: Johns Hopkins UP, 1983.

———. *Notes on the Puerto Rican Revolution: An Essay on American Dominance and Caribbean Resistance.* New York: Monthly Review, 1984.

———. *Puerto Rico: Freedom and Power in the Caribbean.* New York: Monthly Review, 1963.

Lim, Shirley Geok-lin, and Amy Ling, eds. *Reading the Literatures of Asian America.* Philadelphia: Temple UP, 1992.

Limerick, Patricia Nelson. *Legacy of Conquest: The Unbroken Past of the American West.* New York: Norton, 1987.

Limon, Graciela. *The Memories of Ana Calderon.* Houston: Arte Público, 1994.

Ling, Amy. *Between Worlds: Women Writers of Chinese Ancestry.* New York: Pergamon, 1990.

Lively, Penelope. *Oleander, Iacaranda: A Memoir.* New York: HarperCollins, 1994.

Loescher, Gil, and John A. Scanlan. *Calculated Kindness: Refugees and America's Half-Open Door, 1945 to the Present.* New York: Free, 1986.

Lomelí, Francisco, ed. *Handbook of Hispanic Cultures in the United States: Literature and Art.* Houston: Arte Público, 1993.

Lopate, Phillip. *The Rug Merchant.* New York: Viking, 1987.

Lynch, John. *The Spanish-American Revolutions, 1808–1826.* New York: Norton, 1973.

Lyotard, Jean-Francois. *The Postmodern Condition: A Report on Knowledge.* Trans. Geoff Bennington and Brian Massumi. Minneapolis: U of Minnesota P, 1984.

MacKinnon, Catherine A. *Feminist Theory: A Critique of Ideology.* Chicago: U of Chicago P, 1981.

Malamud, Bernard. *The Complete Stories.* New York: Farrar, Straus, Giroux, 1997.

———. *Idiots First.* New York: Farrar Straus, 1963.

———. *The Magic Barrel.* New York: Farrar, Straus & Cudahy, 1967.

Malin, Irving, ed. *Contemporary American-Jewish Literature.* Bloomington: Indiana UP, 1983.

Mandel, Ernest. *Late Capitalism.* London: New Left, 1975.

Marshall, Paule. *Brown Girl, Brownstones.* 1959. New York: Feminist, 1981.

————. *The Chosen Place, the Timeless People.* New York: Vintage, 1984.

————. *Daughters.* New York: Atheneum, 1991.

————. *Praisesong for the Widow.* New York: Putnam, 1983.

————. *Soul Clap Hands and Sing.* Chatham: Chatham, 1961.

Martínez, Oscar J. *Border People: Life and Society in the U.S.- Mexico Border-lands.* Tucson: U of Arizona P, 1994.

————. *Troublesome Border.* Tucson: U of Arizona P, 1988.

McKenna, Theresa. *Migrant Song: Politics and Process in Contemporary Chicano Literature.* Austin: U of Texas P, 1997.

McWilliams, Carey. *North from Mexico.* Westport: Greenwood, 1968.

Medina, Pablo. *Exiled Memories: A Cuban Childhood.* Austin: U of Texas P, 1990.

Meier, Matt, and Feliciano Rivera. *The Chicanos: A History of Mexican Americans.* New York: Hill and Wang, 1972.

Melendy, H. Brett. *Asians in Americas: Filipinos, Koreans, and East Indians.* New York: Hippocrene, 1981.

Memmi, Albert. *The Colonizer and the Colonized.* Boston: Beacon, 1965.

Ming, Bill Ong. *Making and Remaking Asian America Through Immigration Policy, 1850–1990.* Stanford: Stanford UP, 1993.

Minh-Ha, Trinh T. *When the Moon Waxes Red: Representation, Gender, and Cultural Politics.* New York: Routledge, 1991.

————. *Woman, Native, Other.* Bloomington: Indiana UP, 1989.

Mohr, Nicholasa. *El Bronx Remembered: A Novella and Stories.* New York: Harper Keypoint, 1993.

————. *In Nueva York.* New York: Dial, 1977.

Mori, Toshio. *Yokohama, California.* 1949. Seattle: U of Washington P, 1985.

Morrison, Toni. *Playing in the Dark: Whiteness and the Literary Imagination.* Cambridge: Harvard UP, 1992.

————. *Tar Baby.* New York: Knopf, 1981.

Mukherjee, Bharati. "American Dreamer." *Mother Jones* January/February 1997: 32–35.

————. *Darkness.* New York: Penguin, 1985.

————. *Jasmine.* New York: Grove Weidenfeld, 1989.

————. *The Middleman and Other Stories.* New York: Fawcett Crest, 1988.

Muller, Thomas. *Immigrants and the American City.* New York: New York UP, 1993.

Muller, Thomas, et al. *The Fourth Wave: California's Newest Immigrants.* Washington: Urban Institute, 1985.

Nabokov, Vladimir. *Lolita.* New York: Putnam, 1958.

Naipaul, V.S. *The Enigma of Arrival.* New York: Knopf, 1987.

————. *The Middle Passage.* London: Andre Deutsch, 1962.

Ng, Fae Myenne. *Bone.* New York: Hyperian, 1993.

Niggli, Josephina. *Mexican Village.* Chapel Hill: U of North Carolina P, 1945.

Novak, Michael. *The Rise of the Unmeltable Ethnics: Politics and Culture in the Seventies.* New York: Macmillan, 1973.

O'Brien, David J., and Stephen S. Fugita. *The Japanese American Experience.* Bloomington: Indiana UP, 1991.

O'Connor, Flannery. *A Good Man Is Hard to Find.* New York: Harcourt, 1977.

———. *A Memoir of Mary Ann.* New York: Farrar, 1961.

Okada, John. *No-No Boy.* 1957. Seattle: U of Washington P, 1976.

Okihiro, Gary, et al. *Privileging Positions: The Sites of Asian American Studies.* Pullman: Washington State UP, 1995.

Olalquiaga, Celeste. *Metropolis: Contemporary Cultural Sensibilities.* Minneapolis: U of Minnesota P, 1992.

Olshan, Joseph. *Clara's Heart.* New York: Ballantine, 1985.

Ophir, Adi. "On Sanctifying the Holocaust: An Anti-Theological Treatise." *Tikkun* 2 (1987): 63–65.

Ortega, Eliana, and Nancy Saporta Sternbach, eds. *Breaking Boundaries: Latina Writing and Critical Readings.* Amherst: U of Massachusetts P, 1989.

Ozick, Cynthia. *The Cannibal Galaxy.* New York: Knopf, 1983.

———. *The Shawl.* New York: Knopf, 1989.

Palmer, Ransford W. *Pilgrims from the Sun: West Indian Migration to America.* New York: Twayne, 1995.

Paredes, Américo. "The Folk Base of Chicano Literature." *Modern Chicano Writers.* Ed. Joseph Sommers and Tomás Ybarra-Frasto. 4–17.

Passel, Jeffrey S., and Barry Edmonston. *Immigration and Race: Recent Trends in Immigration to the United States.* Washington: Urban Institute, 1992.

Pastor, Robert A. "The Impact of U.S. Immigration Policy on Caribbean Immigration." *The Caribbean Exodus.* Ed. Barry Levine, 245–47.

Paz, Octavio. *The Labyrinth of Solicitude: Life and Thought in Mexico.* Trans. Lysander Kemp. New York: Grove, 1961.

Pérez, Louis A. *Between Reform and Revolution.* New York: Oxford UP, 1988.

Pettis, Joyce Owens. *Toward Wholeness in Paule Marshall's Fiction.* Charlottesville: UP of Virginia, 1995.

Pettit, Arthur. *Images of the Mexican American in Fiction and Film.* College Station: Texas A & M P, 1980.

Portes, Alejandro, and Robert L. Bach. *Latin Journey: Cuban and Mexican Immigrants in the United States.* Berkeley: U of California P, 1985.

Prakash, Gyan, ed. *After Colonialism: Imperial Histories and Postcolonial Displacements.* Princeton: Princeton UP, 1995.

Pratt, Mary Louise. "Arts of the Contact Zone." *Profession 91.* New York: MLA, 1991. 33–40.

Rachlin, Nahid. *Foreigners.* New York: Norton, 1978.

Rebolledo, Tey Diana. *Women Singing in the Snow: A Cultural Analysis of Chicana Literature.* Tucson: U of Arizona P, 1995.

Reeves, Trish. "Interview with Russell Banks." *New Letters* 53.1 (Spring 1987): 45–59.

Refugee Reports. Washington: American Council for Nationalities Service. December 18, 1987.

Reimers, David M. *Still the Golden Door: The Third World Comes to America*. New York: Columbia UP, 1992.

Ricoeur, Paul. *Fallible Man*. Trans. Charles Kelbley. Chicago: Regnery, 1965.

Rieff, David. *The Exile: Cuba in the Heart of Miami*. New York: Simon and Shuster, 1993.

———. *Going to Miami: Exiles, Tourists, and Refugees in the New America*. Boston: Little, Brown, 1987.

Rivera, Mario L. *Decision and Structure: U.S. Refugee Policy in the Mariel Crisis*. Lanham: UP of America, 1991.

Rivera, Tomás. "Chicano Literature: Fiesta of the Living." *The Identification and Analysis of Chicano Literature*. Ed. Francisco Jiménez. 19–36.

———. *y no se lo tragó la tierra: And the Earth Did Not Devour Him*. 1971, 1987. Trans. Evangelina Vigil-Piñon. Houston: Arte Público, 1992.

Robinson, Cecil. *Mexico and the Hispanic Southwest in American Literature*. Tucson: U of Arizona P, 1977.

Rocard, Marcienne. *The Children of the Sun: Mexican Americans in the Literature of the United States*. Tucson: U of Arizona P, 1989.

Rosaldo, Renato. *Culture and Truth: The Remaking of Social Analysis*. Boston: Beacon, 1989.

Rose, Jacqueline. *States of Fantasy*. Oxford: Clarendon P, 1996.

Rosenfeld, Alvin H. *A Double Dying: Reflections on Holocaust Literature*. Bloomington: Indiana UP, 1980.

Ross, Stanley R., ed. *Views Across the Border: The United States and Mexico*. Albuquerque: U of New Mexico P, 1978.

Roth, Henry. *Call It Sleep*. 1934. New York: Avon, 1976.

Roth, Philip. *Goodbye, Columbus, and Five Short Stories*. Boston: Houghton, 1959.

Rouse, Roger. "Mexican Migration and the Social Space of Postmodernism." *Diaspora* 1:1 (Spring 1991): 8–24.

Royce, Anya P. *Ethnic Identity: Strategies of Diversity*. Bloomington: Indiana UP, 1982.

Ruderman, Judith. *William Styron: Literature and Life*. New York: Ungar, 1987.

Ruoff, A. LaVonne Brown, and Jerry W. Ward. *Redefining American Literary History*. New York: MLA, 1990.

Said, Edward. *Culture and Imperialism*. New York: Knopf, 1993.

———. "Identity, Authority, and Freedom: The Potentate and the Traveler." *Boundary* 2, 21 (1994): 1–18.

———. *Orientalism*. New York: Pantheon Books, 1978.

———. *The Word, the Text, and the Critic*. London: Faber, 1984.

Saldívar, José David. *The Dialectics of Our America: Genealogy, Cultural Critique, and Literary History*. Durham: Duke UP, 1991.

———. "The Limits of Cultural Studies." *American Literary History* 2:2 (Summer 1990): 251–66.

Saldívar, José David, ed. *The Rolando Hinojosa Reader: Essays Historical and Critical*. Houston: Arte Público, 1985.

Saldívar, José David, and Héctor Calderón, eds. *Criticism in the Borderlands: Studies in Chicano Literature, Culture, and Ideology*. Durham: Duke UP, 1991.

Saldívar, Ramón. *Chicano Narrative: The Dialectics of Difference*. Madison: U of Wisconsin P, 1990.

Salvo, Joseph J., and Ronald J. Ortiz. *The Newest New Yorkers: An Analysis of Immigration into New York City during the 1980s*. New York: Department of City Planning, 1992.

Sanchez, George J. *Becoming Mexican American: Ethnicity, Culture, and Identity in Chicano Los Angeles, 1900–1945*. New York: Oxford UP, 1993.

San Juan, E., Jr. *On Becoming Filipino: Selected Writings of Carlos Bulosan*. Philadelphia: Temple UP, 1995.

Santiago, Esmeralda. *América's Dream*. New York: HarperCollins, 1996.

———. *When I Was Puerto Rican*. Reading, MA: Addison-Wesley, 1993.

Santos, Bienvenido N. *what the hell for you left your heart in san francisco*. Quezon City: New Day, 1987.

Sartre, Jean Paul. *What is Literature?* 1949. New York: Harper, 1965.

Sato, Gayle K. Fugita. "Momotaro's Exile: John Okada's *No-No Boy*." *Reading the Literatures of Asian America*. Ed. Shirley Geok-lin Lim and Amy Ling. 239–58.

Segal, Aaron. "The Caribbean Exodus in a Global Context: Comparative Migration Experiences." *The Caribbean Exodus*. Ed. Barry Levine. 44–66.

Seidel, Michael. *Exile and the Narrative Imagination*. New Haven: Yale UP, 1986.

Selvon, Sam. *The Lonely Londoners*. London: Wingate, 1956.

Shorris, Earl. *Latinos: A Biography of a People*. New York: Norton, 1992.

Showalter, Elaine, ed. *The New Feminist Criticism*. New York: Pantheon, 1985.

Simmons, Diane. *Jamaica Kincaid*. New York: Twayne, 1994.

Singer, Isaac Bashevis. *A Crown of Feathers*. Greenwich: Fawcett, 1974.

———. *Enemies, A Love Story*. New York: Farrar, Straus, Giroux, 1972.

———. *Lost in America*. Garden City: Doubleday, 1981.

———. *Meshugah*. New York: Farrar, Straus, Giroux, 1994.

———. *The Penitent*. New York: Farrar, Straus, Giroux, 1983.

Smith, Henry Nash. *Virgin Land: The American West as Symbol and Myth*. Cambridge: Harvard UP, 1950.

Smith, Page. *Democracy on Trial: The Japanese American Evacuation and Relocation in World War II*. New York: Simon and Shuster, 1995.

Sollors, Werner. *Beyond Ethnicity: Consent and Descent in American Culture*. New York: Oxford UP, 1986.

Sommers, Joseph, and Tomás Ybarra-Frausto. *Modern Chicano Writers*. Englewood Cliffs: Prentice-Hall, 1979.

Soto, Pedro Juan. *Spiks*. New York: Monthly Review, 1973.

Spivak, Grayatri. *The Postcolonial Critic: Interviews, Strategies, Dialogues*. Ed. Sarah Harasym. New York: Routledge, 1990.

Stavans, Ilan. *The Hispanic Condition: Reflections on Culture and Identity in the Americas*. New York: HarperCollins, 1994.

Steiner, George. *Language and Silence: Essays on Language, Literature, and the Inhuman*. New York: Atheneum, 1967.

———. "The Long Life of Metaphor: An Approach to the 'Shoah.'" *Writing and the Holocaust*. Ed. Berel Lang. 154–71.

Stepan, Alfred, ed. *Americas: New Interpretative Essays*. New York: Oxford UP, 1992.

Sternberg, David Joel. *The Philippines: A Singular and Plural Place*. Boulder: Westview, 1994.

Stonequist, Everett V. *The Marginal Man: A Study of Personality and Culture Conflict*. New York: Scribners, 1937.

Strassoldo, et al. *Cooperation and Conflict in Border Areas*. Milan: Franco Angeli Editore, 1982.

Styron, William. "Hell Reconsidered." *This Quiet Dust and Other Writings*. New York: Random, 1982. 95-106.

———. *Sophie's Choice*. New York: Random, 1979.

Suarez, Virgil. *The Cutter*. New York: Ballantine, 1991.

———. *Havana Thursdays*. Houston: Arte Público, 1995.

———. *Latin Jazz*. New York: William Morrow, 1989.

Suro, Robert. *Remembering the American Dream: Hispanic Immigration and National Policy*. New York: Twentieth Century Fund, 1994.

Sutton, Constance, and Elsa Chaney, eds. *Caribbean Life in New York City: Sociocultural Dimensions*. New York: Center for Migration Studies, 1987.

Takaki, Ronald. *A Different Mirror: A History of Multicultural America*. Boston: Little, Brown, 1993.

———. ed. *From Different Shores: Perspectives on Race and Ethnicity in America*. New York: Oxford UP, 1987.

———. *In the Heart of Filipino America*. New York: Chelsea, 1995.

———. *Strangers from a Different Shore: A History of Asian Americans*. New York: Penguin, 1990.

Tan, Amy. *The Joy Luck Club*. New York: Putnam, 1989.

———. *The Kitchen God's Wife*. New York: Putnam, 1991.

Tatum, Charles. *Chicano Literature*. Boston: Twayne, 1982.

Taylor, Patrick. *The Narrative of Liberation: Perspectives on Afro-Caribbean Literature, Popular Culture, and Politics*. Ithaca: Cornell UP, 1989.

Tein, Jenn-Yun, and Thomas K. Nakayama, eds. *Asian Americans: The Year 2000 and Beyond*. Phoenix: Arizona State UP, 1996.

Thomas, Piri. *Down These Mean Streets*. New York: Random, 1991.

Turner, Frederick Jackson. *The Frontier in American History*. 1893. Huntington, NY: Krieger, 1976.

Tuveson, Ernest Lee. *Redeemer Nation: The Idea of America's Millennial Role*. Chicago: U of Chicago P, 1968.

Ty-Casper, Linda. *Wings of Stone*. New York: Readers International, 1986.

Ueda, Reed. *Postwar Immigrant America: A Social History*. Boston: Bedford, 1994.

———— ed. *Immigration: Dimensions of Ethnicity*. Cambridge: Belknap, 1982.

Urofsky, Melvin I., ed. *Perspectives on Urban America*. Garden City: Anchor, 1973.

Van der Veer, Peter, ed. *Nation and Migration: The Politics of Space in the South Asian Diaspora*. Philadelphia: U of Pennsylvania P, 1992.

Van Slyck, Phyllis. "Repositioning Ourselves in the Contact Zone." *College English* 59.2 (Feb. 1997): 149–70.

Vásquez, Richard. *Chicano*. Garden City: Doubleday, 1970.

Vida, Nina. *Goodbye, Saigon*. New York: Crown, 1994.

Villarreal, José Antonio. *Pocho*. 1959. Garden City: Anchor, 1970.

Waniek, Marilyn Nelson. "Paltry Things: Immigrants and Marginal Men in Paule Marshall's Short Fiction." *Callaloo* 6 (1983): 46–56.

Waters, Mary C. *Ethnic Options: Choosing Identities in America*. Berkeley: U of California P, 1990.

Waugh, Patricia, ed. *Postmodernism: A Reader*. New York: Edward Arnold, 1992.

Weber, David J., ed. *Foreigners in Their Native Land: Historical Roots of the Mexican Americans*. Albuquerque: U of New Mexico P, 1973.

Weinberg, A.K. *Manifest Destiny: A Study of Nationalist Expansionism in American History*. Chicago: U of Chicago P, 1963.

West, Cornel. *Keeping Faith: Philosophy and Race in America*. New York: Routledge, 1993.

West, James L.W. III. *Conversations with William Styron*. Jackson: U of Mississippi P, 1985.

Wiesel, Eli. *The Fifth Son*. New York: Summit, 1985.

Wilentz, Gay. *Binding Cultures: Black Women Writers in Africa and the Diaspora*. Bloomington: Indiana UP, 1992.

Williams, Eric. *From Columbus to Castro: The History of the Caribbean*. New York: Harper, 1970.

Williams, Raymond. *The Country and the City*. New York: Oxford UP, 1973.

Winnick, Louis. *New People in Old Neighborhoods: The Role of New Immigrants in Rejuvenating New York's Communities*. New York: Russell Sage Foundation, 1990.

Wolfe, Alan, ed. *America at Century's End: American Society in Transition*. Berkeley: U of California P, 1991.

Wong, Sau-ling Cynthia. *Reading Asian American Literature: From Necessity to Extravagance*. Princeton: Princeton UP, 1993.

Wong, Shawn. *American Knees*. New York: Simon and Shuster, 1995.

⸺. "Each Year Grain." *Aiiieeeee! An Anthology of Asian American Writers*. Ed. Chan et al. 169–75.

⸺. *Homebase*. New York: I. Reed Books, 1979.

Woodford, John. "Immigrant Author Sees 'a dark side to multiculturalism.'" *Michigan Today* (1992): 14–15.

Wyman, David S. *Paper Walls: America and the Refugee Crisis, 1938–1941*. New York: Pantheon, 1985.

Yamamoto, Hisaye. *Seventeen Syllables and Other Stories*. Latham: Kitchen Table: Women of Color P, 1988.

Index